A Spy in the House of Loud

AMERICAN MUSIC SERIES
Jessica Hopper, David Menconi, Oliver Wang, Editors

A SPY IN THE HOUSE OF LOUD

New York Songs and Stories

Chris Stamey

UNIVERSITY OF TEXAS PRESS ⟨⟩ AUSTIN

Cover photograph © 2015 Carol Whaley; used by permission

Requests for permission to reproduce material from this work
should be sent to:
    Permissions
    University of Texas Press
    P.O. Box 7819
    Austin, TX 78713-7819
    utpress.utexas.edu/rp-form

♾ The paper used in this book meets the minimum requirements
of ANSI/NISO Z39.48-1992 (R1997) (Permanence of Paper).

LIBRARY OF CONGRESS CATALOGING-IN-PUBLICATION DATA

Names: Stamey, Chris, author.
Title: A spy in the house of loud : New York songs and stories /
    Chris Stamey.
Other titles: American music series (Austin, Tex.)
Description: Austin : University of Texas Press, 2018. | Series:
    American music series | Includes bibliographical references.
Identifiers: LCCN 2017055297 | ISBN 978-1-4773-1622-1 (cloth :
    alk. paper) | ISBN 978-1-4773-1623-8 (library e-book) |
    ISBN 978-1-4773-1624-5 (nonlibrary e-book)
Subjects: LCSH: Stamey, Chris. | Rock musicians—New York
    (State)—New York—Biography. | DB's (Musical group)
Classification: LCC ML420.S81127 A32018 | DDC 781.66092 [B]
    —dc23
LC record available at https://lccn.loc.gov/2017055297

doi:10.7560/316221

Contents

Preface
The Story behind the Painting

I RETURNED TO NEW YORK IN 2009, TO PLAY CARNEGIE Hall. I had first moved there from my native North Carolina in 1977, renting a room on Seventh Avenue, around the corner from the great concert hall, a perch from which I had watched as a small group of rabble-rousers at CBGB, a distant watering hole on the Bowery, transformed the rules of what was possible in handmade rock music. I had even waved a few flags in the revolution's march, first with a critically lauded rock band called the dB's and then as a solo recording artist and record producer. Now I was back for a benefit concert celebrating the music of R.E.M., a group of fellow Southerners and one of the most successful standard-bearers for that musical sea change.

Although I once knew every street corner and hotdog stand in Manhattan, I had left in 1992, and the city had shape-shifted several times since then. I had returned this time with my wife, Dana, and my daughter, Julia, and before the concert we went

The dB's (left to right: Will Rigby, Peter Holsapple, Gene Holder, Chris Stamey) at Odessa Restaurant (New York City) in 1979; photo by Stephanie Chernikowski

walking in search of familiar signposts, accompanied by our friends Amanda and Lydia Kavanagh and Amanda's six-year-old daughter, Oona. We ended up at the bar of the Algonquin Hotel, the famed site of another insurrection led by influential malcontents: the Algonquin Round Table of Dorothy Parker, Harold Ross, Alexander Woollcott, et al.

You walk into the room there and immediately see its well-lubricated history depicted in Natalie Ascencios's painting *A Vicious Circle*, which hangs on the far wall next to the kitchen. We had already told ten-year-old Julia about the meaning of its mise-en-scène; she walked over to examine it closer. Oona followed close behind. Julia whispered to her, "There's a *story* behind this painting" and continued to study it. When she broke her gaze, she saw that little Oona was nowhere to be found. After a few frantic moments, the girl was discovered around the other side of the wall, in the kitchen, staring at the hung cutlery, to the amusement of the chef.

When asked why she was there, Oona replied, "But you said there was a story *behind* the painting! . . . I'm looking for it."

This is, first and foremost, my task here: to tell some of the stories behind my own hand-painted songs. Sometimes there will be a lot to say about a lyrical twist or melodic turn, a bit of backstory, specifics that perhaps add to or alter the enjoyment of the tunes. Sometimes I'll include crosstalk, bleed-through, from other music, other's stories, other rooms. Sometimes we'll end up in the kitchen, staring at the knives, surrounded by layers of ghosts, past raconteurs, and fellow travelers.

There is another, familiar story here, however: a coming-of-age migration from a hinterland to a cultural capital. When I was twenty-two and freshly arrived in Manhattan, I suddenly found myself in a band with singer Alex Chilton, and in just a few weeks we were being reviewed favorably in *The New York Times*. One day at rehearsal, I mentioned being surprised that the best and most innovative players around us all seemed to be from out of town. Tom Verlaine and Richard Hell had arrived from Delaware to be poets together and then formed the band Television. The leader of Talking Heads, David Byrne, had entered the fray from Maryland by way of Rhode Island. Chilton, who was himself from Tennessee, told me what he believed: "Listen, good things come from the *provinces*." This is not strictly true, but coming to the big city and holding up a flame against its lights has long been a rite of passage for artists of all sorts. So many of my friends and I, from the Southern exposure of North Carolina, made this voyage together in the late seventies and early eighties, just as Carolina-bred musical giants Thelonious Monk, John Coltrane, Max Roach, and Nina Simone had done in years before. We brought parts of our provinciality with us, some Tar Heel–adhesive determination and innocence, and in return absorbed equal parts of New York's frontier abandon. Whether we stayed for only a short time or never left, we pilgrims in those heady, uncharted days were forever changed by this.

During my days in Manhattan, there were no cell phones with earbuds to blot out the city sounds (the Sony Walkman arrived in 1979 but wasn't ubiquitous for another decade). We all shared the air. And music leaked in everywhere, from huge, swinging portable cassette blasters, club doorways, bodega radios—the whole city was a mix tape. It was a town of loud, then. Every thoroughfare could be an "Electric Avenue," as Eddy Grant's 1983 smash proclaimed. And the DJs in the clubs were curators more than creators, proud of getting the latest platter from London or Athens, Georgia, eager to turn you on to something new. To replicate this flavor of the era, and since all my songwriting in those years occurred in the context of this sonic smorgasbord, I've included some Jukebox sections, my chance to play DJ for you. (And you can even hear the music while you read, in the order it appears, if you like. Go to my artist's profile at Spotify and select the playlist *A Spy in the House of Loud*, or just type http://lnk.to/chrisstamey into your browser.)

———

It's funny how things turn out. I never meant this book to be any kind of memoir. It began solely as an annotated songbook, concise paragraphs attached to sheet music, words and melodies and chords suitable for parlor playing in the old way. But from the git-go, I pretty much failed at the "concise" part. The annotations grew and grew until, in the end, they took on a life of their own. Each chapter here is named after a line from the song that was originally its inspiration.

1 Don't Stop to Think

It's been a hard day As you walk home, you can hear her on the

tel-e-phone, words she said___ in your head So you think back on the

ONE FRIDAY MORNING, MID-MAY 1975, I IMPULSIVELY drove from my creaky little rental cottage in the student ghetto of Chapel Hill, North Carolina, to the Amtrak station in nearby Durham and got on a train to New York. I was following a crush, a young woman with whom I was sharing a rented house that summer. She had told me the night before that she was going to split for a few days, and in my teenage mind, I thought I would go, too. So I surprised her by showing up at the station, unasked but with ticket in hand. This plan, which had seemed romantically undeniable in the wee hours of the previous night, was quickly revealed as absolutely delusional in daylight, and we weren't speaking by the time the train was rolling through Virginia. I think I had thirty dollars in my pocket, no friends in town, and no place to stay as the train arrived at Penn Station.

My old friend Sam Moss was a guitar dealer to the stars, so I called him from a payphone and offered him my only liquid asset at the time, a newly acquired vintage blond Telecaster, at a bargain price. He wired me the money, and that let me scrape by for a few days in Manhattan, until I could use the return ticket. It was a strangely delectable feeling, to be stranded in Manhattan, alone, with few resources and fewer plans. And I found I cherished it; I wanted to feel that way forever: wide open, walking into the unknown, constantly turning corners onto new streets where I was a stranger and every door could open into undreamed-of adventure.

I was already familiar with the town; I had visited it almost every summer since the start of high school, going there with Mitch Easter, a close friend since first grade and at this point a bandmate. We would stay with his dad in Greenwich Village, just south of Washington Square Park, for a week or two, trying to discover more about the burgeoning national music scene and hoping to find our own place in it. Sometimes we would drive up from our hometown of Winston-Salem, North Carolina, in a 1961 black Cadillac hearse filled with amps and drums, thinking that if we got asked to "jam," at least we would be ready. (Do I need to say that this never happened?) Most of those amps in the hearse had originally come from the legendary Manny's Music, and now we could hop a subway and gawk for hours at the store's fabled walls, covered with oodles of black-and-white photos of just about every significant jazz and pop figure from 1935 on.

We even made the rounds of record labels on these trips, with reel-to-reel tapes of some of the original songs we had recorded, both in a Winston basement and at Crescent City Studios in nearby Greensboro. One early stop was at Morris Levy's Roulette Records, where the A&R guy, who might have been the notorious Morris himself, listened briefly and then exclaimed, "That's not a hit! Wanna hear a hit?" after which he dialed up Tommy James and the Shondells' latest.[1] We momentarily intrigued Sire Record's Seymour Stein with a song by Mitch called "Gone Again"—but then came the slightly more complicated bridge; "You blew it there," he informed us, shaking his head. Seymour's then-tiny label was home to the prog band Focus, who had the instrumental hit "Hocus Pocus," and we, with our guitar-harmony acrobatics, felt some kinship there, so the rejection left us crestfallen. (Only a few years later, Sire stopped licensing European prog rock and became instead a champion of homegrown talent such as the Ramones, Talking Heads, and the Pretenders' Chrissie Hynde.) On those summer trips, we saw the town become more dilapidated and dangerous each year, but no less compelling because of that.

That eventful May weekend, after stopping by Western Union to pick up the small amount of cash I got from the sale of the Telecaster, I ended up at a dive bar I had read about in Lisa Robinson's *Rock Scene* magazine to see a double bill consisting of the Planets—a Who-influenced band run by an enthusiastic guitarist named Binky Philips—and Television, a band whose members, wearing cryptically tattered clothes, had appeared in the mag several times, even with no record label and no recorded evidence of their sound. (At this point, even their initial 45 was not yet available.) Since they had appeared in an actual magazine on actual newsstands, I expected the bar, whose awning trumpeted "CBGB OMFUG" (for "Country, Bluegrass, Blues and Other Music for Uplifting Gormandizers"), to be overrun with fans. But it was empty: There was only a lanky dog, a grizzled barkeep, and three or four other spectators, tops, two of whom—singer-poet Patti Smith and, from the popular band Blue Öyster Cult, Allen Lanier—I recognized, also from *Rock Scene*'s pages. It was an early lesson in the disconnection between critics' faves and actual popularity. I grabbed a chair in the corner and tried not to look the greenhorn.

I liked the Planets fine; their music wasn't all that different from some of the Anglophile sounds coming out of North Carolina. They seemed like nice guys. But Television was a shock.

Careless of time, the band let the songs stretch out luxuriously to embrace telescoping guitar solos that sounded more like something from John Coltrane or Eric Dolphy than from Eric Clapton or Mike Bloomfield. The bassist, Fred Smith, plucked very simple lines that anchored the music, leaving the drummer as well as both guitarists free to react to one another. Tom Verlaine, the main singer, spat out the lyrics, which when intelligible seemed to be describing fugue states with images that didn't pander to a lowest common denominator. And his guitar vocabulary was a revelation, drawing from elements of the postmodern "classical" music I was studying as a music composition student at the University of North Carolina. He employed complicated rhythmic constructs and asymmetrical phrases that flowed over the bars, as well as push-pull, violinlike vibrato, virtuoso hammer-ons, and behind-the-bridge extended techniques, but he never defaulted to standard bread-and-butter playing. He seemed not to know the clichés. When he bent strings, it was an anguished sound. When he set up fluttery sections, it evoked Debussy. Richard Lloyd, the other guitarist, had a more traditional, heroic guitar technique, deploying third-finger whole-step bends and familiar box shapes, but he was highly lyrical and able to develop long, dramatic lines over several minutes in a way that reminded me of the earlier Romantic composers—Tchaikovsky, for example, in his so-called *Pathétique Symphony*—and the Impressionist Ravel. He, like Tom, also avoided most clichéd faux heroics, but his playing counterbalanced Tom's esoterica. Billy Ficca, the drummer, really listened to what was going on and had hair-trigger responses to the other players. He didn't play in lockstep with the bass; his kick drum was more of a commentator in that jazzy way, and there was something of Elvin Jones in his top-kit rambles. His hi-hat, however, meshed with the tiny details of the chords' rhythms in a way I hadn't exactly heard before, except perhaps with Dave Mattacks, the drummer in the the British band Fairport Convention, who blended so well with their guitarist, Richard Thompson.

Perhaps most shocking, however, was that Television was really well rehearsed, at least instrumentally. This was hours of

Television (left to right: Tom Verlaine, Fred Smith, Richard Lloyd, Billy Ficca); photo by GODLIS

woodshedding on display. They could walk to the edge of calamity at the end of an improv section and then turn on a dime into a crystal-clear coda. By the midseventies, most popular mainstream bands had affected an intoxicated swagger and laid-back sloppiness that fit with their often boastful "let's party" lyrics. The toastmaster was king; precision was not a priority. At times it seemed like the triumph of Dean Martin, Frank Sinatra's pal, who always pretended to be smashed (and whose vocal affectations Elvis Presley had so admired and imitated). The New York Dolls, another Manhattan band championed by *Rock Scene* and considered by the press to be a radical alternative to mainstream rock, was really much the same beneath the slight shock of their lipstick and faux transgender dress. They were great fun, but no one ever accused them of being overrehearsed. And even the jammy, ever-present Allman Brothers, who were capable of fluid group-improv abstractions, always kept it comfortable and relaxed and then returned to the expected blues-growled lyrics.

Television was not relaxed. They were all wound tight, ahead of the beat, not behind it, and the music was highly dramatic. It didn't prostrate itself to reach you; you had to pay attention, or you would get lost. It was a bit like hearing Esperanto for the first time: Their language was similar to mine, there were regular fleeting moments of clarity, but it resisted easy comprehension. There was an "otherness" about it, and the singer seemed to be looking over the audience's heads into another room, somewhere else, as he sang lines such as "I dig friction," "Elevation don't go to my head," "How'd the snake get out of its skin?," and "I fell into the arms of Venus de Milo."

I stayed for their second set, which went long into the night. Then I returned the next night to listen to two more.

The impact of that weekend changed my concept of what a rock band could be, and it also gradually changed my songwriting and guitar playing in general. I think I was already headed in a similar direction, under the influence of too many undergraduate philosophy classes and midnight cups of coffee, but it was catalytic to see Tom Verlaine and company displaying the courage to express a kind of existential angst more openly than I had yet dared. I wouldn't make the move until more than a year later, but it was at this point that the city shifted from being a place where I would love to live to being the place where I felt I could belong.

———

"On the Brink," a two-and-a-half-minute emphatic electric song I wrote for the Sneakers record that came out the following year, has a little bit of the desperation I had heard that weekend and that I had felt all that year; I was learning to stop imitating, to tell my own stories. "Put the coffee into socket, got the look of a long night," as my song goes, is about right. "Don't stop to think, you're on the brink"—1975 was a year of insomnia.

2   I Love the Sound of the Traffic

I love the sound of the traf - fic   the rat - tat - tat of the train, ___

a rhap-so - dy that's pneu-ma - tic: so new and   strange

I T WAS ALWAYS NEW YORK. MY LIFE BEFORE MANHATTAN seemed simply a coiling before the leap north. I had visited early and often. My dad, Charles Stamey, a farmer's son who, against all odds, had ended up with an MD from Harvard and then built a thriving pediatric practice in Winston-Salem, regularly attended medical conferences there, and my whole family— my mother, Margaret; sister, Cindy; and brother, Kent—would all tag along. My parents didn't fly, so in the late fifties and early sixties we would book a Pullman train car out of nearby Greensboro and sleep through the night in the bunks, rolling over the rails, only to wake in a fantastical terrain among skyscrapers and bleating horns. When one such trip coincided with the 1964

World's Fair, we kids felt like we had spun the clock forward. It was the Unisphere; the Tent of Tomorrow; a boat ride through It's a Small World; IBM's enormous mainframe computer, which could use handwriting as input; GE's Progressland; Ford's Magic Skyway; GM's Futurama. I was only nine years old, but I knew what I had seen. It was the future coming to greet us, and that future's compass pointed always north.

I think it was on this expedition that, after no doubt much pleading on my part, my folks popped into F.A.O. Schwarz and bought me an early Christmas present: a bright orange portable reel-to-reel tape recorder—a toy, really, with three-inch clear plastic reels and big D-cell batteries for juice. Traveling home,

Returning from New York City with a tape recorder; author archives

I spent the night in the upper berth making its wheels go round, muttering secret messages into its tiny microphone, capturing the sounds of the tracks, until the batteries gave way. I thought I had found a way to stop and rewind time itself, the distinction between memory and the now blurring away into dreams along the course of that sleepy night.

I had already declared my intentions as far as music went. At age five, I had found the page in the *Childcraft* encyclopedia that showed a conductor flailing his arms in front of an attentive orchestra. Pointing to it, I told my mom unequivocally that I was going to be a musician when I grew up. (At that point, though, I thought the conductor was giving visual cues for the pitches instead of setting the pace and giving entrance cues: I thought that the higher his hands went, the higher up the scale the players were supposed to play.)

It's funny how life grabs you early. Winston-Salem, then with a population of just over 100,000, was in some ways a solidly blue-collar town. Its central employer was the tobacco giant R. J. Reynolds. But there were nicotine millionaires aplenty, as well as an excellent Baptist-affiliated college, Wake Forest. My best pal in kindergarten, an elite program held at the college that included French and math, was a faculty kid named Ben who was fascinated with theater, had a bedroom decorated with Marilyn Monroe pinups, and would make up elaborate, theatrical plots for us to act out involving spy costumes or superhero capes; as a drama critic for *The New York Times*, Ben Brantley has now been brilliantly describing Broadway and environs for decades.

Radio provided me one of my earliest indoctrinations into the mythos of New Amsterdam. Gordon Jenkins, later the more lush and sentimental of Sinatra's arrangers and also the man responsible for Nat "King" Cole's rich sound at Capitol Records, had in 1946 created a fully orchestrated radio play called *Manhattan Tower*, and the 1956 expanded version of this was broadcast many times over local radio when I was a child. Although the work is often cheesy and florid, it was absolutely captivating to listen to a plot unfold without any visual imagery—no stage, no choreography, just the dialogue, songs, and soaring orchestral commentary. I would sit, glued to the speakers, with my eyes closed and imagine what all these mysterious places might look like if I someday moved to that strange island.

Another defining early moment, for me along with much of young America, occurred when the Beatles appeared on the *Ed Sullivan Show*. But my reaction was a bit atypical: As clear as day, I can recall standing on the walkway to my elementary school in third or fourth grade, talking to my best friend, Mitch. He was saying that he thought the four Brits were really interesting and exciting; even then a budding contrarian, I said something like, "I dunno, it seemed silly to me"—and years would pass before I lost at least part of my skepticism about the Fab Four.

In the time before the Summer of Love, before first folk rock and then psychedelic rock arrived, science was king. The astronauts were the heroes of the early sixties; the space race was on. While still in elementary school, I read every single book on the public library's science-fiction shelves, riveting tales of rocket life by Alfred Bester, Robert Heinlein, Theodore Sturgeon, and the rest. Our family of five and our several cats and many dogs (thirteen adult Afghan hounds at one point) filled up all the rooms in our suburban brick home at 3229 Crittenden Court, in the Sherwood Forest neighborhood of Winston, but Easter, an only child, had free rein over his parents' large, empty suburban basement across the way at 610 Nokomis Court, and it soon became a laboratory and staging ground for experiments rewiring discarded radios and utensils. We shot Estes model rockets with salamander astronauts into "space" above the schoolyard, laughed together over what we could understand of the savage humor in *Mad* magazine, and played at being international spies, tinkering with soldering guns in an effort to make espionage gear worthy of our television favorites, *The Man from U.N.C.L.E.* and *Secret Agent*.

By 1965, long before either of us could play guitar, Mitch and I had both begged Sony reel-to-reel tape recorders for Christmas (a step up from my World's Fair trophy machine) and would put them through their paces. I experimented with recording myself reciting palindromes, to see whether the likes of "radar" or "Peel's foe, not a set animal, laminates a tone of sleep" sounded the same when the tape was running back to front. (To save you time, I'll report: This does not work.) And we tried defeating the erase head's function by covering the head with paper and aluminum foil, which let us add layer after layer on the mono machines without losing what had gone before—a very primitive, hissy form of overdubbing. In addition, I had a magnet shaped like a pencil and could use this to gradually "fade" a recording by slowly moving it closer and closer to the tape as it moved from one reel to the other. I'm not sure when we started experimenting with tape loops, but I think it was around this time as well.

It was the era of the electronic tinkerer, and *Popular Electronics* magazine was the bible. CB radios came into vogue among hobbyists around then, and we would roam the dials trying to connect with other voices in the ether. Mitch even had his own barely legal AM radio station, built from a kit from the Heathkit catalog, with a range of practically two hundred feet. From the top of the cul-de-sac, we would spin "Snoopy vs. the Red Baron," by the Royal Guardsmen, or "Wooly Bully," by Sam the Sham and the Pharaohs, using a microphone to capture the sound from a record player and adding commentary for the near neighbors, all the while keeping an eye peeled for FCC agents with handcuffs. The Guardsmen tune; "Expressway to Your Heart," by the Soul Survivors; and "The Letter," by the Box Tops, were all songs that combined small-combo performances with sound effects of airplanes, traffic, and crowds, and any such extramusical additions always drew me in. I also experimented with my dad's SoundScriber machine, which he used for office dictation. This device etched out low-fi grooves onto fluorescent-green translucent plastic disks, and I would borrow it on weekends to make "records," rubbing the mic and banging on it for my own Foley effects.

The Manhattan I visited with my parents in the early sixties was still that of midtown, all taxis and hotel lobbies. We didn't venture below Fourteenth Street. But I knew there was a different world on the island, south of that border. Music became a way I could peer into it with my imagination. The Greenwich Village folk scene—its beatnik goatees, bongos, espressos, and berets—was a part of popular culture, regularly satirized in Sunday cartoons and TV sitcoms, and the news coverage of the civil rights movement of the early sixties would usually include earnest singers of protest songs with guitars dangling off their shoulders from strands of twine. Washington Square Park was the gathering place by day, and at night the Bitter End, Caffè Reggio, Café Wha?, the Gaslight, Gerde's Folk City, and the Village Gate were among the points of congregation. The ideas of the day—of politics, poetics, art, philosophy—were debated avidly and passionately, with a decidedly liberal, leftist prevailing wind. The musicians of that time revered earlier, traditional forms and tunes, with the Harry Smith 1952 collection *The Anthology of Folk Music* as a vade mecum, but the modern age was finding its way into new lyrics for these old melodies, with "topical" songwriters such as Phil Ochs and Bob Dylan carrying on in Pete Seeger's footsteps.

This Village music was not often heard on the radio, but in 1963 a song called "Walk Right In," recorded by the Rooftop Singers, captured first place on the *Billboard* charts. The lyrics of this compelling folk-style, harmony-rich update of a 1929 country blues song by Gus Cannon seemed strangely apropos:

> *Everybody's talkin' 'bout a new way of walkin'*
> *Do you want to lose your mind?*
> *Walk right in, sit right down*
> *Baby, let your hair hang down*

The Rooftop Singers' version featured an unfamiliar sound—the twelve-string guitar. This was by design: The band's leader, Erik Darling, who created the band specifically to record the song, had to special-order the rare acoustic twelve-strings, matching left- and right-handed models, from the Gibson company; even in New York, they were not widely available. Erik was convinced that the unusual sound would bring him a hit record, and he was right.[2] A year later, both acoustic and electric twelve-string guitars hung on music store walls everywhere. And the Village folkies gradually went electric, following Bob Dylan's at-first controversial championing of the technology and the Beatles' continuing success.

Singer Petula Clark's producer, Tony Hatch, inspired by a visit to New York in 1964, returned to London with a song for her, an ode to downtown that proclaimed it a panacea for loneliness. (Hatch later revealed that he had mistaken the Times Square area for downtown, however. He was about thirty blocks off.) Recorded with an orchestra and future Led Zeppelin leader Jimmy Page on guitar, "Downtown" was an international smash by the start of the next year. It beckoned us all, promising, "Everything's waiting for you." Other bands, too, built signature sounds based around the "jangly," octave-doubling twelve-string, with one notable example being the Byrds, a band based in Los Angeles but led by New York studio musician Jim (later Roger) McGuinn. And a new band from below Fourteenth Street, the Lovin' Spoonful, found success as well, hitting the *Billboard* Top Ten in 1965 with "Do You Believe in Magic?" by using twelve-string simulation: combining an electric six-string with the *brrrrng* of an autoharp.

The Spoonful's John Sebastian and Zal Yanovsky were among the Village folkies who left coffeehouse singing behind and embraced electric music in the middle of the decade. They followed up their autoharp triumph with a clever song based around a totally different instrument, however—the Hohner pianet—and again struck gold, this time with the ingeniously studio-crafted "Summer in the City," which was released on the Fourth of July during the hottest New York summer on record (at that time) and held the top spot nationwide for most of the sweltering August of 1966. And every time it was played, we all were airlifted in our imaginations into the middle of a Bleecker Street evening. It's a fantastic, cinematic record that uses sound effects—car horns from a Volkswagon Beetle, construction-crew jackhammers—and minor-major shifts to put the listener right in the middle of a Manhattan summer. It oscillates between two musical moods. The C-minor first section, which features a descending bass line of straight quarter notes and describes a stressful, steamy day, is followed by an energizing modulation to F major to depict the joys of the night, and then it poignantly returns to minor chords to bemoan, "Don't you know it's a pity . . . the days can't be like the nights, in the summer, in the city."

We all wanted to believe, that August. We all wanted to drop everything and head to the Village to find that magic.

3 In Our Wildest Dreams

Here's where we get off___ you lived right down the street_

in our wil-dest dreams no-thin' can com-pete___

I T WAS PROBABLY 1965 WHEN I SAW MY FIRST REAL RECORD-
ing studio. One summer, my maternal grandfather, Andrew
"Drewsy" Harrill, got permission to visit the backstage studio
of a local radio station near my grandparents' home in western
North Carolina, possibly in Forest City. Cardboard egg crates
were stapled everywhere on the top portion of the walls to
minimize reflections, with pegboard lining the bottom to form
a sort of poor-man's Helmholtz bass trap. I remember only one
microphone, in the middle of the room, perhaps a big, ol' "Elvis
model" RCA 44-BX ribbon mic, and I think they were recording
directly to a lathe, cutting on lacquer for one-of-a-kind records,
although many US studios had been using tape for two decades

by that point, the technology coming courtesy of the vanquished Germans at the end of World War II. The studio was pretty much as depicted in the Coen Brothers' 2000 film *O Brother, Where Art Thou?*, in the scene where the musicians crowd around the single microphone and zigzag in and out to balance the sounds bar to bar. It was an *aha!* moment for me: So this is how it's done!

Ken Easter, Mitch's dad, was an accountant at Western Electric, then AT&T's manufacturing wing, and he sometimes brought home discarded electronics, including on one occasion an oscilloscope that, rigged with aluminum-foil arm straps, quickly became our completely bogus "lie detector." In 1967, following up on a classified ad in the local paper, he brought home some much more interesting devices: a used sunburst Gibson 330 "thinline" hollow-body electric guitar and a brown-tweed Fender Princeton amp. The Ventures were cranking out instrumental versions of the hits of the day, as well as original tunes such as "The 2000 Pound Bee," and Mitch quickly mastered their deceptively simple but precise plectrum technique, which created a rock-solid foundation for the virtuosic level of playing he later reached. Indeed, learning to play guitar before the advent of distortion and compression pedals was a boon; the fuzzier things get, the less one is forced to pay attention to plectrum basics at first. He started learning surf instrumentals, and it looked like great fun. At some point, this agility earned him a Mosrite "Fast Frets" guitar, like the one that the Ventures played, and I loved the cool lines of his next guitar, a jangly "Olympic White" Fender Electric XII twelve-string. But I was still confined to merely tinkering around on the family piano and playing bass in the junior-high orchestra, and I couldn't keep up with him musically for quite some time. In any case, piano was not a practical instrument for high-school combos of that era. Realistic-sounding electronic versions didn't exist yet, and an acoustic piano was just about impossible to transport, had to be tuned regularly and expensively, and couldn't be heard over the guitars and drums. Even when mic'ed and run through a PA, pianos were quickly swallowed up by the ever-escalating guitar stage volumes.

The Loyal Opposition, surf-instrumental rehearsal at Nokomis Court;
Easter archives

It was an era when only a few young players had yet cracked
the physiology of the wrist-twisting, string-bending electric guitar technique now made possible by the new thin wire gauges,
such as Ernie Ball's Super Slinky set. In Britain, Eric Clapton
and Jeff Beck were making inroads, listening to and extrapolat-
ing from rare tracks recorded in the fifties by blues innovators
such as B. B. King, Albert King, and Hubert Sumlin. And in
the United States, Mike Bloomfield had gone to the sources in
Chicago and now had it down pat. Robbie Robertson, with Bob
Dylan's backing band, was also getting it together a bit. But most
of the radio players quickly got into deep water when they tried
to stretch the strings and apply vibrato. Up to that point, guitar
players had produced vibrato just as violinists do, by pulling
a finger forward and back, parallel to the length of the string,
making the pitch go alternately a tiny bit flat and sharp. This
yields a lovely, humanizing effect but not a very dramatic pitch
shift. The new electric players' string-stretching technique, with

the thumb hooked over the neck and the wrist pivoting, allowed bends of a whole step or more and a deeper vibrato. The sustain and compression created by heavier amp distortion allowed for expressive phrasing that mimicked gospel vocal inflections, going up to pitch and then dipping down and back up but not ever above. (A record from a later decade, Bill Frisell's cover of Aretha Franklin's hit "Chain of Fools" on his *Is That You?* album, nicely illustrates a string-bending guitarist mimicking a singer.) To rock ears at that time, amazing jazz players such as Larry Coryell sounded almost clumsy, because they were slow to cotton to the new lazy, thumb-over-the-neck microtonal style.

Mitch's chops soon brought him, and all of us, into contact with another member of the secret society of early rock string-benders, a slightly older and most extraordinary character: Sam Moss, a Methodist minister's son from the small nearby town

Sam Moss, with 1962 (pre-SG) Les Paul; Easter archives

of Lewisville, who lived and breathed guitar and had also broken that code.

Sam recognized Mitch as a fellow devotee and started visiting at the Easter's for days on end. We would all eat the endless cheddar-cheese sandwiches served up by Lib, Mitch's mom, drink Coke after Coke, and listen to Sam spin tales and "bend wire." Sometimes I would spend the weekend with Sam, who was by that point living farther down the road in Taylorsville, near Statesville, and he would patiently show me, a beginner, parts of how it was done. Those lessons have stayed with me.

From the first day we met, Sam spoke in a patois that was his alone, full of implied quotation marks and arched eyebrows around unexplained catchphrases, although some of these came from the black-and-white W. C. Fields movies we would sneak into at Wake Forest College. ("Go away, kid, ya bother me" seemed to fit most any occasion.) He seemed at times to be someone out of an R. Crumb comic, striding confidently through the frames of life while the rest of us waited for page turns. He would talk about "hitting the note" (based on a specific high harmonic that Todd Rundgren, another early adopter of the new vocabulary, had popped out during a solo on the first album by his early band, Nazz), which now applied to any peak moment in life. Anything with inner Aristotelian beauty, from a great chili hot dog to (later) the novel *A Confederacy of Dunces*, was proclaimed "Blues approved." I was under his wing for a while, learning everything from the proper way to drink tequila (with salt and lime on the hand, taught to me while sitting in a '66 Ford Thunderbird on the side of the road) to all the myriad reasons why the Warren Commission had gotten the Kennedy assassination all wrong and all the obvious reasons why Rolling Stones guitarist "Keef" Richards had gotten almost everything right. In short order, Sam became our resident wise man and arbiter of all that was true and good in music, with extra points assigned if it was rooted in the blues.

4   Have You Seen the Last Elite?

Have you seen__ the last__ e - lite__ on Dear-born Street?

Oh, their life__ is so__ com- plete_ on Dear-born Street

A DUCK, TETHERED TO A KICK DRUM BY A FORTY-FOOT piece of twine and flying through the air in time to the pounding rhythm. A 150-watt bulb in a black box, its illumination interrupted by the slowly revolving blades of an electric fan: a poor man's strobe light. Yours truly, cowering in fascination as the cavernous acoustics in the cafeteria of the Bishop McGuinness Catholic high school for girls swallowed up what coherence there was in the improvisatory fury of Captain Speed and the Fungi (pronounced "funky" by those in the know) Electric Mothers. It was 1968, I was thirteen, and Winston-Salem was being forever transformed.

Not that there hadn't been electric guitar music in town

One of a handful of copies of the Captain Speed test lacquers; Easter archives

already. In fact, Easter was now leading the Loyal Opposition, with "girl drummer Robin Borthwick" (the prefix usually included for shock value). Their quartet played precisely picked versions of material from the Ventures' surf-instrumental songbook for turtlenecked partygoers.

But it was nothing like this: the freedom, the volume, the rumble. Psychedelia, on the wings of a waterfowl, had flown into our little tobacco town. We watched Steve Hutchison blur into a many-limbed beast as he rolled around the toms, while Buddy Carlisle traveled all over the neck of a Fender Precision bass (shaped like a "Year Zero"—i.e., 1951—Telecaster) as he sang. Guitarist Mike Greer had taken the underground phonograph sounds of Cream, the Amboy Dukes, Vanilla Fudge, and Hendrix and conjured them into life on his way to transmuting them into the band's "Yesterday's Tomorrow" b/w "Reptilian Disaster" single (of which there were only three or four copies ever made, reference lacquers only). This was a seismic event for our town, and as the dust cleared, everything looked different.

The Imperturbable Teutonic Griffin, demonstrating the potent combination of a Fender electric twelve-string and a Mosrite Fast Frets six-string; Easter archives

Within a year there was a gaggle of brightly dressed, Nehru-collared bands with extended guitar solos, bell-bottom pants, and peace signs. It was a pop-music shift as extreme and rapid as that of CBGB's rise to prominence a decade later. Easter's band, the Loyal Opposition, had evolved in short order into the Imperturbable Teutonic Griffin and then Sacred Irony, singing original songs such as "I See Love" and "I Am Your Doctor" with 100-watt Marshall stacks and wah pedals and ace Ted Lyons (later an influential painter, raconteur, and bluegrass mandolinist) now on the tubs.

Guitar guru Sam Moss still played with the B. B. King via Mike Bloomfield phrasing he had mastered, but now in the context of the sonic wash of Upinshades [*sic*] and, later, on songs from the Beatles' trippy *Revolver*, with the Rhythm Method (a reference to a birth-control technique that seemed anachronistic then, with the recent advent of "the Pill"). A bit later, our own McCartney figure, heartthrob bassist and singer Don Dixon, already a veteran of "beach music" session work in Charlotte, migrated from Lancaster, South Carolina, to anchor Arrogance,

Mike Greer's new, oh-so-heavy (meaning "profound," "ponder-ous," and loud) project, singing both "Maybe I'm Amazed" and the Black Sabbath catalog with equal aplomb. Robin Borthwick now pounded away behind the Shadows of Thyme.

The psychedelic invasion that this earthquake sent rippling out through Winston-Salem that year was an inclusive phenom-enon: If you didn't play well enough to be onstage, you could probably sign on with one of the requisite light shows; no band in town would willingly perform without an overlap of black-and-white cartoons (on actual film) and giant amoebas created by floating oil on water in Pyrex dishes on top of overhead projectors "liberated" from high-school supply closets. I had started taking electric bass lessons at a downtown music store, but my skills had not yet caught up with the rest of the musi-cians in town. So I found my own place in the action by taking one of the stereo tape recorders I had formerly used to record

Don Dixon; photo
by Bobby Bean

palindromes and planting it backstage, with rewired boxes from Radio Shack as cascaded four-channel mixers, to capture the undulating sounds (though not the visual fury) onto seven-inch reels of analog tape. Almost every weekend, there would be the four layers of action: the light-show guys in front splashing away in the water dishes, a pulsating band onstage splattered from head to toe with their strobes and cartoon ducks, the freeform dancers and shoe-gazers in front of the stage, and myself in the hallway behind, watching meters and changing reels.

New York was linked to all this via our ambassador, Ken Easter. AT&T had posted him to Manhattan, and he was living in Greenwich Village's NYU towers, although keeping the family in North Carolina and coming back as often as he could. On frequent trips to Manny's Music (the world's hippest music store since 1935, then located at 156 West Forty-Eighth Street, now demolished), he had made friends with Henry Goldrich, the son of the original owner. The Goldriches had connections to Winston-Salem (possibly through the R. J. Reynolds Tobacco family and its femme fatale, the New York-based singer Libby Holman), and they were pleased to connect with another Winstonite. Tales trickled back to North Carolina of Ken and Henry sitting around after hours while Alan Rogan, the Who's head guitar tech, tried out new fuzz pedals and amps and selected guitars for guitarist Pete Townshend to smash. As did Ken's purchases of the latest thing, the insanely loud high-rise Marshall amplifiers. These were made for an era when bands used PA systems only for the singing, not for a full blend of the instruments. The sound from the stage amps had to reach to the back of the room, making stage volume at ground zero breathtakingly loud. There were also precious few distortion pedals on the market, and the ones that were available—the Dallas Music Fuzz Face; the Jordan Boss Tone; the Maestro Fuzz-Tone, which claimed to replicate the "sound of a thousand woodwinds"—for the most part all sounded like the Ventures' aptly named "2000 Pound Bee," just *buzz buzz buzz*. The high volume was necessary to overdrive the amps themselves, for sustain. This wasn't a problem with the small, twelve-watt Fender amps, but the eight-speaker, one-hundred-watt Marshall stacks had to roar before they would saturate acceptably. Sacred Irony even ended up with a tube Marshall PA, basically a big, trebly guitar amp with mic inputs, which made all the singing sound a bit like Stratocasters feeding back.

Most of the churches in town had community rooms for pot-luck meals after services, and in an effort to contain and control the teenage explosion, these were offered as concert halls on the weekends. It gave a religious tint to the activity, as youth pastors circulated with plates of Nabisco cookies and trays of lemonade through the weaving, free-dancing crowd, watched over by watercolors of saints. This liturgical largesse had a dramatic and unexpected effect. Because the bands felt absolutely no need to play the hits of the day, as they might have felt at bars in other cities, they started writing their own songs and covering obscure underground favorites. It's hard to overemphasize the importance of this: By opening their doors, the churches played a huge role in fostering creativity in the Winston-Salem music scene. Adopting the Captain Speed template, all the local bands were soon trying to write their own original extended takes on such scene hits as the political, apocalyptic "Monster" by Steppenwolf or Iron Butterfly's "In-A-Gadda-Da-Vida" (a phonetic spelling of the singer's mumbled "in the garden of Eden"); the Beatles and the Stones were mostly missing in action, old news. Little could match the excitement of writing a song during the week and then playing it for your musical peers on the weekend. Such things are now taken for granted, but in the decades before indie rock, this was a paradigm shift.

All this was great fun, but I wasn't completely sold yet; on some level, I was still the doubting Thomas who had questioned the worth of that new television boy band the Beatles back in fourth grade. My snobby skepticism about pop records was finally overcome by Lib Easter, who jokingly called herself "the oldest living teenager" and was enamored of electric and acoustic folk rock. One rainy afternoon, when everyone else was practicing in the basement, she took it on herself to play me each track on a flagship Greenwich Village folk-rock release, her current favorite, the third Simon and Garfunkel record, *Parsley, Sage, Rosemary and Thyme*. The duo had scored a surprise hit when the record label, Columbia, overdubbed electric instruments onto their acoustic-guitar recording of "The Sounds of Silence" without the band's input. Now the duo had taken a whole month in the label's Manhattan studio to spend an unheard-of $30,000 using a brand-new invention, the eight-track tape recorder. I sat and listened patiently to Lib's commentary for song after song, and I liked the careful use of language, although the music sounded very restrained. But when it got to "7 O'Clock News/ Silent Night," with the announcer's monotone about Vietnam War deaths weaving in and out of the Christmas ballad, the irony of the sound collage really grabbed me. Of course, the disastrous war and the draft were on all our minds in those years, with the protests, napalm, and body bags on TV daily. Perhaps the song reminded me of the layering I had created earlier by covering my tape recorders' erase heads with aluminum foil. Or of the sound effects added to "Snoopy vs. the Red Baron" and "Summer in the City." But it was the contrast between the deadpan recitation of death tolls and the Everly Brothers–style tenor harmonies that did it: From that moment on, I wanted to make records.

Our scene was heavily influenced by a pair of local 1969 concerts by the Los Angeles–based Yellow Payges, which featured Bill Ham, a guitarist from Fort Worth, Texas, playing their regional hit "Vanilla on My Mind" on a tiny double-cutaway sunburst Gibson Melody Maker. The band's members started the evenings by each coming out and playing an unaccompanied solo and then jamming together before even playing a single song; we all loved that. Their entrances were preceded by offstage announcements, with their manager identifying their home-towns: "From Houston, Texas," "From Dallas–Fort Worth"; I think the bassist was a "Citizen of the World," which instantly went into local legend as something to aspire to. I recorded both their area appearances, and those tapes, passed from hand to hand, became a textbook of sultry guitar phrasing for Moss and Easter and the rest of the local guitarslingers.[3]

———

In addition to being the guy lugging the big Sony TC-660 reel-to-reel tape recorder backstage at the coffeehouses, I was now in a band myself, but on the down-low. Since their fifth-grade year, Peter Holsapple and Kent Schuyler, both a grade behind me, had been meeting to play blues together, inspired by the Paul Butterfield Blues Band's third album, 1967's *The Resurrection of Pigboy Crabshaw*, and a year later I joined them with my new upholstered Hagstrom I electric bass. I don't think this band, later called Soup, ever got much further than Schuyler's bedroom, although there was perhaps one gig at the coffeehouse at Knollwood Baptist Church.

Kent played well but in a rapid-fire, jazzy style that didn't quite mesh with rest of the somewhat jazz-phobic Winston scene. I could tell that Peter, however, had something going on that would connect, and I started mentioning him to the slightly older folks I was recording. He went away to Phillips Exeter Academy for one year, starting in fall 1970, where he formed a band called the Oirolf P. Florio Memorial Blues Band (or simply Oirolf Florio—palindromes everywhere) with future Tom Petty keys player Benmont Tench. But he was back for good the next summer, and Ben came up from Florida to visit with him for a few weeks. Tench and I sat around one afternoon with pairs of headphones and marveled at the intricacy of the new MC5 album, *High Time*; everyone loved the "Five." When he commented at the end that "it was a really great, dense mix," I eagerly concurred, wondering secretly what a "mix" was and what would make such a thing great.

At Sam Moss's suggestion, I set up a jam session à la *Super Session* (an iconic Al Kooper, Mike Bloomfield, and Stephen Stills record) in the living room at my parent's house with Peter, Benmont, and Sam, as well as Mitch and some of Sam's other cronies, and recorded the results. (My parents must have been out of town.) Because the guitar chairs were full, Ben and Peter switched off on keys, and although we were already prepped for the former's music chops, Peter's natural feel for the instrument thrilled us all on James Taylor's "Steamroller Blues" and a few other tunes. This became known as the Hot Wheels Session, because during breaks everyone would play with my brother's new toy Mattel cars. After this, Benmont went back to Florida, to eventually join up with Tom Petty in Mudcrutch and then the Heartbreakers, and Peter became Winston's first-call pianist for a while.

Although any music called "psychedelic" would get our immediate and full attention, my peer group was just young enough to be charged with keeping our embarrassingly stoned older musician friends from walking into traffic under the influence of psychedelic drugs, and this had a dampening effect on our own desire to join that part of the action. I had tried smoking pot once, at the Shack, a den of iniquity that headquartered local garage-rockers Little Diesel and the Weasels, but it didn't take. Perhaps it was also more of that contrarian streak, but Mitch, Don, and I ended up with a lifelong affection for mind-expanding music but no significant experience of the associated substances.

In most other ways, however, we were eager to take part in the action. I was letting my hair grow long (even over the tops of my ears) and wearing bell-bottom jeans, having started back in 1967, when the covers of *Newsweek*, *Time*, and *Life* began displaying the Summer of Love in every grocery store. I had subscribed to radical mags such as *Old Mole* (Boston) and the brand-new *Rolling Stone* (San Francisco), although I stealthily had them coming to Easter's parents' address, as they would have been hard to justify to my less open-minded family. And everything was changing in the South; the jocks from the football team who had taunted and punched us musician types one year over our long hair and paisley had walked in to school the next fall shooting two-finger peace signs, wearing fringed leather jackets, and sporting a new, hip vocabulary. But I still kept up

Sacred Irony, at a West Forsyth High School dance; Easter archives

my membership in the high school chess club, a social set completely different from the musician's gang that hung out at a set of steps sardonically dubbed Combo Corner—"Combo" implying a band from the dorky turtleneck-and-surfers era. *Our* bands were proudly called *groups*.

———

In Winston-Salem, lineups were forever shifting. By 1972 Don Dixon's Arrogance, older than the rest, had relocated to Chapel Hill for college and, with the addition of Robert Kirkland as a harmony partner and songwriter, had found a new Crosby, Stills and Nash–influenced attitude. And Sacred Irony had lost steam after a soul-crushing boondoggle in July 1970, when they and their hearse full of gear were bumped from a much-anticipated headline slot at North Carolina's Love Valley Rock Festival on the final night because the headlining Allman Brothers wanted to jam a second time. Peter Holsapple, Mitch, and I, along with a powerhouse drummer with double kick drums named Bobby Locke, took over the name of a meticulous cover band called Rittenhouse Square that was disbanding, playing our own music under that banner. But the more we wrote, the more we wanted to record.

After enduring a difficult, expensive all-night session at professional Greensboro recording studio Crescent City, which yielded a rare but dubious twelve-inch EP of juvenilia that goes for lots on eBay and that we would prefer to just go away forever, we went back to the Easters' basement lair on Nokomis Court, a corner of which had been walled off and refurbed as a practice space some years before. In February 1972, with money saved from playing clubs, I bought a modern miracle: a consumer four-track reel-to-reel tape recorder, the TEAC A3340. It was such a liberation from the two-track machines available to consumers up until then. Those extra two tracks and the Simul-Sync heads changed everything for us; we could now overdub. It was, as far as I know, the only such machine for miles around, since I had bought it from Manny's the first week it came on the market. The next two years were spent mostly in that basement trying to figure out how pop records were created.

There were no textbooks to tell us anything about this, no classes to take then; it was all trial and error in endless hours of experimenting over terribly inaccurate monitor speakers and with often dreadful results. The same quest for knowledge that previously had us putting salamanders inside model rockets and sending them into space—with, of course, capsules that separated and parachuted the amphibians down safely (honestly: parachutes)—now had Mitch and me rewiring scrap Altec Lansing PA mixers and recording secret backward messages. By then, he played guitar, bass, pedal steel, drums, and some keys, all well. I played electric bass well; piano, too; and a bit of basic guitar, although I improved quickly down there in the lab. The two of us would fill four tracks on the TEAC, mix them down to the two tracks of one of the remaining earlier stereo machines, and then move that mixdown reel back to the four-track and thus be able to add two more to it. We would listen to a new commercial record, speculate wildly how they had created it, and then try it ourselves. Peter loved live performance, though, so he faded from the tedious basement recording scene, returning to play with his younger peers in Little Diesel, now the city's premiere garage band, and that was the end of Rittenhouse Square.

The basement band didn't really have a name as far as I can recall. Faye Hunter, Mitch's girlfriend, became the third member of our squad, adding flute, enthusiasm, and sometimes bass to the productions and helping consume the endless bowls of popcorn and bottles of Coke or Tab, but with Mitch now serving as both the drummer and the main guitarist, playing live was out of the question. And there wasn't time in any case; songs started pouring out and begging to be assembled with tweezers on the TEAC.

The three of us produced many "albums," running off four or five copies on stereo reel-to-reel tapes of maybe eight new songs each, with ourselves as the only audience. But the music was not totally unheard. The student radio station at Wake Forest University, WFDD, was all classical until 10 p.m., when *Deaconlight* ignited with freewheeling underground rock until perhaps midnight. And it was brilliant: We could mix down our newest recording, hop in the car, drive the two miles to the station with a reel of tape, and then hear them play it over the air that same night, sometimes even as we drove back. What a thrill this was! There was no competition at all, no one else was bringing them "indie" local music, and there was no station prohibition against it. I can't imagine what the student DJs thought, although I suspect they didn't even listen before airing these tapes. And the station broadcast all over the metropolitan region, a big step up from the Heathkit AM radio transmitter that had struggled to reach even to the bottom of Nokomis Court eight years before. As a private, Baptist-affiliated college (not yet a university), Wake Forest hadn't even allowed *dancing* on campus for many years. Yet here they were, playing our bizarre recordings without a second thought.

———

Sgt. Pepper's Lonely Hearts Club Band had been a four-track production in the style we were using, with multiple generations being copied between two machines, but we preferred the exaggerated, treated tones that their fellow Brits the Move were achieving on songs like "Brontosaurus" and "It Wasn't My Idea to Dance." We tried to make everything stylized and monstrous like that. Unfortunately, neither of us had sung much in the bands we had been in, and we had no technique to draw on, so we left this dreaded part until last, using the one remaining track for all of the singing, which was often the downfall of these recordings. These multitrack tapes still reside somewhere in the vaults at the Fidelitorium Recordings studio in Kernersville, North Carolina. I haven't heard those songs since high school (hindsight makes me pray that no one else ever does), but I do remember a few titles of mine: "In a Chinese Restaurant," a densely chromatic, very short a cappella cluster piece where I warbled all the parts; an ominous one, "The Birds of Prey"; and "Ships," a long, minor-key Tchaikovskyesque instrumental written on piano and then orchestrated with lots of guitars filling in for the imagined woodwinds and strings.

"Dearborn Street," an attempt at a denunciation of the upper classes in the style of the Kinks' "A Well Respected Man" or the Who's "Substitute," might have been my best song from that time, but all I can remember about it now is the chorus ("Have you seen the last elite, on Dearborn Street?") and a riff based on a parallel-thirds descending guitar line. The indisputable culmination of the Nokomis studio era was an epic song from Mitch called "The Train Stops Here," which satirized the joys of post-Woodstock communal living with lines such as, "Are you coming, my dear? We have waited many a year for the birds and the plants and a bedful of ants . . . We'll live on dirt and eat leaves for dessert. . . ." It featured every instrument in the basement, including pedal steel and electric sitar, topped off with Faye's whistling flutes. After this opus, it was all downhill, and when college beckoned at the end of 1973, the great Nokomis basement sound lab was shuttered, once and for all.

Jukebox

Just Tryin' to Tell a Vision

"Little Johnny Jewel," Television,
seven-inch single, Ork Records, 1975

In the fall of 1975, everything changed.

With albums, you often feel like someone is trying to sell you something: a concept, an attitude, a haircut, a concert ticket, a marketing plan. With singles, someone is trying to *tell* you something: They are urgent, brief, to the point, a horseback ride across enemy territory with a crumpled-up piece of paper in a back pocket. And in the days of vinyl 45s, the brave little disks underwent a kind of torture to get their message across: A needle scratched the music into spiraling lacquer furrows on an aluminum disk, which was then given electroshock treatment until the grooves had been rendered onto metal plates that could squeeze out multiple copies of encoded plastic pucks with big holes punched in their centers.

I was studying orchestration and writing Webern-derivative

woodwind miniatures at the University of North Carolina when a record slipped past the guards of Official Record Label Land and, via tiny ads and sympathetic reviewers and against-the-grain pictures in *Rock Scene* magazine, infiltrated small pockets of underground rock aficionados nationwide.[4] A few years later, it was to be the album *Marquee Moon*, released by a division of Warner Bros., that would make the headlines and go on to find acclaim as one of the best rock records ever. But it was Television's "Little Johnny Jewel," recorded on a consumer-level four-track tape recorder identical to the one Easter and I were slaving over in North Carolina, that started the American indie-rock revolution.

Having seen the band blaze live some months before, I sent a check for two bucks to the bizarre-sounding Ork Records, and sometime later the postal carrier dropped it off in a plain brown wrapper. The recording inside was crude, ungroomed, and unfiltered but also poetic, punctuated, and improvisational. For the most part, it was quite different from the guitar-pop records on the Ardent label I had loved in high school, especially in the singing, which was more like talking, but there were still those over-trebled guitars; that fluid, reactive drumming; and, most crucially, the sense that the singer wasn't lying, that he, like his song's protagonist, was instead trying to express something visceral, something real.

The song describes a character named "Johnny Jewel" who is "tryin' to tell a vision" (a great play on the band's name, with the latent suggestion that this was also possibly their mission state-ment). Attracted by the "rush and the roar," he goes down to the airport, where, as if answering yes to the question posed earlier by "Walk Right In," he "loses his senses." Then a guitar solo seems to take over this conceit, spending the next three minutes musically depicting Johnny's loss of sensibility. (At the time, it reminded me of "Psychotic Reaction," a 1966 single by the Count Five that also evokes an altered state with distorted guitars, although in a more cartoonish fashion.) It wasn't jazz, but there was a similar quality of careful attention during this instrumental section, with the drums almost duetting with the lead guitar, phrase for phrase, as the bassist stuck to the simple underlying riff. Mitch Mitchell had done something similar when drumming with Jimi Hendrix in the sixties, but to my ear, this interplay was more interlocked and attentive than theirs had typically been.

Releasing "Little Johnny Jewel" on a seven-inch 45 rpm disk yielded an unintended consequence: At seven and a half minutes, the entire recording was too long to be etched onto a single side. It was thus broken into two halves, "Part One" and "Part Two," with the track fading out at the end of the first side and then fading back in at the start of the second. I loved how the story continued after an intermission, even though the break was most likely a byproduct of the medium's constraints and not part of the original conception. This interruption seemed to connect the record to the storytelling of an old radio play, where a plot would be interrupted by a commercial, which made the song more of a narrative. It faded away, and yet as I got up to actively participate in the "performance" — to lift the needle, flip the record, and then lower the tone arm — it would seem to still be playing in my imagination, as if it were reverberating somewhere in the cosmos all the while. I remembered the sixties television program with Bill Bixby, *My Favorite Martian*, which proposed, ludicrously, that sound waves of conversations on Earth were perpetually traveling out there, somewhere, ever deeper into space, and that Uncle Martin (the Martian) could use his alien ears to find a conversation from the previous day, which might be echoing out past Neptune by that point. Somehow this vinyl fading-in-and-out also reinforced my impression that this was, as Atlantic Records' Ahmet Ertegun famously said later, "not Earth music" — and that the single had been launched from the planet of New York to see if there was other intelligent life out there, beyond its orbit.

5 The More You Learn, the Less You Know

Put on a new face, we'll go for a walk on the main-stream bou-le vard__

Girl, with your che-mi - cal eyes, you can look so hard_____

I N MAY 1975 I RETURNED TO CHAPEL HILL AFTER THAT
first visit to CBGB and resumed my awful job, forming hamburger patties by the hundreds from dubious slats of raw beef.
I worked by myself, in a back room at the Carolina Coffee Shop,
on the main drag. A waiter there, Rob Slater, was also from
Winston-Salem, and from mutual friends I discovered that he
was an enthusiastic guitarist. I had been in innumerable rock
groups in high school, but always as a bassist. I had to some
extent turned my back on popular music when I first began my
formal music studies at UNC, finding little that spoke to me
in those days. Now I had taken up guitar almost exclusively to
more easily accompany myself on the songs that were once again

Chris Stamey and Robert Keely, at a Sneakers rehearsal, with gloves on the wall, 1976; photo by Buzz Spector

spinning 'round my head. I had also gradually resumed recording with Hunter and Easter, who had relocated the Nokomis base- ment gear to Chapel Hill in fall 1974 after some time in Illinois.

Slater and I started a band, Sneakers, along with Little Diesel alum Will Rigby on drums and another Winston friend, Robert Keely, on bass. We sought mostly to embellish some of my lat- est Kinks-style tunes with complicated guitar figures and meter shifts. Sneakers was already out of step with the other local bands, and we rarely played in public. When I described what I could remember of the Television sets to the rest of the group and started to tug the band's arrangements in that direction, there was no fear of jeopardizing our audience; we had none.

My other job in those college years was assisting Don Dixon in his recording endeavors around Chapel Hill. It was a great way to learn. While still in high school, Don had connected with producer Wayne Jernigan at Reflection Sound Studios, a pro stu- dio in Charlotte that specialized in gospel and Carolina "beach" music, and he knew how things were really done; he was way beyond the rest of us in this regard. Don and I used my trusty four-track TEAC to record bands in nightclubs for a show on local Winston radio station WAIR, and we also recorded ad-hoc sessions in living rooms, producing demo tapes for boogie bands that wanted to impress club owners with their cassettes. One memorable example was a 2:18-long T. Rex–influenced production called "Galaxies of Love" by a local rocker named Wayne Hurst. Don always had the best tricks to get the most out of our primitive gear, and he was generous about sharing what he knew. Sometimes we would record bands in the daytime at the Cat's Cradle, the local rock club (still going as I write), using the stage as the studio and the bar as the control room.

Late in the summer of 1975, we set up the gear at the Cradle, then located at 405 W. Rosemary Street, and recorded some members of an acoustic band called the Red Clay Ramblers. Don then had to fly to New York to oversee a mastering session for them at Sterling Sound, and he invited me along. Sterling had mastered all the recordings in the Nonesuch Explorers series of world music, and I knew those sounded great. Don had carefully guarded the Ramblers' master tape all the way up, as we all believed that unseen magnetic emanations from motors lurked everywhere, ready to erase our work. We made it there safely, and as we waited for the elevator, he pointed out that the Nonesuch series' mastering engineer, Robert C. Ludwig, was now on the wall directory under a brand-new company name, Masterdisk, and Don said we should remember that name. The Sterling engineer, who I believe was George Marino, put the tape on his machine, which he calibrated to our squealing alignment tones, and, after turning a few knobs, carved out grooves in soft lacquer on an aluminum version of a potter's wheel. The process was fascinating to watch, and it started my lifelong fascination with the art of mastering.

I hung out for a few days in New York, making sure to see Television play again. Back in Chapel Hill, it was a few weeks before boxes of the finished seven-inch records arrived from United Record Pressing in Nashville and shortly thereafter appeared for sale at the local Record Bar. It wasn't until I saw this stack of dominoes fall that I realized that I had all the pieces to "seize the power" and put out my own songs—I had Don's recording savvy, Sneakers to rehearse and play the music, Cat's Cradle to record in, and URP to make the vinyl. I could make my own "vanity records" (as they were quite accurately called); I didn't need to convince the Seymour Steins to broker them for me. As comical as this sounds now, when it can seem like just about everyone has a self-released record or a streaming site, it was then a revelation.

I can't overemphasize both how liberating this was and how unusual it seemed then. Sure, indie labels had flourished in the fifties and sixties, although they usually had to hook up with major distributors and record pluggers if they were going to get anywhere. But by the seventies, it was virtually all major corporations again, most of the radicals, such as Elvis Presley producer Sam Phillips at Sun, having cashed in their chips. And even in the early days of rock, the artists themselves were not the ones pressing records and then getting to a national stage. Close to home, Dixon's band, Arrogance, had in fact self-released an album that sold well locally, but it had not gone further. Mitch and I had thought the only way to get our recordings through the gate was via the corporate A&R men. Still, there were a few recent glimmers of hope on the national horizon. Patti Smith had released "Hey Joe" b/w "Piss Factory" in 1974, but that was really done by her management, the Wartoke Concern. The single by Television came in 1975 and was the true declaration of "indie-pendence" for us, as the band had created and released it themselves, although it had their manager/confidant Terry Ork's name on it. Pere Ubu, from Cleveland, seemed to us to be kindred spirits, perhaps because they were also from the provinces; they put out several distinctive 45s, starting with "30 Seconds over Tokyo" at the end of 1975. But that was about it, as I recall.

So we began. I knew enough about the physics of records to know that if the seven-inch disk ran at 33⅓ rpm instead of the usual 45, I could get a bit more time on each side, although that many revolutions would require cutting the disks with very shallow grooves. Such shallow grooves would result in attenuated bass response (the grooves being too shallow for the big waves), but Sneakers was all about the treble anyway. We ruthlessly edited the structure of six songs so they ran for only two minutes each to stay under the maximum of about six minutes per side for a seven-inch double-sided EP. We arranged the songs in advance, planning on cramming them as full as we could with sitars, car horns, toy pianos, tambourines, and guitars, guitars, guitars. Almost all the instruments had to be played simultaneously onto two tracks of the TEAC four-track, since Don didn't want to lose a generation of tape by copying from one hissy semipro machine to another in order to overdub. So we practiced the six songs endlessly in bassist Keely's dorm room at Duke University.

Once we felt ready, we persuaded the owners of Cat's Cradle to let us again use the club as a studio space. Starting early one summer morning, we took hours to load in, set up all the equipment, and test the mics. Easter, not yet a full member of Sneakers, had joined us on the session to play quiet nylon-string guitar on the live takes, sitting in the bathroom the whole time, for sonic isolation. Friends Robert Kirkland, from Arrogance, and Chris Chamis were given percussion instruments to wave and bang, details that would have typically been added at the very end of a normal multitrack recording process. Will, Rob, Robert, and I were on the stage. But around 2 p.m., when we finally finished the tech and had run down just one or two of the songs, the guy who mopped the club showed up. I guess there were some crossed signals, but it was a filibuster: He planted his wet mop and would not surrender the floor. Cleanliness trumped godliness. Worse, Mama Dip's Kitchen, next door, was also unhappy with the lunchtime racket, so we dejectedly tore down everything and moved to the bedroom of Slater's girlfriend, where we set it all up again, squeezing everything around her bed, with Mitch now in a different bathroom. Finally, around midnight, the initial tracks were done.

After recording these instrumental "beds," we were able to use the two remaining tracks to capture all the singing and filigrees, some of which was done during off-hours in Dixon's home-base pro studio, Reflection, in Charlotte, where I sang with the worst head cold of my life. The rest—electric sitars in harmony, car horns, toy pianos—was done on headphones in Don's tiny apartment while (as I recall it) his first wife, Phyllis, kindly put up with us as she watched *Kojak*'s Telly Savalas ask repeatedly, "Who loves ya, baby?" with that Tootsie Pop hanging out of his mouth. It was Beatles-style four-tracking, pre-*Sgt. Pepper's*, in that you could fill the gaps between vocal sections, but all solos had to end abruptly to make room for the lyrics to follow on the same track; there was no way to overlap them.

The song "Condition Red," like most of tracks on the Sneakers EP, couldn't, in the allocated two minutes, actually capture the extended, free-form improvisatory aspect of those live Television gigs I'd seen, although I think some later, never-recorded Sneakers material did catch this flavor. To fit six songs into twelve minutes on the disk, we had to make them concise and play them fast. There was no time for group improvisation. That song was as close to an anthem as that record got, however. I had admired the lopsided structure of the Raspberries' power-pop single "Go All the Way," with its astonishingly short verse and then lots of chorus repetition, and I wanted to try that. It's not the cleverest arrangement on the record (that honor probably goes to "Driving") or the catchiest (that would be "Ruby," with Robert Keely singing lead). But it's the song I come back to the most. It reminds me of the urgency of that summer, of that time alone in New York, no direction home. There's no instrumental intro, not even a groove at first; all the guitars and drums and singing hit together, as hard they can, with no warning.

Toward the end of high school, I had been especially enamored of the obscure first two records by Memphis's Big Star, the flagship band of Ardent Records there. A song called "When My Baby's Beside Me" was a radio hit in Winston (although nowhere else, it seems), and the album, *#1 Record*, which I purchased surreptitiously for a dollar from a DJ at WTOB radio, had a depth that revealed itself over the hundreds of spins we all gave the disk in those years. The second release, *Radio City*, which seems to have gone directly to the cutout sale bins at the local Kmart, was even more compelling, with the exciting "September Gurls" next to experiments such as "She's a Mover" and "Morpha Too." But now I wasn't paying that much attention to them. My college listening centered more on the density of George Crumb's *Black Angels*, the minimalists Steve Reich and Terry Riley, and Lou Reed's palette-cleansing *Metal Machine Music* with its endlessly looping lock groove on the vinyl double album's side 4. But in the lyrics for "Condition Red," I did steal a line from the Memphis crew . . . not from one of their songs, but from one of the secret messages scratched into the inner-groove serial-number area of the vinyl. No, not PRUDENCE or CHASTITY (other cryptic messages appearing there; those turned out to be the names of cats belonging to Chris Bell, one of Big Star's guitarists), but the kind of slogan a young college student could fully savor: THE MORE YOU LEARN, THE LESS YOU KNOW. The choruses of "Condition Red" are kind of silly, but I still like the song's three verse couplets:

> *Put on a new face,*
> *let's go for a walk on the mainstream boulevard*
> *Girl, with your chemical eyes, you can look so hard . . .*

> *Sound of the city,*
> *the feeling you get in your bones, it's always new*
> *Everything you see reflecting your point of view*

> *Throw out the textbook,*
> *the more you learn the less you know, I think it's so*
> *Condition red, let it go to your head so slo-o-ow-ly*

Don balanced and mixed the four tracks, added some reverb, and then sent the master tape directly to United in Nashville

Sneakers record-cover picture; photo by Buzz Spector

(no custom New York mastering for us). After the pressed disks arrived, they went into hand-addressed manila envelopes and then out into the world, inside a picture sleeve with high-contrast B&W photos, shot for free by "Buzz," a nice guy who worked at the local bread shop. His photos made us look like squinting, gawky, slightly dangerous renegades, almost as tough as we had hoped to be but much, much tougher than we were. The photos probably did as much as the music to propel that release. (I lost touch with the photographer for decades, until 2007, when I was asked to contribute to the soundtrack of *The Rise and Fall of Books*, Jake Gorst's film about an acclaimed professor of photography at Cornell—lo and behold, it was the same Buzz Spector, now a major figure in the field.)

Of course, Sneakers had to follow suit and put their own inner-groove message on the EP. I think it was fashion-conscious

Will Rigby who gave us "UP WITH DRESSES" on the A-side and "DOWN WITH PANTS" on the B.

————

For the Sneakers EP, a few new, rebellious rock music magazines in New York and California made all the difference. These publications went out of their way to encourage and give favorable—often hyperbolic—reviews to these poorly distributed new indie records. Detroit's *Creem* had probably started this, and Greg Shaw's *Bomp!* (originally *Who Put the Bomp*), the Anglophile *Trouser Press*, and then *New York Rocker* followed suit. Some of the record stores imported the UK music papers *Melody Maker* and *New Musical Express*, and they, too, might kindly review a self-released record that came in the post. It was all about mail order. There were only five or six retail stores that even had those tiny dividers at the back of bins to make a space for the five or six independent releases they might carry, Bleecker Bob's in Greenwich Village being a notable example. There wasn't a name for this microgenre—"punk" and (heaven forbid) "New Wave" were not yet commercial tags; perhaps the record-store dividers read US INDEPENDENTS, which sounded good to us. The new mags might slam an expensively produced commercial release with a big promotional budget and then, in the next paragraph, heap praise on a basement recording that sounded like it was coming over the telephone but that in some way was deemed to show promise. And then they would print the mail-order address and the price. In many ways, the Sneakers record was much less ambitious than were the rather experimental recordings Mitch Easter and I had created, one instrument at a time, in basements and living rooms; it was mostly a live performance by players who had little session experience and had spent the day hauling gear from one location to another before finally getting to play music. Tempi fluctuated a bit, and there were some flubbed notes and flat singing. But somehow it clicked, and there we were with a toehold on the national scene—though still unable to draw flies in our hometown. The Sneakers record arrived at just the right time to get rave reviews; it had its merits, and there was an undeniable core enthusiasm in the grooves, but it got a huge boost from having little competition. I think, in fact, it helped open the door a little wider for the indie revolution that was to spread so far and so fast in the years to come.

After some of these reviews swelled our heads, in June 1976 I borrowed the family station wagon and headed north once again. Walking in unannounced to Max's Kansas City, at Eighteenth and Park, I buttonholed manager Mickey Ruskin and got a booking—Sunday, Sept. 12—for Sneakers at the club, which seemed cooler than cool to our set because of its reputation both as a hangout for Andy Warhol's demimonde and as the site of a 1972 live recording of Lou Reed's last appearance with the Velvet Underground. It was incredibly exciting to be booked there, so much so that, upon leaving, I drove the old Buick up Broadway for several blocks, chattering away, before I noticed the police sirens and I realized that Broadway . . . only went down.

6 Pavement Slapping My Feet

When I walk down the street,   pave-ment slap-ping my feet

sun feels like the way_____   I think of you__

WHEN I FINALLY MOVED FROM CHAPEL HILL TO MAN-
hattan, in the early days of 1977, I felt like I was running away to join the circus. As it turned out, the only
job opening was for the Guy Who Gets Shot Out of the Cannon.
Everything seemed to be happening at once.

This was the dawn of the pop-music auteur era, as the sun
finally began to set on a period when the corporate-sponsored,
producer-dictated, formulaic, clichéd, mostly monosyllabic rock
and pop music of the seventies—which often seemed to be made
both for and by party-goers sedated by combinations of IQ-
lowering Quaaludes and liquor—had reached a societal satura-
tion point. It had taken a while to tame the explosive, genie-like

energy once exemplified by Elvis, Hendrix, and Dylan, to codify it and put it back in the bottle, but by the early seventies, once the increased income streams made it worth the effort, corporate powers had found a way to market a leashed version of that initial fury, and the most successful rock musicians often seemed complicit. Watching the leather-pants-clad stars in the cavernous civic centers with their fog machines, flash pots, and theatrical blood was fun for a while, but once you returned home from the arena to the privacy of your turntable, and heard the empty boasts and sloganeering, it was harder to accept their pomposity. And for many musicians, it was hard to imagine ever wearing those kinds of tights.

A few new New York bands had turned their backs on all that and were trying to write their own rulebooks, in the margins, on the edges of town. They often had only a limited musical vocabulary, but it was their own. And others outside the world of rock were doing so, too: Philip Glass, Laurie Anderson, Meredith Monk, and Anthony Braxton were all taking stands apart from the established order, making it up as they went along. All that, then, drew me toward the city. And as much as I had loved my time in Chapel Hill, it was a too-safe haven. I had spent almost four years there studying rules—of music theory and composition, recording, guitar playing, songwriting, living—and now, at age twenty-two, I figured that was enough; it was time I tried to break some.

On an earlier trip, I had met jolly impresario Terry Ork, and his Ork Records was the coolest game in town. The label had flung out the Television single, which was infiltrating the musical landscape everywhere it was spun—so strange, so cool, so cryptic, so trebly. Terry now announced he wanted to sign me to his label, and in that first month, he also talked me into temporarily joining the Erasers, a tentative "baby band" with a great name borrowed from Robbe-Grillet. Terry also had me playing guitar briefly with Lester Bangs, the outspoken rock critic from *Creem* magazine, which we had all read avidly in high school. I was also close to Jim Green, Dave Schulps, and Ira Robbins

Charles Ball and Terry Ork; photo by GODLIS

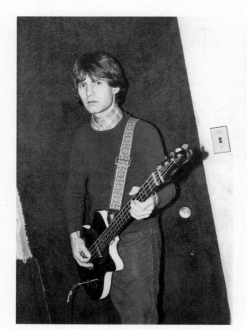

Original single sleeve for "The Summer Sun"; photo and design by Julia Gorton

Chris at a Chilton rehearsal, March 1977; photo by Julia Gorton

at *Trouser Press*, which had reviewed Sneakers. I ended up renting a bedroom from Jim and his mom, in the back of a spacious, elegant apartment in Alwyn Court, 180 West Fifty-Eighth Street, around the corner from Central Park. Hanging out with those folks meant there was always some new record release or art opening to scurry off to. And then a song to write, late the same night.

Right away, Terry asked me to help him put together a rhythm section for Alex Chilton, who was releasing an EP on Ork. Although Chilton was still best known for his low, bluesy singing on "The Letter" (the huge 1966 hit by the Box Tops), I had loved his involvement in those first two Big Star records and then marveled and puzzled over every inch of my bootleg cassette of the band's then-unreleased *Third* album. It was easy to say yes, though my huge grin made it hard to speak at all.

Alex called a few days later, from "Meh-fis," and interrogated me; when he said he often preferred a woman on bass, I suggested he ask Tina Weymouth, part of a new trio called Talking Heads, which was starting to get some ink at the time. But he liked the astrological implications of my birth date and decided to give me the gig. I enlisted the only good drummer I knew of in town, a Jersey guy named Lloyd Fonoroff, who played in a Fairport Convention cover band my housemates knew of. And Alex's brief promo visit turned into a magic year of playing and hanging out and recording together.

Chilton had already turned away from the big crowds, leaving the Box Tops' sixties teen idoldom to live in Greenwich Village in the early seventies; meeting Roger McGuinn, Lou Reed, and Loudon Wainwright there; and then returning to Memphis to make, with the other members of Big Star, two records of the confessional folk- and Beatles-influenced music that, although often sounding like radio music from the sixties, was 180 degrees from the boisterous seventies hit parade. My friends and I, playing in garages nearby in Winston-Salem and making our own tentative steps toward writing and recording songs, had been cheered to find this music was coming from our very own South;

otherwise, it was all Allman Brothers and Marshall Tucker jams where we lived, leading us to turn our ears primarily toward England for what we considered smarter stuff. Ardent, Memphis's aptly named state-of-the-art label and studio, was an ideal breeding ground for young, would-be auteurs: The studio's visionary owner, John Fry, invited the band members—Chilton, Chris Bell, Andy Hummel, and Jody Stephens—to show up for private early morning classes at the studio, no matter how hungover, so they could learn how to run the refrigerator-size analog tape recorders and transistor outboard gear for themselves. When they completed his "course," Fry gave his inmates keys to the asylum—in this case, literal keys to his world-class recording complex.

Faced with minimal sales and the continuing dumbing-down of rock, Big Star had slowly condensed down to two remaining members, Alex and Jody Stephens. By 1975, finding themselves without a record distributor and thus unconstrained by any real hopes for commercial impact, Alex and Jody (together with Alex's girlfriend, Lesa Aldridge, on "Downs") wrote the sprawling, muse-inspired third record, heavily influenced by Reed's Velvet Underground recordings; along the way, the group's new producer, Jim Dickinson, showed Alex his guidelines for smashing every rule in sight. With Carl Marsh's inventive, precise chamber-music arrangements added in among noise clusters and feedback, the trio achieved a new level of text painting, where the sound of the tracks matched the lyrical intent as closely as possible, even at the expense of traditional production values. As the *Guardian* later opined: "*Third* is an album of soft moonlight and deep black holes. . . . It's an album that sounds as if it was being demolished even as it was being recorded, where a heart-stoppingly beautiful melody might at any moment be washed away by a scree of white noise." This courageousness was promptly rewarded with a new level of major-label rejection for the band. *Third* (as it became known), although now regarded as a landmark, desert-island disk, was widely deemed unreleasable, even unlistenable in some quarters, upon completion.

Alex Chilton, just arrived in New York City in 1977, at Terry Ork's loft; photo by Julia Gorton

Arriving in New York two years later, Chilton was both dejected by the recent collapse of his fiery romance with muse Aldridge and invigorated by a new start in the big town, where the bohemian, "downtown" impulses on parade resonated with his own upbringing in a Memphis household filled with painters, jazz musicians, and free-thinkers of every stripe. He had a depth of knowledge far beyond most of the scenesters but was still sympathetic to inspired amateurs and wide open to new possibilities. I watched his every move, hung on every sardonic phrase and every high, trebly note, as we played the circuit together that year and he slowly found his footing in the scene.

Several recent books and articles have painted the time Alex and I spent playing together in Manhattan as his "lost weekend," filled with nonstop drinking, carousing, and depression. I recall things differently, but I could see that it was not an entirely happy time for him. And perhaps he had good reason for that. Charles Ball, Ork's partner in the label, represented him for management, but Charles had never done anything like that before and was unable to do much for Alex's career; he, like Terry, came from the world of film, not music.

Chilton and Aldridge finally broke up for good after she visited during the citywide power blackout in July 1977, leading him to sadly insist to me that "there is no such thing as [true] love" as we listened over and over to Zombies' singer Colin Blunstone sing "I Don't Believe in Miracles."⁵ But there were great times as well that year. It felt like a new start for both of us, like the clouds were lifting. Later, after having read some of those dark histories about this time in Alex's life, I was starting to think I was viewing my memories through the proverbial rose-colored glasses when I stumbled on a rehearsal tape that confirmed the upbeat attitude I remembered. It came from a time after our first gig—with almost no rehearsal—at the

Chris, Lloyd Fonoroff (drums), and Alex Chilton, in rehearsal; photo by Ebet Roberts

Lower Manhattan Ocean Club, the record of which (on Norton Records) is, sadly, the only commercially available evidence of a band that improved greatly thereafter. The later rehearsal tape I came across in 2015, however, reveals three players thoroughly enjoying running through not only Big Star material but also outliers such as "Neon Rainbow," by the Box Tops ("My mother's favorite song," Alex says); "You Like Me Too Much" (a George Harrison Beatles song); the very difficult "And Your Bird Can Sing" (also Beatles); and Alex's unreleased "Windows Hotel" and "She Might Look My Way"—as well as swapping lots of carefree chatter about songs we loved and displaying a general optimism about what was to come. We thought we were about to take the world by storm, as evidenced in Alex's new song that declared our vision of ourselves: "Shakin' the World (from 34th and Lex)." I found an innocent and somehow charming dialogue about stagecraft on the cassette as well. Here's a sample. We are discussing how to approach the upcoming first gig at CBGB:

CHRIS (HESITANTLY): Oh, one thing I was thinking about was maybe not having [Big Star classic] "September Gurls" second, because of the capo [change and retuning] . . . maybe having three songs we could go fast on.

ALEX (IN A SLOW DRAWL): Yeah . . . [but] we might need a break there for crowd control, you know? Really, I believe . . . I *believe* that we are gonna start causing hysteria."

LLOYD FONOROFF (RAPID-FIRE): Yeah, I do, too, with all this hype . . .

CHRIS (INTERRUPTING WITH A WARNING): The thing is, Alex . . . at CBGB's, there are going to be a bunch of journalists who aren't going to jump up for anybody . . . at the front row.

ALEX (CONFIDENTLY): [Even senior journalist Robert] Christgau jumps up . . . I've *always* made journalists jump up, they're easy! . . . Really, if we could . . . book *Shea Stadium* right now, we'd *pack* it!

LLOYD: Really? With these kind of reviews? . . . [then sin-
cerely and unironically agreeing, summing up] You might
be the next *Springsteen*, the way things are going.

————

Alex was not my only mentor in those first months. Before
moving to town, I had corresponded with a writer named Alan
Betrock, and we soon became neighbors in a new apartment
building, at 89 Bleecker Street, between Mercer and Broadway.
An authority on early sixties girl groups, such as the Shangri-
Las, Alan also was the editor and instigator of the influential *New
York Rocker* magazine; under his steady hand, this publication
tried to be the "paper of record" for the new music (in contrast
to the cartoonish *Punk* magazine, also on the newsstands). He
had a keen ear—he had picked Blondie out of the club rabble,
even recording (and later getting me to mix) "Heart of Glass"
in a demo years before it became their worldwide smash. Alan
often stood at some remove from the bedlam in the scene his
magazine covered; he had a sage, historical perspective that most
other rock writers lacked. I would take the elevator up two flights
to his apartment, filled with movie posters and artifacts, and
listen carefully as he played me the latest of the ever-widening
stream of eccentric, self-released promo vinyl that arrived daily
for *New York Rocker* to review, as he smoked clove cigarettes one
after another. Terry Ork could sense what was exciting about
a live performance, but Alan always looked for musicality and
melody underneath it.

Every visit to Alan's would include a show-and-tell of obscure
B-sides and Phil Spector trivia. Spector, who was the greatest of
the early girl-group producers and who also worked on several
Beatles-related projects, is considered to be a California guy, but
his career had started when he left Los Angeles after high school
and attached himself to the coattails of New York producers
Jerry Leiber and Mike Stoller. Spector got his break when he
cowrote and then produced, in just an hour or so, the extraordi-
narily evocative hit "Spanish Harlem" for the Drifters, the first

record of his to feature the "boom, bah-boom" *baion* rhythm that he was later to elevate to Wagnerian heights. I had known little about Spector before moving to New York, but Betrock was a world-class authority. The whole mystique of Spector's traveling to the city and making his mark there filled my imagination, and I think this was when I began to dream concretely of becoming a *producer*—music's equivalent of a film director.

Alan played me the Rosie and the Originals song from which John Lennon (an avowed fan of the band) had lifted the "Imagine" piano riff. Another time, he pulled out a reel of master tape in the very rare three-track format: It was an unreleased, unmixed Phil Spector master he had somehow acquired, and we looked in vain for a studio to mix it in; no one still had a machine of that sort. It was with Alan's aesthetic in mind that I wrote a new song called "The Summer Sun," a Shadow Morton kind of thing, for sure, a quick scribble and scratch on the back of an envelope. It was turning summer in New York, and all we did was walk in that town, having no money for anything else most days. "Pavement slapping my feet" indeed—the city seemed to be rising up to meet me.

———————

Chilton also heard the girl-group aspect of "The Summer Sun" when I played it for him, but he had done hundreds of shows opening for the Beach Boys, singing "The Letter," "Cry Like a Baby," "Neon Rainbow," and a string of other Box Tops hits, and had even lived at drummer Dennis Wilson's house for a while, with cult-leader Charles Manson in the household as well. (Alex had said later that if he ever wrote an autobiography, it would be called *I Slept with Charles Manson*, as he had awakened one morning at Dennis's to find Manson snoozing alongside him.) Indeed, Brian Wilson had been calling him recently, imploring him to drop everything and fly to Las Vegas to sing lead on an arrangement the eccentric Wilson had elaborately created of the old nursery song "Shortnin' Bread"; we both shook our heads at this. And so Alex found the Beach Boys side of the song when he produced it for Ork Records early that year, up at Trod Nossel Studios in Wallingford, Connecticut, where Ork had a production deal. The two of us played all the instruments and sang all the parts, with Alex turning compressor knobs until they cried for mercy and commanding that we "sing like hounds" on the backup "ah-oop" vocals.

He arranged the tune on the spot so that every instrument had a purpose, his drumming hitting only the crucial beats, his concise guitar solo a marvel of economy in the parallel-thirds style of the aforementioned "And Your Bird Can Sing" (the tune that was also the template for the slashing-quarters rhythm-guitar groove of his own classic "September Gurls"). I just stood back and watched, trying to absorb as much as I could.

———

It was a time when lines were being drawn in pop music culture, and I think this was on my mind. The jets' exhaust trails were chalk marks scratched across the sky, daring us to cross them; the Bleecker Street sidewalk at my front door split funky downtown Soho and Tribeca from the elegant uptown chauffeur scenes and then dead-ended into CBGB; the day was something you endured until the nighttime came alive. I was reading about Zen Buddhism and loved the idea of koans, of having a couplet that didn't make literal sense but could make another kind of sense, which (I'm somewhat chagrined to admit) is probably why the Eiffel Tower (instead of London Bridge) is falling down in the song. But it's mostly a song of hope, the hope I felt then, that there is the "warmth of the sun" there to be found, even if "some are always cold."

Alex and I were both tickled pink with this studio work and also with the flip side, "Where the Fun Is," an older song that I had conceived as a Left Banke–type harpsichordy tune until Alex filled it with guitar feedback and abstract ARP synthesizer wiggles and squiggles. It was here that he showed me how to achieve fluid orchestration-like effects by adding texture and color via overdubs without even listening to the other instruments, a method similar to William Burroughs's cut-up techniques for generating poetry, giving kismet a way to contribute. I was to use what I named *wild synch* a lot over the years as a way to "let God into the room" during sessions that felt too regimented; I don't know whether it is simply Ouija-board thinking, but it seems to work more often than not. And it is hard to forget Alex's ideal scenario for synthesizer overdubs: "Chain a chimpanzee to the keyboard and put peanut butter on the knobs," he prescribed (not that our limited budget had either zoological or cleaning allotments). Jackson Pollock, John Cage, and others had trod aleatoric waters before; these were not new ideas, but they were new to this situation. As an assistant to Dixon, I had already learned some of the right ways to do things (not that Don wasn't highly creative as well); with Alex, I was learning how right it could sometimes be to do it wrong.

In fact, "Where the Fun Is" may have been our favorite of the two productions. But "The Summer Sun" was a defining moment, for him as a producer and for me as . . . I wasn't sure what. "If I'm lost, I've won" was the motto then. I was only six months into New York, and the pavement stretched out ahead like a yellow-stained brick road.

7 Eyes Submerge Your Face

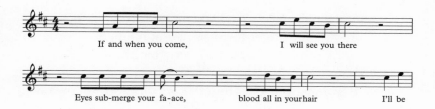

If and when you come,   I will see you there

Eyes sub-merge your fa-ace,   blood all in your hair   I'll be

BY MID-1978 I HAD BEEN IN NEW YORK FOR OVER A year, perhaps the longest year of my young life. And once again, everything was changing. For one thing, despite many memorable adventures together, the group with Alex had failed to find a solid foothold. He had returned to Memphis early that year to record *Like Flies on Sherbert* in the new, adventurous style he had found on Manhattan stages. For another, I'd now started a new band, the dB's, that was up for trying anything.

There was a pretend band name even before there was a band, though: "Chris Stamey and the dB's," a bit of a joke, implying "and the drums and bass," that superfluous apostrophe suggesting a dash of "Booker T. and the MG's" as well. It was a shingle

Richard Lloyd; photo by GODLIS

Television's Richard Lloyd and I had hung out for a one-off collaborative single called "(I Thought) You Wanted to Know." (The abbreviation denotes deciBels, a unit of loudness equal to a tenth of a Bel, and also references something Alan Betrock had written about me in *New York Rocker*.)

With Alex gone, I was left to find a way forward on my own. Lloyd was a man on the scene in those days, outgoing and ambassadorial in a way that would later remind me of R.E.M.'s Peter Buck. In contrast to his bandmate Tom Verlaine, who was viewed by the public as being cloaked in an inscrutable reclusiveness (perhaps parallel to R.E.M.'s man of mystery, Michael Stipe), Lloyd was approachable and forthright. I believe making the single was originally his idea, but it probably came from some late-night bar conversation we had. Although we were not then close, I had met Richard previously through Terry Ork and Charles Ball. Please remember: Despite its escalating national press coverage, this scene was really tiny. There might have been two or three hundred band members, photographers, and regular club-goers involved by 1977. We would all run in to one another regularly, at gigs, at art openings, and especially walking, since most of us were pedestrians. One time stands out, however, like a souvenir from a dream.

In the small hours of one night in January 1977, at a party held at the apartment of Ball's girlfriend, Joanna, Richard arrives with a square, flat package under his arm. Probably everyone in the room has heard Television play in the bars many nights, and we know almost all the songs in their shifting live iterations, but none of us other than Ork has heard anything of the versions they have been recording for Elektra/ Warner Bros. up at the funky little A&R Recording near Manny's— and Ork has been noncommittal about the album's direction. The band had originally wanted it to be produced by Rudy Van Gelder, he of A Love Supreme *and other classic jazz small-combo releases. They had compromised with the label's wishes, however, and instead selected as a producer a credentialed rock recording engineer, Andy Johns, who had worked with Led Zeppelin and the Rolling Stones and whose older brother, Glyn, was the first-call recording engineer and producer in England. Johns ended up walking out on the project after the first week and splitting for California. Unfazed, Television had continued the rest of the month, without even telling the label that they lacked a producer, and then had coaxed Johns back to mix once they were done overdubbing.*

A shadowed Lloyd bends to put the lacquer test disk on the turntable at the candle-lit party. The needle drops, and we all hear Marquee Moon *for the first time. It is heavenly, transporting; and the unexpected thing is that it sounds like the band we know, sans any studio pomp and makeup. It isn't fake or pumped up with studio effects. It is as familiarly alien and evocative as a good set at CBGB. Somehow they have managed to get through the major label trenches with that wonky, unique sound intact. The vibe in the room that night is that of "home team makes good," and this lasts for most of that first side, heads bobbing along, until we hit the long, reggae-like dream of the title song, which obliterates all our preconceptions and blows our minds.*

The next year, 1978, when Lloyd suggested that he and I record a song of his for my little shoebox record label, Car Records, I leapt at the chance, even though his contract with Elektra ruled out his doing live promotion of it. I liked him a lot. He had a quick wit and an earnest, inquisitive manner, and he seemed dedicated to constantly improving his playing. He had enjoyed some rock stardom following that candle-lit party in 1977, touring Europe and America, though (unbeknownst to me) he had also started the heroin habit that would almost kill him several years later. He wasn't allowed much creative input into the composition of the Television songs, and he had written that tune I liked a lot, the aforementioned "(I Thought) You Wanted to Know," in the hospital while recovering from an early overdose. I was bussing tables at Spring Street Bar in Soho to support myself, and I was willing to add extra shifts to raise the several hundred dollars it would cost for studio time at Bob Blank's up-and-coming Blank Tapes, in Chelsea. This was to be my first deluxe production for my own label: a solo single by Richard Lloyd.

The two of us recorded the song track by track, just as Easter and I had done years before at our basement studio in North Carolina, with Lloyd on all the guitars and initially drums (later replaced by the Marbles' David Bowler); besides contributing some of the engineering, I covered the bass and piano parts—and suddenly the lead vocals, too, because Elektra's legal department now also vetoed Richard in this role. (He had originally told me that *he* would be singing, which had been part of the attraction for me.) To get around the lawyers, Richard used several aliases on the final release, including Marvin Gardens, from *Monopoly*, and the evocative Clyde McFettered. Even though it was not my first choice to have my own next record as an artist feature a song that I hadn't written myself, there was no question of simply letting it drop; I had spent probably $400 at that point! That was a fortune to me in those days. And it came out great, electric guitars alternately swirling and droning, with a punchy, somewhat Stonesy rhythm part and a lead theme that made a meal out of a simple major scale. The questing lyric was decorated with surprise Jeff Beck–like dive-bombing in the middle;

overcompressed low piano octaves, like those of Jimi Hendrix's "Crosstown Traffic"; a vibraslap; and one of Lloyd's trademark ascending-to-the-heavens Stratocaster melodies to close it out. Though it was certainly over the top in places, the fun we had creating it shone through.

As Richard couldn't legally promote it as a solo release under his name, we now decided that it would be a "Chris Stamey and the dB's" single, which left me stuck for a band. But in records begin responsibilities (to paraphrase Delmore Schwartz), and my favorite players from my high school days, drummer Will Rigby and Gene Holder (on bass, although he was then a more adroit guitarist than I), heeded my call and joined me in New York to flesh out those initials for some promotional live shows. The band thus went from "pretend" to "almost there."

The new trio of Will, Gene, and myself gathered in a rehearsal space in the Westbeth arts complex at 55 Bethune Street, near the Hudson, where we laid down our first recording: the single's rough-hewn B-side, "If and When," captured on my old TEAC.

The original trio lineup of the dB's (left to right: Gene Holder, Chris, Will Rigby); photo by Myra Holder

(At the same session, we also tracked "We Should Be in Bed," later compiled on *Ride the Wild TomTom*, as a backup choice.) And they stayed on to play a "few promo shows" with me that June. In the same way as a single publicity gig with Chilton turned into over a year of playing, the promo shows with Gene and Will turned into a Tar Heel collaboration, a band.

It was a busy summer. Television's second album, *Adventure*, was released by Elektra in April 1978, and the band played a fiery three-night stand July 29–31 at the Bottom Line, a venerable seated concert venue in the NYU complex. They had toured Europe to acclaim, and at the two nights I attended, the group had never displayed more confidence or ensemble precision. I was surprised, then, when a few weeks later Richard called me from Big Apple Studios, where he was producing the Erasers, and told me that he and Tom had amicably decided to break up the band. So an era ended.

Around Labor Day, Alex drifted back to town for a brief stay, and Will and I backed him up for a few shows at Max's Kansas City. But then he was back to Memphis, to (Sam) Phillips Recording, where he was still at work on the *Like Flies on Sherbert* record, cutting some of the material he and I had played together the previous year, although many cool tunes from that time, including "(I Get a) Contact High (with You, Baby)," "Executive Suite," and "C-A-T Spells Cat," were never heard from again.

The trio version of the dB's was augmented midfall by the multitalented Peter Holsapple, who had been unhappily ensconced in Memphis since May, on the periphery of the Chilton crew, working with engineer/drummer Richard Rosebrough. We had intermittently received word on Peter's progress there, and Will had been keeping him abreast of what we were up to. In September, Alex himself had dropped by during one of Peter's sessions at Phillips, and the two, with Rosebrough, had cut Chilton's "Tennis Bum"; Chilton somewhat shockingly detuned Peter's bass guitar slightly as tape was rolling, saying afterward, "Tuning is such a decadent European concept," which quickly became an ironic catchphrase for us all (especially useful on

Peter Holsapple with the white Strat in a promo for the release of his single "Big Black Truck"; photo by Judy Schiller. Front and back of "Big Black Truck" single; author archives

hot club stages where guitars would often not hold pitch for the length of a single song). Peter's prep-school friend Benmont Tench happened to be in Memphis that day and stopped by that session to say hello and soak in the scene. The next evening, Peter watched Ben play a gig with his new up-and-coming band, Tom Petty and the Heartbreakers. And the very next morning, he left Tennessee detuning behind and traveled north to answer our summons. The dB's became a quartet, and that became the combination that achieved critical mass.

———

Peter originally signed on as just the dB's' organ player, giving us a lineup reminiscent of the one that Question Mark and the Mysterians used for "96 Tears." (A Holsapple solo single for Car

Records, the very cool rockabilly track "Big Black Truck" backed with "96 Second Blowout" and "Death Garage," had already been in the works and was released that fall. The A-side had been initially cut with Alex in Connecticut back in 1977, although he wasn't credited on the release for legal reasons, and it was finished without him.) We liked the variety of sounds that Elvis Costello's new band, the Attractions, was getting out of that combination, and we had also seen Chilton's songs bloom live once organist/pianist/singer Fran Kowalski made Chilton's Kossacks (the name Alex later used for our band together) a quartet in the spring of 1977. The "organ combo" sound was being celebrated then, as well, by the club dance and party smash "Rock Lobster," the first single by a band from Athens, Georgia, called (with yet another superfluous apostrophe) the B-52's, a group that seemed to play the Mudd Club every month or so in 1978. Their fast-paced, infectious tune, an example of what would have been called a novelty record back in the fifties, framed absurdist recitatives of aquatic scenarios with Farfisa organ lines, surf guitar figures, Theremin-like vocalese reminiscent of Yoko Ono, and . . . no bass guitar at all. It was a very clever record, especially striking because it seemed devoid of that sense of desperation and angst so intrinsic to the underground at that time. Instead, it was simply an invitation to propulsive fun, an invitation that was accepted by my girlfriend Jamie Sims's NYC dance troupe, the Cosmopolitans, who started performing in clubs with several songs in that same Farfisa-and-surf style. (Their "[How to Keep Your] Husband Happy" b/w "Wild Moose Party" was to garner significant airplay in Manhattan by 1980.)

But Peter's days as merely an "organist sideman" were brief. I was reminded at the time of the ironic and hilarious press release from back when Crosby, Stills, and Nash added their *Y*, something like, "We needed a nonsinging, nonsongwriting sideman . . . *so we got Neil Young.*" Like Neil Young's in CSN, Peter's own songs were too strong to keep him long confined to that organ chair, as was his superb guitar playing. He also had a strong, pleading, expressive voice and a high range, which immediately helped offset my quieter, more folky style of singing, partly the product of an asthmatic childhood. So the molecules shifted, and we all found a new chemistry together as a band with two solid songwriters in a town where (apart perhaps from Broadway) songwriting was not highly valued on its own.

I had known Holsapple the longest of the three other band members. We were in the same schools, although both he and Rigby were a year behind Holder and myself. Peter and I had played blues together in Soup, trying to find a way into that deep music, and he had exposed me then to a lot of great records, including those of the Beach Boys and Peter Green's early, bluesy incarnation of the seventies pop band Fleetwood Mac. In the course of living-room conversations about those rich thirteenth and half-diminished harmonies typical of Brian Wilson and, earlier, the Four Freshmen, I had discovered that he also was a talented (albeit self-taught) keyboardist, perhaps partly through the influence of his brother, Curtis, a classically trained pianist and organist, and I had made it a point to proclaim his talents to the other players I knew. Peter remembers his nervousness when, in order to make such introductions, I had brought him along to a combo rendezvous at a Burger Chef one Winston afternoon around 1969. Guitarists were found on every corner then, and there was a lot of snobbery and one-upmanship there; players would turn away from the stage during the tricky bits so that the others couldn't watch their fingers and figure out their hard-won techniques. But a high school pianist with a great ear who could sound like both Nicky Hopkins, of British session fame, and Leon Russell, of Los Angeles's so-called Wrecking Crew, was rare indeed. Peter had entered our combo scene as an ivories-tickler, not a string-strangler.

The first time I saw Will Rigby drum in Little Diesel was with charismatic, powerhouse singer Bob Northcott singing and Peter on guitar, not keys. It might have been at a lawn party in the afternoon, with burgers on a grill, boiled peanuts as appetizers, and a pickup game of softball; there were a lot of these. The Mica-Sonic-brand kit that Will used was small, hardly pro, and he sat on an antique stool with a ball-joint pivot base, which let him swivel around erratically as he executed his painterly yet surprisingly bombastic tom fills. He was very skinny, somehow both looking and sounding like an exclamation point come to life. Will was a rhythmic stylist all his own, but his performances had the same kind of swing and joi de vivre that Easter and I loved in Bev Bevan's tracks for the Move. It was a combination of professional technique and first-time fervor, as if to say, "Hey, guys, look: I just got a drum kit for my birthday!" He played like it was fun, like it was "play." As I recall, some of the older players in town didn't quite get Rigby's swinging style and fluid tempi, but I thought from the first that he had a distinctive touch with a sharp intelligence behind it. No one else sounded like Will.

Gene Holder and I had been in the same grade level, but he had moved to town in high school. He and I had met in typing class during tenth grade. I recall thinking him to be a somewhat intimidating figure at first, with a motorcycle and matching jacket, as he would regularly bum typing paper from me. He was a bassist as well, though, and soon we had become friends. I quickly discovered the kind soul under the James Dean exterior. His home, downtown at 1308 West Fourth Street, quickly became a hangout for all of us.

Mel Holder, his Philadelphian mother, seemed to love having a full house of rockers, and we all loved her, too. Their house came to join Mitch Easter's basement at Nokomis Court as gathering places. She operated a very popular women's hair salon out of the front, and this became a "friendly nation" for styling the ever-longer locks we were all sporting. For guys in those days, having hair over your ears was a way of drawing a line in the sand, of choosing sides between cultural factions, especially in the South. Strangers would actually walk up to me, pull out knives, and say, "Cut that hair, boy, or I'll cut your throat." So finding a place where you could get a slight trim without risking a barber going rogue and carving your head into a Marine 'do was crucial.

Gene's deceptively easygoing, wisecracking demeanor had turned out to hide a razor-sharp brain and a fascination with the details of musical instrument construction as well as performance. His playing abilities grew rapidly, alongside his encyclopedic knowledge of vintage Fender and Gibson guitars. In the era before the Internet (and before George Gruhn's compendium *Gruhn's Guide to Vintage Guitars* first codified the landscape, in 1991), it was still possible to find various "eureka!" collectable instruments by tracking down rumors and watching the newspaper classifieds, and Gene excelled at that game. In short order, he had found a fellow instrument aficionado in Sam Moss, and the two of them had spent most of the seventies playing in bands together and finding hidden-treasure sunburst Les Pauls under backwoods bunk beds.

That summer of 1978, then, I found myself reunited in this strange Northern metropolis with friends who had shared a previous lifetime in small Southern towns. It was a powerful feeling. We knew each other so well that we could skip many of the first steps to any relationship and get right to the essence. There were also no places to hide, no pretenses that would work with this crew; we had already shared so many of the grand embarrassments of adolescence. Standing in rehearsal rooms and staring at one another with instruments in hand, we were thus left to wonder, *Where do we go from here?*

———

"If and When," the flip side of that first single, pre-dates Holsapple's arrival. The recording features piano, but it's Rigby who plays the ivories. Its melody ascends to a ninth on each phrase, giving the lines an open-ended, wistful quality. The concise, awkward lyric could fit on a postcard and is indeed a kind of invitation, sung instead of stamped and mailed, to my future wide-eyed girlfriend Carol Whaley, asking her to "come visit" me in the "dirt and debris" of the Bowery. At that point I still had Alex's distinctive fifties-vintage maple V-neck Stratocaster guitar with the metallic-white refinish, and its brilliant treble overdrive was augmented during the live-band take by a gnarly old pencil mic that had come with the stereo Sony tape recorder

I had first used to record bands in Winston years before. We then overdubbed the piano and vocals all at once onto the remaining single track of the TEAC four-track. I realized later that the melody was probably some kind of lift from "all the leaves are brown," the start of "California Dreamin'" by the Mamas and the Papas, which was appropriate, as this was "New York Dreaming." But there was little of the West Coast to be found in the sonic onslaught of the performance. It sounds like the room we played it in, all exposed concrete and bare lightbulbs. When I played the finished track for Richard Lloyd, he suggested that it become the single's A-side; I disagreed, thinking it to be too raw, better for the B-side. But now I find myself drawn to that rawness, that reveal. This was the honest sound of the dB's in that first incarnation, as a trio. (To my surprise, I later found that the song also works well as a quiet, fingerpicked acoustic number.)

> *If and when you come, I will see you there*
> *Eyes submerge your face, blood all in your hair . . .*
> *Walk, we'll walk the town, the dirt and the debris*
> *We won't have to think, and you won't look at me . . .*

8   Caress and Spite

Dy - na - mi - ite___   late   last   ni - ight___

Jet   face   whi - ite___   So   po - li - ite___

ON THE ONE HAND, THE NEW YORK UNDERGROUND
music that coalesced around CBGB in the late seventies shunned the pomp and technology of mainstream
rock and pop—no stacks of synthesizers, no Peter Frampton
making his guitar talk. No click tracks! But machines started
to infiltrate. Suicide, a duo based on low-tech electronics, a
Farfisa organ, and drum-machine beats, was playing the same
clubs, and many, including Chilton, loved the desperate, lonely,
nihilistic sound they had found. Brian Wilson, now considered
practically a Howard Hughes–like recluse, unveiled an album,
The Beach Boys Love You, that was often propelled by isolated
snare and kick beats instead of a full drum kit. Philip Glass was

Scott Litt at Ramport Studio (London); courtesy of Will Rigby

Cover of "Dynamite"; author archives. Boss Tone fuzz box; author archives

The dB's at Rhythm Alley in Chapel Hill, North Carolina; photo by Malcolm Riviera

dividing his time between driving a taxi and writing music that *sounded* like it was made by computer sequencers. And I had a new tune I was eager to record.

Another year had flown by. It was now the summer of 1979, and the four corners of the dB's were working together well, with regular club dates, lots of woodshedding, and a new batch of songs under our quickly tightening belts.

I had already spent a lot of time with an old modular Moog at music school in North Carolina and had no aversion to patch cables and oscillators. So when, that same year, Gary Numan used synths to create the worldwide smash "Cars," which became unavoidable at New York hangouts such as Hurrah and the Mudd Club, I was drawn to the strange, robotic sound (if not the song).[6] Now, though, I cringe to think that I was trying to do something similar with "Dynamite"—but by using live players to imitate those machines. Fortunately, we were kept on track by the ever-present, intoxicating influence of New England's NRBQ, one of our favorite bands, and Gene and Will found a teetering, but not toppling, groove. The way that NRBQ would shift between a swing feel and a rock-solid beat, keeping listeners on their toes; the way they would do just whatever they liked, whether it was the theme from *Petticoat Junction* or a Sun Ra tune, and always with an irresistible verve and superior musicianship—these qualities were highly influential to our New York scene, as they were to be later for fellow "Q" fan Ira Kaplan when he and Georgia Hubley put together Yo La Tengo. (When I could, I would later hire NRBQ's Terry Adams for my own records. Sessions with Terry would be hat-driven, à la Thelonious Monk: Terry would select just the right chapeau to fit each song before he played on it.) In fact, looking back, I think the dB's "punk roots" at that time were actually NRBQ and Richard Thompson as well as Television, and with a little of Peter's faves Kid Creole and the Coconuts—not really very solid ripped-shirt credentials. And there's a lot of NRBQ in "Dynamite." Something about the repetitive (but not computer-sequenced) Ace Tone organ chirps makes me think that Lucky Peterson's 1969 hit, "1, 2, 3, 4," might also have been a part of the equation.

There is no real narrative to the song's lyric. I had seen a newspaper report about an IRA car bombing around that time, and perhaps that was a small part of it; the catchphrase of comedian Jimmie "J. J." Walker (a drawled "dy-no-miiiiite") might have played into it, too. "Dress in stripes" came from Rigby's grooming suggestion that vertical stripes made you look thinner—not a worry that he himself had. "Caress" was a drawling spin on my first name. I don't think it will reward much further scrutiny, however. But it's a good example of writing with a *sound* in mind.

I had some ideas first, specifically for the machiney groove, the "96 Tears" *tap-tap-tap* of the Ace Tone, the verse's chords, and a few key lyrics. Peter and I quickly fleshed out these ideas right before the two of us demoed it (afterhours on desks in the *New York Rocker* magazine office). In addition to helping with several of the lyrics, he was the one, I think, who came up with the three-bar organ hook, with a high G drone that rubs first against an F♯ and then against an F♮. The sound wasn't complete without running the organ through an Orange Squeezer compressor, an obscure, dinky, lo-fi metal cube—heard previously on the guitars of both "Reeling in the Years," by Steely Dan, and "Sultans of Swing," by Dire Straits—which exaggerated the natural "vacuum cleaner" wheezing tones of the organ. (Decades later, the dB's were to record an ode to the mighty mini Orange Squeezer on the *Revolution of the Mind* EP.)

Another technique we used on that record was crescendo-decrescendo glissando harmony singing, a slow vowel-sound morphing with a bit of doppleresque pitch bend that we faded and bent into lines, sometimes turning our heads from the mic as we swooped. It had the effect of natural tape flanging (again, humans imitating machines) and was a bit reminiscent of airplanes nosediving—which became evident when I later played it for Jake Riviera in the London offices of his then red-hot indie Stiff Records (home to Elvis Costello and Nick Lowe). Jake and all his minions spontaneously spread out their arms and pretended to fly around the room. The clubs at that time often had dub reggae on the DJ menu, and the solo section comes from that influence. The clubs' sound systems usually included a Roland Space Echo tape delay, and in sections like this, the house's sound guy could twist its knobs and have a little fun with us.

Apart from "Dynamite," Peter and I rarely wrote together in the dB's; in fact, we were friends but not all that close during those chaotic, heady times. It's absurd, I know, but having been one year ahead of Will and Peter back in school, Gene and I seemed to carry that division in our social lives into our early twenties. That said, Peter would certainly help me fix a clunky line or two, as would the others, and his arrangement contributions were consistently stellar surgical strikes. For my part, always wearing the de facto producer's nosey-parker hat, I would often propose restructuring ideas for his tunes. The incident I remember most fondly was when I suggested that he could expand his miniature diamond "Big Brown Eyes" from one minute all the way up to a whopping two minutes and two seconds simply by having an extra three-line verse and more than just one chorus. I don't know whether this made it better art, but it did mean that generations of music lovers could hit the repeat button only half as often.

———

The mixing session for the studio version of "Dynamite" was one of the first times the dB's worked at Power Station studios, over on the far west side of Midtown, at 441 W. Fifty-Third Street. Tony Bongiovi, the studio owner, had been just a kid with a stereo tape recorder when, back in the sixties, he called the office of Detroit's Motown Records, home to the Jackson Five, the Supremes, Marvin Gaye, Stevie Wonder, and many other amazing talents. Bongiovi actually got the kingpin, Berry Gordy himself, on the phone and said something to the effect of, "Mr. Gordy, Sir, I have figured out how you are making those records!" After Gordy stopped laughing, which might have taken a while, he chatted with the young upstart and then, when that summer came, flew Tony from California to Detroit, where he became an intern helping to create the "sound of young America," playing tambourine for the Supremes and watching from the (dirt) ground floor as the Motown team created one perfect AM radio hit after another. Bongiovi later graduated to working for Hendrix's producer, Eddie Kramer. Having decided then to venture out on his own, he found a business partner, Bob Walters; together, they took an unused power station on the Upper West Side and, in an era of deadened, lifeless recording spaces, created a new New York studio with a unique wooden cathedral ceiling and a brilliant, focused sound. Bongiovi filled every room with newly popular vintage gear—Neve mixing consoles and stacks of twenty-four Pultec equalizers, one for each track—and was able to command top dollar for the space. I loved the place and hung out and worked there every chance I got.

The dB's had been impressed by the way the studio's head engineer, Bob Clearmountain, had mixed Tom Verlaine's first solo record, and our coproducer, Alan Betrock, had a connection there, but when we asked the studio manager for Bob, we were told that, in addition to paying for the studio time ($300 an hour?), we'd have to pay him a side fee of $200 *a song*. Well, we certainly weren't going to work with a *crook*! No way. We thought it outrageous, unheard of, to have to pay "extortion" like that. If you know much about the tech side of making records, you are laughing at us; you know that Bob, a most kindly and musical fellow, an awesome talent, and 180 degrees from a crook, soon moved into the hit-maker stratosphere with "Start Me Up" and "Miss You" by the Stones and *Avalon* by Roxy Music, as well as hits for Chic, becoming (for good reason) the "Dean of Mixers"; he is still at it, and I believe gets something like $10,000 per song these days.

So we were offered a young engineer named Scott Litt instead and told we didn't have to pay a tariff for him, because he was a bit fresher to the game. From the first, though, we knew there was *magic* in what he did. The effervescent, bouncy quick mix of "Dynamite" that he did in only two hours was the same as the one that was later released. He became not only a great friend but another great mentor for me, and he and I occasionally collaborate on projects even to this day. And in a few years, Litt, too, was no slouch, with a meteoric career since then, as both a mixer and producer for Nirvana, the Stones, R.E.M., Bob Dylan, and many others.

The mixing itself went pretty smoothly, the only hitch occurring when I innocently asked to plug a tiny guitar effect—my pocket-sized pet Boss Tone fuzz box with its two controls, "Attack" and "Volume"—into the console's patch bay, thus giving us a knob on every single channel that could selectively "fuzz out" the instruments. (Distortion, of course, was not yet generally considered a desirable attribute, to say the least; grunge, rap, and indie sounds were at least a few years away.) The call went out over the intercom for "Maaaal-*colm!*" (Malcolm Pollack, head studio tech at that time), and I remember it as if a SWAT team then descended on the room; the surgeons discussed and figured out that the precious Power Station Neve board could probably survive the Boss Tone invasion.[7]

Gene Holder and I traveled to London together that year in an effort to find label interest for this new adventure. Two years earlier, I had met a drummer named Chris Hughes (later producer of Tears for Fears' amazing smash shuffle "Everybody Wants to Rule the World," which he cowrote, and also producer of Wang Chung's similarly insistent hit "Dance Hall Days") at CBGB one night when he subbed on drums with the Kossacks. Hughes and Alex had walked in right off the plane from a London recording session at which they had covered "Can't Seem to Make You Mine," the snarling classic by LA-based sixties acid-rock band the Seeds (and, like "I Don't Believe in Miracles" earlier, another choice of Alex's that seemed to me to be related to the end of his relationship with Lesa Aldridge). On this UK trip in 1979, Gene and I now spent time with Hughes at the Putney headquarters of Electronic Music Studios (EMS), where he was on staff; the three of us laid down some nutty keys demo tracks, including a version of a future dB's song, "Espionage." EMS synths were crucial weapons in the music of the effete potentates of the "other side," the reviled post–Syd Barrett version of Pink Floyd, kings of melodramatic arena theatrics. But the keyboards were great fun, in part because they traded patch bays and cords for a plug board, using cribbage-like pins in tiny holes to control the various parameters.

Holder and I shared a bed-and-breakfast floor on that trip with iconoclastic *New Musical Express* writer Nick Kent and his then "American girlfriend," an unknown Akron, Ohio, songwriter named Chrissie Hynde, who had not yet found British allies with whom to form the Pretenders. I didn't see her again until 1986, when I visited London sessions for *Get Close*, a record she and the other Pretenders were making with coproducers Bob Clearmountain and Jimmy Iovine. She picked up a copy of *Raw Power* by Detroit's Stooges, waved it in the air, and told me adamantly that this was what it was "all about"; as if to provide contrast, keyboardist Bernie Worrell, my friend from New

York sessions and touring, was in the next room adding big, airy digital synthesizer layers to clean, mainstream (but great) rock tracks—nicely illustrating the era's struggle to find a meeting place for human and machine.

9

I Loved You, and You Did, Too

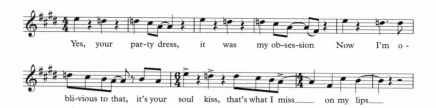

Yes, your par-ty dress, it was my ob-ses-sion Now I'm o-bli-vious to that, it's your soul kiss, that's what I miss____ on my lips____

T HE LOWER MANHATTAN MUSIC SCENE OF THE LATE SEV-
enties and early eighties sometimes seemed a tale of two
cities, two artistic impulses: one was esoteric, adventurous,
and sometimes difficult; the other, exoteric, all flailing arms out-
stretched to the lowest common denominator. There was a frequent disconnection between the former scene, toward which I
gravitated, and the latter, the only part of the scene that the magazines regularly portrayed. It was easy for the mass-market press
to describe the visuals of the sweat-filled, fisheye-lens pictures of
the Dead Boys and the Ramones at CBGB alongside visits from
British acts such as the Sex Pistols and the Damned and present
it all as merely a sociological movement of less-than-coherent

anarchists and determined primitives. (Of course, the Ramones were better songwriters than the rest of these, but their songs were still based on traditional rock chord progressions, often from the early sixties, just played faster and louder than ever before.) The outrageousness and the revolt against everything that had gone before, both in rock music and in polite society in general, made for good stories and better photo spreads in the checkout lines at grocery stores. But mass-market periodicals could not, or would not, allocate space to describe the specifics of music by Television or the sonic innovations and continuing evolution of Talking Heads; it was much simpler to dash off a few paragraphs about the Sex Pistols' spitting confrontations with audiences and record labels or Richard Hell's ripped clothes and eye-catching song titles.

There was thus a "purloined letter" aspect to the other kind of new music: It was hidden in plain sight. This blindness was understandable. It had happened earlier in history, for example when the shock tactics of a few of the Dadaists, in both France and New York, got the press and masked the more rigorous and interesting work done by other adherents. (Pere Ubu, the Cleveland, Ohio, band that was an early influence on this scene, took its name from a character in Jarry's Dada classic, the play *Ubu Roi*.) Perhaps this side of other cities, other scenes, also remained hidden to outsiders; I don't remember much of the exploratory side from the West Coast, for example, but perhaps it was there and just never made it across the country to me. One exception was Steve Wynn's ensemble the Dream Syndicate, which got going a bit later, in 1982; with Karl Precoda as lead guitarist, they aspired to the same kind of improvisatory electric-guitar performances as the Velvet Underground and Television. In fact, the band's name came from a Manhattan source: Tony Conrad's sixties just-tempered minimalist-drone ensemble, which included La Monte Young and future Velvet Underground members John Cale and Angus MacLise. And Sacramento's unabashedly intelligent Scott Miller was restlessly inquisitive, first with his 1982 band Game Theory and then with the Loud Family. In England, both the Clash and Elvis Costello and the Attractions were making consistently innovative recordings, but they were fronted by skilled songwriters, Joe Strummer and Costello (aka Declan MacManus), respectively, who had learned the craft in the pub-rock days, *before* being swept up in the late-seventies palace rebellion of punk. Their bands were putting very interesting new clothes on a body of work still based on traditional, tonal, verse-chorus-bridge styles.

All participants in the late-seventies New York scene seemed to agree, though: The old guard had become bloated, cartoonish, and widely co-opted by a search for maximum corporate profits, and we wanted none of it. Abandon ship; to the life rafts all. There was a big gap between the scarf-draped rock stars' lives and stories and our own. A basic lack of lyrical honesty prevailed in that more celebrated world, along with a musical staleness and derivativeness. We all wanted to reexamine, to question, what had become the flash-pot-lit rules of pop and rock music. Hidden behind the press summaries of the new music's sensational punk-horror scene, however, was the fact that many of the players involved had brought with them excellent skills and a sincere desire to find a new place for electric music to go. Though it was "out with the old," it was also "in with the new."

One such group coalesced around Giorgio Gomelsky, a British promoter and record producer who, in addition to producing the Yardbirds and Rod Stewart in the sixties, had worked with many of the more avant-garde European (largely British) progressive, or "prog," acts, including the Soft Machine, Gong, Henry Cow, and Magma. Flush with Yardbirds royalties in 1978, he had relocated to Manhattan and opened the Zu Club, which became headquarters for Material, an adroit foursome composed of Bill Laswell (bass), Michael Beinhorn (synthesizer), Fred Maher (drums), and Martin Bisi (audio engineer). Material's scene with Gomelsky became a magnet for many other players with great chops and open minds, including keyboardists Bernie Worrell (and later Herbie Hancock); guitarists Nicky Skopelitis, Fred Frith, and Buckethead; saxophonists Archie

Shepp and Henry Threadgill; and drummer Anton Fier. The core membership of Material had a far-reaching effect on New York music for the next decade, as the four, along with Fier, became influential producers, working successfully (and separately) with artists ranging from Iggy Pop to Whitney Houston to Miles Davis.

Another group that seemed determined to look under rocks for a new sound was called DNA. I got to know their approach well, as the dB's shared bills with them in several venues, including the fast-rising, forward-thinking Tier 3 club, just below Canal Street at West Broadway and White, and even once at Squat Theatre on Twenty-Third Street, a black-box space run by a Hungarian theater troupe of the same name. DNA frontman Arto Lindsay's parents were missionaries who by that point had landed in North Carolina (although I met him in New York). But as a youth, he and his family had spent a lot of time in Brazil, at the heyday of the Tropicália movement, where he

DNA (left to right: Arto Lindsay, Ikue Mori, and Tim Wright); photo by Laura Levine

had absorbed both that gentle, harmonically rich music and the Portuguese language.

There was nothing gentle or lilting about the sound produced by DNA, however. Their sonic onslaught featured repetitive drum and bass riffs played by Ikue Mori and Tim Wright (late of the aforementioned Pere Ubu), over which the bespectacled, bookish Arto pulled, pushed, banged, and slapped a detuned Danelectro electric twelve-string guitar and screamed/sung/spoke mostly incomprehensible lyrics, some of which might have been polylingual and some of which were alingual, just screeches and squawks. It was fascinating to watch as well as to hear. The band was extremely tight and well rehearsed, the bass lines were often quite difficult although repetitive, and the guitar phrases, reminiscent of both England's Derek Bailey and an active construction (or demolition?) site, were riveting, though they were never quite the same two times in a row. Their orginality is evident on this lineup's only release, an EP called *A Taste of DNA*.

Arto occasionally hitched a ride with me to North Carolina when he went to visit his parents, and I always greatly enjoyed his company. In 1981 he became part of John Lurie's early "punk jazz" group, the Lounge Lizards. He and I worked together on the eponymous first Golden Palominos record, on which I added piano overdubs while the tape was running backward, a specialty of mine at the time—I could somehow mentally keep track of fairly difficult chord progressions in reverse by thinking of the past as the future. (I was the first-call guy in town for this effect; unfortunately the calls were very few.) I met with Arto a few times to set some of his Portuguese lyrics and poems to my foggy notions of Brazilian guitar progressions. Together with keyboardist/composer Peter Scherer, he would later form Ambitious Lovers and make a completely different kind of music, highly tonal, with the Brazilian (and some Al Green) influence much more to the fore, a seductive rather than confrontational music, with regular chord progressions; melodies in his lilting, affective voice; and samba and bossa nova rhythms. This was quite a contrast to his first band: DNA was as sonically abrasive as (or perhaps more abrasive than) the less accomplished garage-punk bands that had begun flocking to town, but this kinship lay only on the surface; Arto's trio was trying to find the "new."

Where to begin, as far as a first "taste," you ask? Let me suggest "Blonde Redhead," a favorite of mine in the club days. It's a rhythmically smoother ride than some, and the bass also walks away from the wild(er) side by playing both a moving line and bass chords. DNA: building blocks of life. All together now: "*Waaauuueeeeaaa-aaaye* . . . I got a snake on my mind."

Not all studios in New York City in the late seventies were uptown palaces where tomorrow's hits lived. Power Station and Bearsville Sound Studios (in upstate New York, near the artists' enclave of Woodstock) were at the top of the ladder, but for most projects, I could afford only to dart in and out of them quickly. In this precomputer time, it took a sizable investment in equipment just to open your doors as a studio, whatever the location. There was cheaper real estate downtown, at least, home to several studios I sometimes used: Big Apple Studios (later Greene Street Recording), where Alex and I made the punkabilly "Bangkok" for Charles Ball's new Lust/Unlust Music company; Blue Rock Studio (where I could afford only the listed rate for sixteen tracks, even though there was only the one tape machine; making it twenty-four tracks would have involved only swapping out the other modular head block in a few minutes and at no cost to the studio—absurd and mean-spirited); and Blank Tapes, one of the better small rooms, run by Bob Blank, where I had recorded with Lloyd and where Talking Heads worked on their second record and Kid Creole and the Coconuts created their distinctive polyrhythmic hits. And there was also a new place, Zeami Studios, just south of Big Apple, at 102 Greene Street, in Soho.

Zeami had a Mellotron, a rare bird, and this was pretty much all I needed to hear before booking time there. Mellotrons are early analog-tape sampler keyboards, low-fi and with wobbly pitch—the sound of "Strawberry Fields Forever" and Big Star's "Kanga Roo." When I first started college, these devices had the music faculty up in arms, worried they were going to put real violinists out of business—which was about as likely as a windup toy monkey with a tiny snare drum putting a real drummer out of work. In fact, the Mellotron sounded nothing at all like a real string section, and in that lay its sonic glory.

The new studio had a few drawbacks. For one thing, communication was difficult; the young, all-Japanese staff was eager to please, but the language barrier was high. Most studios had a patch bay, basically a junction box with cable jacks used to string electronic devices together. But at Zeami, when I could finally make myself understood about something like a prefader send to an outboard reverb unit, they'd smile, nod, and then, before I could stop them, raise the hood of the mixing console and resolder the innards on the spot to make me happy. (On a console, if a sound is routed *prefader*, the volume fader of its track can no longer attenuate its volume. Most studios have easy ways to do this with patch cables or built-in switches.) Then, if the routing didn't sound right in the mix after all, they'd tilt open

The Mellotron at Ardent Studios; photo by Jody Stephens

the hood again, and solder fumes would again fill the air. Slow going, at best.

Zeami was where I produced a six-song demo for an energetic crew called the Fleshtones for Michael Zilkha's ZE Records, an upstart label that had signed James White and the Blacks, Suicide, and Was (Not Was) and liked music that was pushing the edge. I had earlier produced a high-concept *Discofier* record for ZE that was made from just tape loops, short strips of analog tape connected in a circle with sticky "splicing" tape so they would play endlessly; this particular recording consisted only of kick drums playing at different tempi, maybe four minutes of looping for each tempo, so that enterprising DJs could play the kick drum record on one turntable—just the *whomp whomp whomp*—and play classical or other non-dance music on the other to expand the horizons of dance at Hurrah and the Mudd Club. This was before affordable drum machines, of course. At the time, I had thought that Rachmaninoff or Stockhausen, or both at once, could work just fine on the dance floor if the added kick drum was consistent enough and loud enough—boy, does this concept sound dated now! But these were early days.

The Fleshtones featured the charismatic Peter Zaremba as lead singer and were kings of the party wherever they played, which usually seemed to be Club 57 on St. Mark's, a film-and-music venue located in a Polish church basement and designated as a "social club," and everyone loved their energy and fervor.

They were a rock 'n' roll band in an era when that was an odd thing to be; I remember Zaremba giving me a "Blind Men and the Elephant" speech over curry one night, saying that whereas Bruce Springsteen might have taken the timpani and pomposity from fifties-era Phil Spector, the Fleshtones instead took the fast tambourine and the background singing from the Spector pachyderm. I was still in my post-Chilton mode that year, where no amount of compression was ever enough, and the final mixes I did for them probably reflected that aesthetic, although I have not heard these since. (Alex later admitted that he used to be like a "kid in a candy shop" with compressors—as evidenced, e.g., in his production of "psychobilly" band the Cramps—and I had learned well from him.) The Fleshtones didn't sign to ZE with that material, but they ended up on I.R.S. Records, and Peter became the host of a variety show, *The Cutting Edge*, on MTV. The Fleshtones tour internationally to this day, still swinging from the rafters everywhere they go.

I had produced bands before, although this might have been the first time I claimed the title. Not only had I made any number of live coffeehouse recordings and, along with Mitch Easter, numerous Nokomis Court self-productions, but also, in high school, I had produced the first and only record by Will and Peter's protopunk band, Little Diesel and the Weasels. In the summer of 1974, home from college, I had pushed my bed to the side, used nails to hang my tiny tweed Fender Champ and Princeton guitar amps on the wall to gain more floor space, and squeezed Rigby's Mica-Sonic drums into the corner. The whole band played together in that ten-foot-square box, without headphones. It was awesome! I had captured it all on the TEAC, mixing the tracks in the same room, and the band members distributed it to friends it by copying it themselves, one by one, onto eight-track cartridges, a format that was then available in cars. (The record was remixed and reissued on CD and vinyl, on Telstar Records, in 2006.)

———

Working at Zeami had some difficulties, but in 1979 their Mellotron made it just the right space for tracking a fast-paced jam called "Soul Kiss," a dB's take on the sort of sixties psychedelia found in the *Nuggets* compilation. We were prepared to put up with a few solder fumes if we could get our hands on the Mellotron's pitch knob.

During the first years when I was bouncing around town at night, I was also attending college in daylight, earning a philosophy degree at New York University under, among others, William Barrett, whose *Irrational Man: A Study in Existential Philosophy* had been a landmark tome in the early sixties (and

DB1·2·3 : dB's Da Beat D Bowie

16th February, 1980 New Musical Express

THE
dB'S

black
and white

soul kiss

■ *Single Of The Week*
**THE dBs: Black And White
(Shake import).** Chris
Stamey's dBs (short for
decibels) pull another cracker
out of their ample bag. It's
almost a year since 'I Thought
You Wanted To Know,' and
that's a good ten months too
long. 'Black And White' brings
more than enough verve and
intelligence to bear on its
alloted three minutes —
creating a furious, condensed
motion in the space between
Stamey's guitar and Peter
Holsapple's vocal. The A-side
is pop that doesn't treat the
genre as something facile.
The B-side ('Soul Kiss') takes
off its jacket, gets raucous,
and forgets its limitations.
   One side is pop. The other is
adult pop. This is the sort of
thing that could make people
want to grow up to form a
group.

Chris Stamey: Manhattan says hi.

Pic: Myra Holder

New Musical Express *(London) review ("Single of the Week"); author archive*

who had been a friend of Lou Reed's teacher Delmore Schwartz
in the early days). Although I had satisfied the requirements for
a music degree at UNC–Chapel Hill, I had never completed the
swimming requirement and a few other things; however, I had
taken enough philosophy classes along the way to transfer to
NYU and graduate with a BA in philosophy. "Soul Kiss" was a
kind of reverse sexual innuendo—I knew that the term was used
for French kissing, but after having spent many collegiate hours
debating Aquinas, Socrates, Plato, et al., I was thinking more of a
connection that was soul to soul, essence to essence. I can't claim
that this is clearly presented in the lyrics, but that's the skinny.

   The song leaps out of the gate with no intro, just as "Condition Red" had done back in 1976.

> *Yes, your party dress, it was my obsession*
> *now I'm oblivious to that . . . it's your soul kiss,*
> *that's what I've got on my mind*

But the first section was in some ways just a front end to its "Part Two" (shades of "Little Johnny Jewel"), where the improvisatory Captain Speedish fun was to be had. (I'm not sure why it name-checks both Deuteronomy and Spandex in whispers there; maybe the contrast between the two was important?) Of course, it is wrapped in the language of the time. The song includes a bass riff that sounds like something our friend George Scott III might have played in the Raybeats, a wonderful, all-instrumental surf band (the dB's felt a kinship to the Raybeats, who prefigured today's Los Straitjackets). The guitar solo quotes liberally from the music that was everywhere in those years—by this I mean, *of course*, the theme from *Star Wars*. Looking back, the lyric seems a bit vague, but "I loved you, and you did, too" is not a bad line.

10 Exhilaration; or, Gorging a Neuronic Aperture

Ne- ver_ too cer- tain_ what is_ to fol- low_

Ex- hi - lar - a- tion,_ then comes the pres- sure_

HOW DO ARTISTS MANAGE THEIR JOINT COMPULSIONS TO create and to eat? We know how it worked with Mozart, under royal patronage. And Bach, under the wings of cathedrals. Universities have been our new kings and priests in recent centuries, musicians trading tutorial duties for a stipend and access to student performances of their new compositions. In North Carolina, the church coffeehouses had given us the freedom to play rock music we wrote ourselves, but there was no way to earn a living from this without going north in search of a contract with a major corporate record label, and these were few and far between.

The new New York music that coalesced in the late seventies

and early eighties, which thrived in the shadows of society and valued raw, untutored expression over technique, had little initial appeal for the labels, the modern equivalent of those patrons from an earlier era. Instead, it relied on the model of the *Benevolent Innkeeper*.

It started with Hilly Kristal's largesse, at CBGB in 1975. The club preferred bands to play music they themselves had written, but even better, they could possibly end a gig with a small bit of cash—all the door income, perhaps a few hundred instead of a couple of tens and ones. This was a pivot point: Unlike other bar owners, who would barely tolerate perhaps one or two originals during the expected regurgitation of the day's top hits, Hilly, the sole proprietor, *expected* bands to play original material. Next up in this lineage was Jim Fouratt, who booked live music into an uptown dance club called Hurrah (he then moved on to Danceteria, part of a succession of landmark New York venues he managed). Jim raised the bar by deciding to pay the local bands on the same scale as he did the English imports who were starting to pour across the water, perhaps $500 or even $1,000 for a single set, shocking amounts at the time. Soon the competition, including the Mudd Club and the Peppermint Lounge, had to follow his lead. And suddenly there was just enough money changing hands to bring managers into the act, most notably Robert (Bob) Singerman's Singermanagement.

Operating out of a loft space on the second floor of the Cable Building at 611 Broadway, Bob, too, thought that musicians deserved better pay, and the dB's, the Raybeats, Lydia Lunch's Teenage Jesus and the Jerks, the Fleshtones, and the Bush Tetras soon were under his umbrella. In contrast to the power brokers then doing business on the scene, people such as Seymour Stein, Marty Thau, and Richard Gottehrer, Bob was our age and had an upbeat, "Can't we all just get along?" style. Like us, he was also learning and making it up as he went. He soon reached out to his former college roommate, a Californian named Frank Riley, and Frank gradually took over the booking side of things.

In 1979 probably no more than twenty venues in America

were sympathetic to the new music, and in this pre-email time, Frank wrote all their phone numbers in teensy horror-vacui penmanship on a single piece of paper. Then there were thirty . . . forty-five . . . that dog-eared piece of paper became a spiderweb of ink, iconic to us but decipherable only to him. Then, one day, after a disagreement with Bob, the piece of paper and Frank were gone; he became Venture Booking, on his way to his current reign at High Road Touring in the long-running role of "coolest indie agent ever."

Bob also aligned briefly with Steve Ralbovsky, who was managing Television and clearly even then a young turk on the way up . . . Steve wasn't there long. He went from the Cable Building to CBS, A&M, Mercury, and RCA, always working within the system yet signing rebellious youth (the Strokes, the Beastie Boys) at every turn.

The loft space at 611 was shared with the New York chapter of the Association for the Advancement of Creative Musicians (AACM), which meant that forward-thinking jazz icons such as Anthony Braxton, Leroy Jenkins, George E. Lewis, and members of the Art Ensemble of Chicago (including Lester Bowie) were passing us in the lobby on a regular basis. I loved the group improvisations of the Art Ensemble in the same way others liked the Grateful Dead, and I wrangled tickets to them every time I could. The proximity to all these accomplished players was inspirational; even though the music sounded quite different from ours, their willingness to play "outside" and to search for new combinations of sound was something the dB's valued and tried to emulate, especially in live sets late at night at Tier 3 or the Squat Theater or in songs such as the proto-feminist blues "Baby Talk."

The word about the new music was spread nationally through the indie bins in independent record stores and by individual clerks there who made it a point to proselytize in behalf of underdog records they loved. But it traveled much more quickly through the work of a group of freelance New York photographers who captured the energy and attitudes visually. Ebet

Roberts (*The New York Times*), Stephanie Chernikowski (*Village Voice*), Roberta Bayley (*Punk*), Laura Levine (*New York Rocker*), Julia Gorton (Ork Records and her own *Beat It*), David Godlis (now just GODLIS), Marcia Resnick, Phil Marino, and Bob Gruen: these were a few of the photojournalists who used their cameras in those first years to document and emphasize the often striking in-your-face wildness of the players, as well as the fashions and haircuts that were evolving in the audience along with the sounds. Without their photographs, it is unlikely that much of this would have traveled far from the Bowery.

Although the eventual rush to sign punk and so-called New Wave acts to contracts with "telephone-number" (i.e., seven-digit) advances had not begun, there was still a kind of corporate support available: A&R staff had credit cards for expenses that were hardly monitored at all. Elektra Record's Karin Berg was fascinated by the new scene and regularly hosted groups of us at all-night eateries such as Phebe's, at 361 Bowery, picking up pretty big tabs. Berg had been a writer for the radical *East Village Other* weekly and for *Rolling Stone* when she met Chilton on his first sojourn in Manhattan, in 1970, and they had become close. Now she was a talent scout for corporate Warner Bros. but still maintained her edgy, adventurous taste. She was all over town, at CBGB, rival rebel bar Max's Kansas City, the Bottom Line, and the host of other clubs that sprung up seemingly overnight in those years. Soon we became friends, and for the next decade, we would meet up at regular intervals at small restaurants such as Sevilla, the classic Spanish joint on Charles Street, and Tex-Mex hotspot the Cottonwood Cafe, at Bleecker and Bank. She and I would gossip and critique the latest twists and turns of the scene, always on that corporate credit card. She was a big fan of Neil Young and, I believe, some sort of liaison between him and the label, but more famously she signed Television when no one else would, as well as several huge hit acts: Dire Straits, the performance artist and musician Laurie Anderson, Devo, and Hüsker Dü. She was additionally involved with the careers of the Cars, R.E.M., and closer to home, the very accomplished Marshall Crenshaw, who came to her attention via an EP released by my old friend Alan Betrock on his Shake label. She had paid for professional demos for Chilton and the Kossacks that first year at Todd Rundgren's studio stomping ground, Secret Sound, although in the end she didn't send these further up the corporate ladder, perhaps feeling that songs such as "She's a Little Fishy" ("swimming around my fishbowl, blowing bubbles . . .") were not Alex's best way forward into Warner Bros. She seemed to have the Midas touch, yet it was always with artists who were different from the pack in highly musical ways. Karin lived on Horatio Street in the West Village until her death, in 2006. I valued her friendship and cherished her integrity.

It was still an era of scrounging for gigs and only distantly dreaming of the validation of major-label record deals. One morning in September 1979, however, the scene did take off. The dB's and other Singermanagement acts—along with the likes of Richard Lloyd's new quartet; singer James Chance and his manager, Anya Phillips; and the Fleshtones—climbed into a rickety, highly dubious chartered plane that looked like something out of a fifties movie and flew, white-knuckled, to Minneapolis, where the Walker Art Center's Tim Carr had organized M-80, a two-day music festival in a mud-floored steel field house. It culminated in a performance by "DOVE, the Spirit of Love" (really Devo under a previous contract restriction), who wore golfing outfits and, as I recall, sang the chorus of the old folk song "Worried Man Blues" ("It takes a worried man to sing a worried song") for quite a long time, as well as a Dylan song, "Gotta Serve Somebody," rejiggered, buffet-style, as (I think) a rebellion of the food-service industry: "You gotta serve yourself." It was a bad gig for the dB's, though. We didn't yet own a single guitar tuner (new, expensive technology in those days), and the metal cavern housing the event made it too noisy to tune acoustically before we got onstage. Still, it felt like a validation of the American scene: Something was happening here. Rock festivals were a well-established phenomenon by then, but they were still associated with hippie bacchanalia; such a gathering of tribes of this rebellious outsider music gave all of us hope.

This also brought Minneapolis closer to Manhattan in the years to come. In addition to Tim Carr, Peter Jesperson and Dave Ayers (both with Twin/Tone), as well as lawyer George Regis, developed music-biz connections integral to the city's scene. We soon found ourselves playing on Manhattan stages and at backyard beer fests with Minneapolis-based musicians including Steve Almaas (from the Suicide Commandos, later the Crackers) and Danny Amis (who replaced our friend George Scott in the Raybeats after George's fatal overdose on August 5, 1980). Joining Regis on the scene as one of a new breed of sympathetic lawyers was a North Carolinian named Josh Grier, who had previously run indie label Dolphin Records there. Josh was soon sagely representing me as part of a songwriting axis that eventually included Jeff Tweedy and Wilco, Bob Mould, and Ryan Adams.

Back in New York, however, the revolution was becoming diffuse. It was not rock but disco, in the form of the insistent international hit "Heart of Glass," that elevated Blondie above the pack. Talking Heads also followed this road eventually, although coloring the disco rhythms in fascinating ways. Nowadays *Marquee Moon* is a fixture on "best of" lists, but neither it nor Television's follow-up, the also superb *Adventure*, had the hoped-for impact on the culture at large, although perhaps the inherently esoteric and personal impulse behind the music somewhat dictated that result from the start. The Ramones sallied forth on their minimalist mission and conquered some territory, but they were a straight-line rocketship and did not expand far from their initial template. Poet/provocateur Patti Smith's momentum was derailed by a fractured spine from a stage fall, although she later had some radio success with "Because the Night," a Bruce Springsteen collaboration initiated by her producer, Jimmy Iovine.

And those were the "success" stories. There was never a mass-market option for the even more esoteric and often severely minimalist explorations of the No Wave movement that followed the CBGB first wave and was documented by ZE and by Charles Ball's Lust/Unlust Records. These folks made concise statements and then moved on, their art seemingly designed to frame solitary moments instead of careers—with some exceptions: Ikue Mori and Arto Lindsay, from DNA, still have their hands in music, and rapier-witted Lydia Lunch transitioned to riveting spoken-word performances and is now also a self-empowerment counselor in California.

———

After the release of "Heart of Glass," Talking Heads were not the only members of the downtown Manhattan community to try on some of the trappings of dance music. I agree with Eric Clapton that musicians shouldn't try to dance. In any case, I'm remarkably bad at it, despite forced attendance at cotillion classes in middle school; I've been told that my signature moves resemble the animated gopher's dancing in *Caddyshack*. In terms of writing danceable songs, though, I got the part about the pounding four-to-the-bar kick drum, and as with the kick-drum disk for ZE, I then thought that you could get away with harmonic murder as long as that big beat never faltered. As realized on the dB's first album, the song "Cycles Per Second," with its lyric about manic depression, sounded like solely the manic part of the equation, although we did decorate that constant kick drum with some fancy trappings. First, we taped a great live-in-the-studio performance of the reasonably complicated song, with Peter once again playing the ever-so-strange Ace Tone organ, bending its pitch by flipping the power switch back and forth, the same way he would mimic the seagulls on our frequent live cover of the Beatles' "Tomorrow Never Knows."

Rather than have the band repeat the title at the end of the song, I made a slightly wonky tape loop of it, cutting off a sliver too much of the tape, so that the sound went off the rails in a way that matched the subject matter. But it still didn't quite convey how thoughts can spiral out of control, so we put the tape at half-speed and did overdubs in real time, making them come out twice as fast and up an octave on playback (Les Paul had pioneered this technique, which was also used to good effect for the guitars on the early KC and the Sunshine Band records). We also added layers without listening to the other tracks at all, as Alex and I had done in Connecticut for "Where the Fun Is." Once we had several tracks of this randomized aural spaghetti, we could run mixes where someone randomly pushed faders up and down, "never too certain" what was going to pop out of what we called the *party tracks* in a given mix pass. This, along with the same airplane-flange harmony singing that we'd sported on "Dynamite," added a Hanna-Barbera quality to it all. We mixed it with Scott Litt at Power Station in the room that Chic used, but somehow it never became the new "Good Times." It's a dizzy spin, though. Its propulsive, muscular drums and bass riffs hoist aloft a flanging, elongated, harmonized high melody. It's one of the tracks that I think still hold up well today—if you're in the mood for a little insanity with breakfast.

> *Never too certain what is to follow*
> *Exhilaration, then comes the pressure . . .*
> *From A to Z in cycles per second*
>
> *Talk in a riddle, several hertz*
> *Some, hypnagogic, turn for the worse*
> *Having a good time (in) cycles per second . . .*
> *—Tell me how to make it stop*

11 Just Like Yesterday

Far a-way and long a - go, I knew you when Far a-way and long a-
go, the dreams we planned Far a-way and long a-

HERE WAS A PINBALL MACHINE IN THE CORNER OF CBGB
that was farthest from the stage, and when the band playing was bad, uninteresting, or both—which, to be honest,
was not so rare an occurrence—many of us would end up there.
Of course, no other realizations ever seem quite as profound (at
the time) as those that come at the end of a long night at a bar.
But when a skilled player like Dee Dee Ramone nudged it just
the right way, making all the lights go off at once, I would see that
old pinball machine as a metaphor for what great rock records
should do: trigger some kind of instant deep-brain response,
bypassing the critical faculties, beyond analysis. Just neurons
flashing all over the place. And these were the kind of records we

The pinball machine at CBGB in action (left to right: David Johansen, Jon Tiven, Dee Dee Ramone, Andy Paley); photo by Bob Gruen

all wanted to make; we wanted the skilled hands to create more of the rare enablers of sonic euphoria. We wanted to shove the machinery. To make the lights flash off and on.

Songwriters had originally been akin to playwrights: both creating words and notation on paper that then waited to be brought to life by musicians or actors, and differently each time. At Tin Pan Alley or on Broadway, the sheet music or play script was the end product of the creator's process. Multiple performances generated from these would be separate, unique events. But shifts in technology always change art. With the advent of the motion-picture camera at the turn of the twentieth century, for example, the creative birthing no longer ended at the script. Movies were in the hands of directors, and the final success—whether or not the cerebral lights started flashing—was ultimately attributed to their efforts. In some cases, they were complete auteurs, writing the scripts and holding the cameras as well as barking the orders. It was the same with pop music: The whole process of audio recording had meshed with that of songwriting by the end of the sixties. Thanks to multitracking, imagination had found a wider, richer playing field.

The rock 'n' roll composers were, as a group, the first to think of songwriting as "writing records," where a particular snare-drum flourish, echo effect, distortion pedal, or backward vocal sound might be intrinsic to the composition—or might even inspire it. And growing up with multitrack recording enabled this auteur spirit. Songs would, to some extent, be "through-composed," the earlier tradition's repeated eight- or sixteen-bar fragments replaced by hands-on variations in the stanzas: an additional half-bar in the second verse; a surprise turnaround in the bridge; a sudden breakdown, where perhaps the drums would be muted and the rhythm guitar, now drenched in echo, would come to the fore. These shifts became part of writing the song-as-record. Though the chord progressions and melodies might be getting simpler, the arrangements would be full of surprises. With all the parts now on separate tracks, one could "punch in" a detail for a few seconds, trying it several times until it sounded just right.

As teenagers during long evenings at the Easters' house, fueled by Coca-Cola and popcorn, we would try to decode how UK hitmakers such as the Who, the Move's Roy Wood, and producers Mickie Most and Tony Hatch were achieving their effects. And every week in the sixties brought new horizons. The Zombies' *Odessey & Oracle*, the Beach Boys *Pet Sounds*, the Mothers of Invention's *Freak Out!*, and the Jimi Hendrix Experience's *Are You Experienced?* are just a few instances of this. No longer was the studio there merely to accurately document and then reproduce a performance; it had become a laboratory in which to realize sounds that before then might have existed only in the imagination—sounds, for example, that might have happened separately at all times of the day or night over the course of weeks or months only to be played back, in synch, all at once. In the world of so-called concert music, musique concrète artists such as Edgard Varèse and Karlheinz Stockhausen had been creating with tape since the forties. In the early fifties, influential New York composers Earle Brown, John Cage, Morton Feldman, David Tudor, and Christian Wolff had banded together for their Music for Magnetic Tape Project. Les Paul had paved the way on the pop charts as his wife, Mary Ford, sang over his spectacularly multitracked guitars, sometimes from a microphone placed over the kitchen sink so that she could resume washing dishes right after cutting a vocal. But now the "sounds of the studio" became part of the essential vernacular of successful pop artists. "Taking it further" was the unspoken imperative: Where could this music go? What could it become?

In the summer of 1967, the Beatles' *Sgt. Pepper's Lonely Hearts Club Band* had been heralded as a prime example of this new kind of art. And it is indeed a good example in several ways, not the least being that its aural cinematography, which was both extremely vivid and varied, overwhelmed its songwriting to some degree. The band's previous releases had better songs: The tracks on *Sgt. Pepper's* didn't work as well as most of those on *Revolver* or *Rubber Soul* when stripped down to just words, melodies, and chords, the Tin Pan Alley ingredients. Rather, the later album offered a compelling listening experience because of the ways its songs were realized in production (as well as how well they were played and sung, of course). "Being for the Benefit of Mr. Kite!" and other such unique recordings were effective because of the way they were arranged and then captured electronically, not necessarily because of any peak of lyrical or melodic skill (the lyrics in this case coming mostly whole cloth as "found art" from a circus poster). Instead of frontloading the process by first refining the words and melodies into sharp focus, the Beatles' songwriting for *Sgt. Pepper's* had left things more open, left more room to weave studio sounds in between the lines. You might even argue that the new aural moviemaking worked *best* if the song itself had come out of the oven only half-baked, if it left a lot of room for production.

By the time I reached Manhattan, I wasn't thinking of songwriting any other way. A song was a script for making a record.

The new technology also meant that, if you were patient enough, you could end up sounding like a better musician than you really were. And thus some of the incentive to really master an instrument was lost. With multitrack recording, it became common to play difficult parts phrase by phrase, performing each one the best you could before moving to the next. A section could also be captured in several long takes, or "passes," which were later compiled, or "comped," into one near-flawless track. Later, samplers and computers were to provide an easy way for audio from acoustic sources to be replayed or manipulated, an approach that would evolve into computer recording of longer and longer sections. Samplers were not widely available, however, in the early eighties, but there were still ways to create similar results: For example, a massed vocal harmony laboriously created for a song's first chorus could be mixed down to another tape recorder and then reused, "flown" back into other sections multiple times. This was a matter of trial and error, hitting "PLAY" on the second machine at just the right time to synch with the appropriate spots on the primary master tape reel. Instead of performing a musical line each time it was repeated in the arrangement, the artist might say, "Okay, that's good. Now just fly it in everywhere else and let me know when you are done; I'll be in the lounge." The engineer would sit there and hit the start buttons over and over, leaving time for the motors to come up to speed, until luck prevailed and the section was inserted correctly. In effect, when used in this way, the tape recorder itself became a crude early sampler, one triggered by an engineer's finger instead of a midi signal or mouse.

At the same time, consumers were beginning to expect recordings to be free of even small mistakes. This encouraged a uniform mediocrity, a blandness, in contrast to the thrill of a risk-taking performance that might have some rough edges but is emotionally more gripping. Radio liked this. Many commercial stations preferred music that sounded as glib and polished and unthreatening as the commercials that were paying their bills— that is, they wanted the songs to sound more like the jingles. This way, it was all of a piece, making the commercials seem more believable as the songs became less so.

Judging just from records, it became hard to distinguish highly skilled musicians from those who simply had large budgets and could hire a highly skilled technician to help them pull the wool over our ears. This led to some real surprises in concert, at least until similar cosmetic technology was added to stagecraft as well. At the same time, as per the Peter Principle, many of the best of these technicians—the recording engineers—were elevated to the status of record producers ("producer" being the equivalent of the cinema's "director"), even though they might have had little or no preparation for making solely musical decisions when they first walked into this new role. Previously these had been very distinct tasks, with a producer functioning as a conductor and arranger, saying when performances were in time, in tune, and in keeping with the arrangement. They would give general instructions to the engineer but rarely would touch the equipment themselves. Now, however, these sonic cinematographers were suddenly being crowned the directors of the new audio movies. Consequently, records started to be more about a "bitchin', gonzo snare sound" (something the engineers excelled at), an old tube microphone, or the latest digital reverb device than about creating specific arrangements using a wide variety of instrumental colors (something most engineers had never been trained in). And they were more about evolving technological ways to fix performance shortcomings than about techniques for coaching better performances in the first place.

I got very good at the earliest methods of error correction. Working with two- or four-track, quarter-inch analog tape in North Carolina, I had learned how to disengage the tape recorder's take-up motor and, by grabbing the tops of the left and right reels, "scrub" a section of the tape backward and forward across the playback head, first fast and then ever slower, zeroing in on one sharp musical transient at a time, until it was clear where a sound started or ended in the tape's metallic oxide. Then I could mark the spots with a wax pencil, pull that section of the tape over to an aluminum editing block, and use a straight razor to make a precise cut in the appropriate diagonal guide trough of the block to physically isolate that section. Such pieces, whether a few inches or many feet long, could then be excised or reconnected in a different sequence with adhesive splicing tape. Often they were draped around my neck, one by one, until all the pieces were ready to be hooked together, the strands looking for all the world like dark-brown dreadlock hair extensions.

Once I started working in professional New York studios in the late seventies, I found that the two-inch-wide tape used for twenty-four-track recording and the faster professional speeds of fifteen or thirty ips ("inches per second") created a wider margin of error for such slicing and dicing—the faster the tape, the more real estate it used up for each second of sound. It was still a risky business. Tape editing, though, had a serendipitous side effect: An edit that sounded a bit clumsy at first might sound slightly better the next day, because the magnetic particles on both sides of a cut would pull on each other overnight, averaging out, crossfading together, and thus softening the sound of the cut. Because of this, engineers playing edits for clients often resorted to a fallback trick, coughing at exactly the right time to cover a dubious edit and hoping that the fault might have melted away by the next day. I would make so many cuts, both tiny slices to fix timing errors and long combinations of the best parts of different takes, that if you were standing next to the tape machine, the splices sounded like playing cards stuck in bicycle wheels as they rolled past the capstan and tape guides.

These editing sessions were often solitary, all-night affairs that happened after already long days in the studio. It was expensive to have a group of musicians in town and at the ready for the initial "basic tracks"; to minimize recording time and expense, they would expect to hear something impressive each morning so they could decide whether an edited version of a previous day's track was good enough for them to move on to other songs. For more complicated fixes, there was the more esoteric *window editing*, a technique of locating little noises on the two-inch tape and then cutting out a tiny square hole at just that one moment, measured out to fall on just that particular twenty-fourth of the tape's height, leaving the other twenty-three tracks of instruments untouched. The dark brown tape would roll by on the machine, and suddenly little patches of light would shine through. (Later the recorders were modified for *spot erase*, and window editing went the way of the dodo bird.)

There was no "undo" button if a razor slipped. In *Tape Op* magazine, the veteran British engineer Phill Brown told a story of doing an edit on the multitrack tape of what was to become a classic reggae track, Bob Marley and the Wailers' "I Shot the Sheriff." Both his hands were engaged in the editing when a band member put a cone-shaped spliff between Phill's lips and then immediately walked away. An ash from the burning joint flew off before he could free his hands, and he watched, aghast, as it burned through the plastic tape in the middle of one of that song's signature tom-tom fills. He coolly asked the band for a little more time for the edit, pretending nothing was wrong, then scrambled frantically to find an outtake reel with a similar bit that he could cut in before they returned, thus saving the future hit recording. They never knew.

These editing options and the ability to add instruments one by one on individual tracks created another major change in record-making: the dictatorship of the click track. Skilled musicians playing together interact with one another, and tempi can fluctuate constantly. In fact, this ability to collectively intuit the ebb and flow of these slight adjustments in pace is part of their high level of musicality. A given bar or phrase will speed up or slow down very slightly based on what is being played and where it's headed in the overall unfolding structure. These shifts might be very subtle or they might be extreme (as in a lot of Romantic and midcentury-modern symphonic music); in either case, they can add a lot to the musical shape, to the music's dramatic impact, flow, and excitement. Even in a pop song with a basically constant tempo, there might be some tempo variation in an improvised drum fill, some toms perhaps, leading into a chorus.

When drummers play without a click, they almost always either drag dramatically at such points or speed up, depending on the specific music. In addition, the following chorus will often be slightly faster, perhaps with everyone then slowing down for the next verse—or not; as the tension builds, the overall tempo of the song might keep increasing up to the end.

To give two examples close to home for me, the iconic Big Star track "September Gurls" and Chris Bell's later "I Am the Cosmos" are, I think, both "pinball lights going off" achievements, and both end at a pace considerably faster than the one at which they begin. And a third, admired from afar and highly recommended: *The Low Spark of High-Heeled Boys*, a 1971 album by British sixties icons Traffic with American Jim Gordon on drums, which ebbs and flows in wonderful ways, just the sound of great players enjoying each others' company, live in the studio. Tempo shifts like these are not flaws; they are a natural way to suggest excitement or relaxation, just as the tempo of our breathing changes with our emotions or physical activity. But if the musicians are adding their parts separately, the interaction between them is gone, and if there is no precise headphone reference, everyone's microshifts in tempo land in different places, making for a sloppy and unmusical result. The drummer, whose track is already on tape, has left the building, and the others cannot react to a piano player coming in a month later. It just doesn't work.

Multitrack recording's solution was to have strict time, a recorded metronome's metallic *click, click, click* on one track as a reference (not to be used in the final mix). All the parts, starting usually with the drums, would then be played in lockstep with this unvarying pulse. This was a great asset for editing and for overdubbing inexpert musicians, one that engineers loved. And if the song was restructured after being recorded, with a verse cut or a chorus doubled, there were no unhappy sudden speed changes. Studio drummers learned to work around this. For example, if they wanted a fill to sound like it dragged (in a musical way), they would start it a fraction early and then slow it down a bit in the resulting extra space, ending the lick right on the beat. Similarly, electric guitarists might compensate for the lack of a chorus accelerando by stepping on a boost pedal and making their sound get louder or "tougher" instead. Even before computers became a part of studio work, of course, it was technically possible to create guide click tracks that varied in tempo, and some of us would often try to keep this natural flow by studying rehearsal recordings, averaging from several performances the places where a given section was faster or slower, and then creating a detailed "tempo map" that might increase or decrease just a few beats per minute, section to section. It takes a lot of time to do this, though, and sometimes there just wasn't enough. But over the years, as unvarying time became de rigueur and almost a requirement of commercial radio singles, and as listeners became accustomed to the very comfortable sound of a fixed pace, this level of finesse became unnecessary and even counterproductive. An important musical element was mostly lost, unmourned, on the cutting-room floor of history. And now that recording is overwhelmingly on computers and hard drives instead of tape, the "eyes" have it. The ease of working to a visual grid on a screen makes any future rebellion against the click track's dictatorial rule even more unlikely.

The constant aerobic tempi of dance music, especially disco, is often blamed for the click-track's current pervasiveness, but it's worth noting that Earl Young, the Philadelphia drummer for the Trammps who is often credited with originating the sixteenth-note off-beat-accented hi-hat and four-to-the-bar kick patterns that defined disco, wasn't using a click on those first records. And classic Chic songs like "Good Times" and "Le Freak," which led the disco revolution then, were not cut to a click track, either: Guitarist Nile Rodgers, bassist Bernard Edwards, and drummer Tony Thompson counted off and played the music together as a *band*, in the traditional way.[8]

_____

If you hang out in recording studios, especially in these digital days, you'll hear a lot of talk about creating "warmth," a buzzword that means different things to different people. (I usually think of plaid flannel pajamas.) When the term refers to the distortion characteristics of tube equipment and analog tape, which is the common usage, there is a lot going on under the hood. Overloading the medium of tape with high input produces odd-order harmonic content not present at the source. It skips over every other note in the overtone series after the fundamental. So a solitary note C might end up with a quiet high G, the twelfth scale step up, and if it's in a C chord that has a G right above the root of C, this G will have its own odd-order harmonic, a D, resulting in a C^9 chord; that is, the quality of the chord, the distribution of notes, changes very, very faintly, becoming richer, more complex, a tiny bit denser harmonically, as the overloaded magnetic signal magnetizes the oxide on the tape. If you are familiar with the effect of moving the various drawbars on a Hammond B-3 organ up and down while you hold a single note, thus changing the proportion of the organ's simulated overtones, you recognize a similarity in how this works; the Hammond circuit mirrors the overtone series and lets the level of the various add-on pitches be shaped to taste. In addition, tape machines offer alignment options in their internal amplifier circuits that alter overall frequency-response curves, yielding potentially pleasing anomalies in the bass and the treble. (Distorting old vacuum-tube gear, such as the classic Teletronix LA-2A compressor, creates even-order harmonics instead, so that first C would add another C an octave up from it, instead of the G that tape adds. You still get subtly richer chords, but they are different chords from the ones that tape distortion creates.)

These timbral shifts are part of the picture, to be sure, but only a part. To my ears, the biggest factor in the equation comes from the aforementioned speed/pitch variability, the motor-fluctuation "chorusing" called wow and flutter, which is usually neglected in the discussions of aural warmth. Vinyl records on turntables also exhibit this slight speed inconsistency. So when you use a record player to play an album originally recorded on tape and then etched into a rotating lacquer in mastering, you have a triple whammy of undulation, of pitch-variation "warmth." Such variability is especially kind to productions that have a lot of slightly out-of-tune elements; with everything warbling a bit, these become less noticeable.

Happily, the New York music scene of 1976 seemed refreshingly free of the seventies' sterile, cosmetics-driven trend toward false perfection, as if it had never happened. For one thing, the musicians and the labels were poor and couldn't afford to make records over the course of months; studio time was measured in hours. For another, they didn't want to be prettified and radio ready; they were glad to keep the sharp edges. And for a third, most of them seemed unaware that these modern techniques even existed: This was the recording studio as Polaroid camera. Impulse and instinct were all, and the past was past, although the shadow of Sam Phillips sometimes seemed to be lurking, that early rock 'n' roll aesthetic of "getting real, real gone" and capturing a moment.

After all is said and done, it still comes back to that pinball machine at CBGB: If a loop, a chant, and a laptop are tools that can make all the lights at the back of your brain go off at once, that can make you suddenly wake up and feel alive in the world, then they are intrinsically the right ones. And they are even more right if they are what's in front of you when inspiration strikes. I remember a long Internet chat on "the best kind of snare drum." Lots of posts, lots of brands, lots of opinions. Then Anton Fier chimed in: "I always think that the best snare drum for the job is the one that's in front of me at the time." It's hard to argue with him on this, and I think the basic idea applies here, as well. As producer Jim Dickinson used to say about guitarists, "Tone comes from the fingers." It's about capturing moments more than about technology. The best engineer is the one who dashes across the room and hits the record button just in the nick of time when something great is starting to happen in the room, no matter whether or not every mic is set up just right yet.

12 Who Will Baudelaire?

Ev - 'ry hair in place, stroll_ a - cross a lawn

Stop_ to catch the sun___ There, and then___ it's gone_

THE ARTISTIC LIFE IS A NOMADIC ONE, AS I FOUND OUT from the very beginning. And the story of my tenure in Manhattan is as much one of *where* as one of *what* and *when*. "Location, location, location": There's a lot of truth in that. I lived so many places in that decade and a half . . .

My first digs were in Jim Green's amazing building, listed on the National Register of Historic Places: Alwyn Court, at 180 West Fifty-Eighth Street. I had really started at the top there, lodgings-wise, only to spiral downward ever after. Sometimes compared to the more renowned Dakota (which was home to Leonard Bernstein, John Lennon and Yoko Ono, and Judy Garland), Alwyn, built in 1909, is a smaller but equally stunning edifice with terra-cotta gargoyles and cherubs on the exterior, a doorman, a wood-paneled elevator, and huge rooms with views of Central Park. It towered above the Petrossian Restaurant, with its world-famous caviar menu, which may further clue you in on the rarified terrain. My personal answer to the setup for the old musician's gag, "How do you get to Carnegie Hall?," was, "Just walk around the corner."

After that temporary rental expired a few months later, I next moved to a new building at 89 Bleecker Street with my girl-friend, creative choreographer Jamie Sims, who not only was the leader of the Cosmopolitans (formerly the Cosmopolitan Dance Troupe) but also had been a fellow composition student at UNC. Our second-floor apartment sat adjacent to the NYU residential towers where Ken Easter had hosted my summer visits, around the corner from Singermanagement in the Cable Building, and also just down the street from CBGB. What could be better? In any event, I had grown weary of hiking sixty blocks in the middle of the night as I made my way from the Bowery clubs up to Fifty-Eighth Street, which I did on those many evenings when there was no taxi to be found there on the Bowery or no money left for the fare.

And it was from 89 Bleecker that I operated my boy-in-a-bedroom indie label, Car Records. The label had started out in 1976 as Carnivorous, for the Sneakers EP, but after making all those hamburger patties at the Carolina Coffee Shop, I had given up on meat and needed to make a change. I had watched the Ork guys make so much noise with so little, and from them I had absorbed the basics of manufacturing, press mailings, and distribution. In those first years, Car had no business plan beyond haphazardly releasing a few records by my friends, including Holsapple's "Big Black Truck." I was surprised, then, when Chilton showed up at the Bleecker apartment one spring day in 1978, on a brief trip back from Memphis, to pitch a song to me for release on Car. He had reconnected down there with Big Star's other main songwriter, Chris Bell, who had played him a passion project called "I Am the Cosmos," which Alex thought I should put out as a single.

Chris Bell, used for the cover of "I Am the Cosmos"; photo by David Bell.
Alex and Chris at 89 Bleecker Street; photo by Stephanie Chernikowski.

The thing was, Chilton didn't have any sonic evidence to back up this opinion (in that era, the evidence would have been a cassette tape). So he grabbed my guitar from the corner and sang me the song, starting with its first sad, lovelorn lines: "Every night I tell myself, 'I am the cosmos, I am the wind,' but that don't get you back again." Then Alex stopped cold and laughed out loud at how perfect and yet pitiful, how "Bell-like," that couplet was. He said he thought it was Chris's crystallization, his "River Deep, Mountain High," his highest achievement. I agreed it was great, but I wanted to hear the actual track. I still didn't have much to go on, frankly, making it hard to commit the full (read "almost nonexistent") resources of my company to the project.

We called Bell in Memphis, and a few hours later, he drove over to Ardent Studios there, put the master reel on the tape deck, and held the phone to the speakers as the music blared out. Of course, the result sounded pretty much like crap, given the state of telephone fidelity and the overloud playback volume in the studio. Nevertheless, this somehow did the trick for me, and I "signed" him on the spot for an advance of $200 but commented, "Maybe you should speed it up when you cut the disk. It's a bit draggy"—ah, the audacity of youth. In fact, Bell did speed it up slightly in the end, as if following instructions from a real record exec instead of a star-struck kid in a boho apartment. And it actually was better that way; whew!

A cassette of the recording arrived in the mail several weeks after the phone call; it took that long because, Chris said, he was having trouble "finding the right packaging"—I was never sure what this meant. Fortunately, it sounded great on the little tape, too, as mixed by Beatles engineer Geoff Emerick—a saturated, 3-D explosion of analog sound, the interlocking guitars and Hammond organ and Richard Rosebrough's drumming mostly routed through the myriad tubes of Ardent's legendary Fairchild compressor, which the studio, called Shoe, had borrowed for the session. And then it became phenomenal on the final lacquer and pressing, cut by mastering engineer Larry Nix, who was then riding high on the success of having mastered the international novelty smash "Disco Duck," quite a different kettle of fowl.

Bell's cassette also held a number of choices for the B-side of the vinyl single, tracks he had been recording over the years at Ardent and elsewhere, of which he preferred the rockin' "Fight at the Table." But I held out for the acoustic ballad "You and Your Sister," another amazing song and a glorious, delicate contrast to the roar of the A-side, with a chamber-pop string and winds arrangement by Bill Cunningham (from the Box Tops) and, in their only post–Big Star studio reunion, high harmonies by Alex himself. I owe Chilton for all this; he went out of his way to knock on my door and help his somewhat estranged brother in arms, and getting a chance to make this release happen still means a lot to me. For the approximately seven hundred folks who bought that little record later that year, and the international reviewers who gushed over it, and the many thousands more who have later thrilled to it in international reissues, life was perhaps never quite the same. Big Star's producer, John Fry, told me that this little record was one of the two things in the world most precious to Bell right before his fatal auto accident later that year, a kind of validation for him after his dismay over the relative obscurity of the first Big Star record. It's a powerful, unforgettable, angst-filled landmark track that has since cast a wide shadow. There's really nothing quite like it.

My relationship with Sims foundered at the end of 1978, and she kept the Bleecker Street apartment. I began a new one with another recent North Carolina immigrant, ebullient photographer Carol Whaley, and became a house-sitting king between tours, notably, on several occasions, at a beautiful Grand Street penthouse owned by a former state comptroller. It seems to me now as if I lived on every block below Fourteenth Street at one time or another, in the span of the next several years. If there was no house-sitting to be had, I might end up for a few nights on the dB's rehearsal-room couch or even back in Winston to visit my parents.

But by 1980 there was a giant hand tugging at the edges of Manhattan, tilting it, rolling all us loose cannons toward the west. Hoboken had been a speakeasy town during Prohibition, when New Yorkers would take the ferry across to Washington Street; at the time, the street had more bars per block than any other in the country, or so the legend goes. (Brooklyn was not then considered an option; it was several decades away from being *Brooklyn*, the hipster bastion. I don't think I had call to go to Brooklyn for music more than twice during the whole time I lived in the North.) *New York Rocker*'s Glenn Morrow, who had grown up in New Jersey, probably spurred the rock scene's migration to Hoboken, taking an apartment there that featured bullet holes and a blood-stained crucifix above the bed and starting a Hoboken-based band called simply "a" with future Bongos leader Richard Barone.

Housesitting for the rich and powerful was not something I could consistently rely on, so after too many couch surfs, uncomfortable stints crashing with Carol in houses she shared with several housemates, and even a short sojourn living in an old station wagon parked on a derelict block near the World Trade Center, around 1983 I took half of a two-room apartment in "Hob" with then *SoHo Weekly News* rock critic Ira Kaplan. As the original tenant, he had the bedroom, which he had decorated with piles of *The New York Times*, books, and manuscripts he was copyediting for Random House (the favored freelance gig for many of the musicians in our circle). I had a mattress in the kitchen, a suitcase in the corner, and a coffee cup in the kitchen sink. At a certain point, the stacks of papers in Ira's room parted enough to let sunlight shine on a corner where resided an old Stratocaster with a hand-painted American flag. I took that sad guitar, cleaned it up with steel wool and linseed oil, restrung it, and did a bit of a setup on it; I think I had the selfish idea that Ira might let me take it over down the line, as I was missing Alex's old Strat, which had now gone to live with Ivy Rorschach, of the Cramps. Instead, the flag Strat's new playability seemed to revive Ira's interest in playing it himself . . .

Hoboken has one central, razor-straight, mile-long north-south artery, the aforementioned Washington Street; at that time, all the other streets were residential capillaries. We were centrally located on Washington, between Fifth and Sixth Streets, right above Benny Tudino's, a pizza place whose somewhat inexplicable popularity was, years later, to become more clear when the owner's son ran into flames to recover a hidden cache of dubiously sourced, possibly ill-gotten cash and, in doing so, made the cover of the *New York Post*. At one end was the PATH train station and ferry terminal, where our huddled masses arrived from New York. Toward the other end was Maxwell's, where the Fallon family was trying to revive a bar patronized mostly by workers from the Maxwell House coffee plant next door on the Hudson River, the source of the burnt java smell that slithered into everything in those halcyon days. Steve Fallon was soon

Steve Fallon at the front door to Maxwell's; photo by Michael Galinsky

to become, for all of us, the champion Benevolent Innkeeper of the eighties.

Steve started letting Glenn and Richard's band "a" play in the bar, though they had to set up on the floor because there was no stage at that point. Slowly other bands appeared, including the dB's, who were booked and even driven there from Manhattan by Morrow himself, who borrowed his parent's station wagon for the haul. When Fallon eventually cleaned up the neglected back room and installed a stage and rudimentary PA, leaving space for at most two hundred packed patrons, the bookings snowballed, a result due in no small part to the fact that, no matter how small the door take might be, there was always a good, hot Maxwell's meal as part of the deal. The big leagues and the labels remained in Manhattan, where I still spent most of my days, but Maxwell's became the nocturnal social center in many ways. R.E.M., Hüsker Dü, the Replacements, and other such bands might play in New York City, but after the gig they would often hightail it to Hoboken and Fallon's second-floor apartment, the de facto dressing room for the club, where they would hang out all night, playing records, drinking cognac and beer, and soaking up Steve's fervor and the latest gossip. And others, such as the Feelies, would loyally choose a Maxwell's gig over one in New York.

Other Hoboken venues occasionally had bands, but Maxwell's loomed huge above the rest. I remember playing a New Year's Eve gig there with Anton Fier's Golden Palominos (who were using the alias the Diving Ducks), and the place was packed. Between sets I would walk down a block to the tiny Elysian Fields bar and catch sets by the absolutely legendary and crucial Hubert Sumlin, lead guitarist for Howlin' Wolf and originator of some of the expanded guitar vocabulary, the swoops and scrapes and strangleholds, that Jeff Beck and Tom Verlaine later built on. Sumlin was playing his elderly heart out to an audience of no more than ten, tops. It's not that the Ducks weren't also playing well, but this was another reminder of the lack of correlation between the excellence of the music and the size of the audience. This experience stuck with me for a long time.[9]

But Hoboken had attractions beyond the nexus of Maxwell's and its convenient public transportation into the city; specifically, it satisfied two other requirements for an evolving rock scene: cheap, roomy places to live and a place to record. The former was a relief after the closet-size, overpriced options in Manhattan; railroad-style apartments with amazing frosted-glass sliding doors and ornate wood carvings were plentiful. The latter was found at Water Music, a bare-bones studio started by the hardworking New Jersey band Cries with a small cash settlement from a traffic accident. Savvy lead singer and studio kingpin Rob Grenoble was a master of by-your-bootstraps creation, and Water soon acquired a classic API board from Sunset Sound in Los Angeles, as well as other great old gear, tubes and discrete-transistor stuff that had temporarily fallen out of favor with most of the big studios. It was homey and comfortable and run by all the excellent musicians from Cries, including James MacMillan and Robert Miller, so there was musical as well as technical expertise behind the board. Both Peter Holsapple and I were treated as honored guests each time we booked there.

It didn't take long for a Hoboken Wrecking Crew of studio-caliber players to swirl around the studio, often helmed by guitarist Dave Schramm, and one of the discoveries was Jane Scarpantoni, who played cello with Maxwell's regulars Tiny Lights. Most of the folks in this scene didn't read musical notation, the reality behind an old, clichéd joke: "How do you make a guitarist be quiet? Put sheet music in front of him." Jane read well, however, and she could also wing it without written music, improvising parts with solid voice-leading. She would go on to

Track sheet from Water Music; author archives

have a stellar career, first as soloist with John Lurie's jazz-punk Lounge Lizards and then as the cellist of choice for hit records by R.E.M., Bruce Springsteen, Lou Reed, Nirvana, Indigo Girls, Natalie Merchant, and Train, but all that was then still before her. At that point, I hadn't been around a capable string player for a long time, and as soon as I heard her play, I decided to one day write a song featuring her.

I didn't get my chance to do that until several years later, on *It's Alright*. The idea of doing something in the Impressionist mold appealed to me, because I loved Debussy, Ravel, and Fauré. I settled on the idea of a pastoral, Satie-like song with a lyric based somewhat on Seurat's *Un dimanche après-midi à l'île de la Grande Jatte*, kicked it off with a melody that began on the sixth, and called it "The Seduction of a Sunny Afternoon," later shortening the title to merely "The Seduction" (the longer title reminded me too much of the Kinks). The tabla on the eventual recording didn't quite fit the Parisian vibe, and the harmonies Chilton added late one night were more We Five, but the cello lines were lovely mixed in with the pastoral acoustic textures.

> *Every hair in place, stroll across a lawn*
> *Stop to catch the sun, there . . . and then it's gone*
> *Every eye upon her now,*
> *Who will buy this day of days? The seduction.*

Walking down the street one day shortly after the record's release, I ran into Michael Hill, a music journalist and Maxwell's regular who had recently become a Warner Bros. executive under Karin Berg. He told me that his favorite on the album was "The Seduction" and added, "Hey, that song reminds me of Seurat's painting." And I felt like I had gotten through there after all.

13 Cut It Hot, Cut It Up, Cut It Clean, Cut It Slow

Five four_ one, five oh_ two—what is_ the num- ber? Six - teen_ West Six - ty— what

street is the street? Ask for_ Jill,_____ ask for_ Jill_____

NO MATTER WHERE I SLEPT AT NIGHT, THE DAYS WERE taken up with music back in Manhattan. When I look back on all that I was involved with at the end of the seventies, some of it, including portions of that first dB's record, *Stands for deciBels,* has not worn well for me, frankly, although there are still moments worthy of pride. We always did the best we could with the materials and skills we had. "I'm in Love," for example, sounds like it was written while distracted, in transit, scattered. The song got lost in an overly fussy period production, for which I have the lion's share of the blame. Years later, I was pleased when the band retooled it for concerts by lowering the key and eliminating some overly melodramatic arrangement twists and

The dB's on tour; photo by Phil Marino

turns; lo and behold, it emerged as a much more effective tune, somewhere between Nick Lowe's early band, Brinsley Schwarz, and the Association.

The only track on *Stands for deciBels* that I now return to with unqualified pleasure is Peter Holsapple's wistful ballad "Moving in Your Sleep."

> *Now I've got you, I can watch you*
> *Moving in your sleep*
> *Now that I've found you, I can surround you*
> *Moving in your sleep . . .*
>
> *We are driving, on a highway*
> *Night is growing deep*
> *See the ocean, ocean highway*
> *Clutching to your sheet*
> *There may come a day*
> *When I must go away from here*
> *. . . Remember me*

Who can disagree with Ralph Waldo Emerson? "Beauty is its own excuse." George Jones, the iconic country songwriter, had stage banter that went something like, "First we're going to play some *fast* songs, then we'll play some *good* songs" (meaning, the slow ones, the ballads). Peter's ballad is a *quite* good song framed by a very colored production, and in this it connects to the experimentation that was rampant at the Nokomis Court studio years before. It's such a good match among subject matter, melodic and lyrical construction, and sonics. It sounds like it was written in whispers and then immediately recorded, all while sitting in bed next to a sleeping lover, as if there were no gap between that first glimmer and the final needle drop.

In fact, it was carefully shaped along the way. With Will at the drums, we squeezed into a hallway during our 1979-1980 sessions at Blue Rock Studios to get away from the usual studio ambiance. Peter played acoustic guitar and the delicious piano filigree. Gene took over on electric guitar, including the hint of a guitar solo (I muted out the first part of his solo when I mixed it, somewhat to his chagrin, to keep the mood strongest; his solo now emerges like a message from a Magic 8 Ball, and I can no longer recall what that missing first part was like). I played the cheap beginner's Sears Silvertone bass that I had used with Chilton all along and that I still use sometimes to this day (a variation of the one Jack Bruce used on the influential second Cream album, *Disraeli Gears,* and the same model that NRBQ's bassist, Joey Spampinato, always played). That bass's choked, tuba-like resonance was quite different from the tone of the commanding grooves Holder played on his Fender Jazz bass; it was more like the sound of a Höfner—hollow, with the lowest tones unsupported because of the instrument's body shape. I doubled some of it, pizzicato, on cello. Peter's achingly McCartneyish vocal was mixed through a Fender Twin Reverb guitar amp with the reverb turned up, a then rule-breaking move that made the performance seem distorted as if by all-too-imperfect memory. The filtered harmonies are Will's, I believe, though the "oo-wah" doo-wops that suddenly appear at the end of the bridge

Gene Holder and Chris (in the trunk with a nylon-string guitar) in Europe in 1981; photos by Will Rigby

were probably massed Holsapples, and it's certainly Peter who whispers "I love you" as the waves recede at the end. I'm sure that at some point in the process, we mentioned producer Jim Dickinson's sonic shades on Big Star's *Third*, especially its most languid songs, such as "Big Black Car" and "Dream Lover," which I think were known to us then only from the cassette bootleg copies we all had played to death. (That kind of floating piano playing, oozing in and out of the mix, inspired our later regular use of the adjective *Dickinsonian* to describe any sparse, high, rubato element.) But the production of the track didn't need these cross-references for justification; it all sprang from the images inherent in the song. And by that point, we could all understand what it felt like to abruptly leave a new love five hundred miles behind.

———

And go away we did. All over the United Kingdom, then by train to Amsterdam, and then Stockholm—a real tour in Europe; spring 1981 was a triumphant blur for the dB's. Nothing world-shaking, but in Stockholm, our record went into the Top Twenty for a while. And the band had already done a much-anticipated session at Nick Lowe's London-basement studio, Ampro, with an engineer/producer named Roger Bechirian. He had worked with Elvis Costello as well as Lowe, and we had high hopes for collaborating with him on a new, infectious pop song of Peter's, "Judy." It didn't hurt that some of the T. Rex singles we loved had been created in that basement, with the great Tony Visconti producing. Roger had provided some good ideas, but we didn't consider his production a fully arranged, finished record, and the mix he had delivered had a kick drum loud beyond all reason, or so it seemed to us. So on the train ride back from Stockholm, in an open car next to weary travelers trying to sleep, we wood-shedded vocal harmonies in order to bring the song into focus and then added them to the track, without Bechirian, once we arrived back in London. This pretty much saved the production in our view; it certainly dialed it back to the kind of pop song that the lyrics and the playing had implied. The label's staff, who had not heard it before we added the harmonies, loved it and wanted us to make a whole record with Roger, but we felt that he had left the song half-baked for us to finish. When we told them we wanted to work with Scott Litt instead, there was a bit of a tussle. They insisted we do a trial run.

So we found ourselves back in New York after the tour with something to prove. It would have been a good move to select a song that was a match for "Judy," something immediate, catchy, another one of Peter's tunes. This would have been fine with me. But I had been working on an idea the band liked, a song based on a minimalist ostinato composed of some syncopated guitar major-second double stops (sometimes matched by a flip-flop drum pattern); I wanted to see how long we could keep shifting the other instruments around this unchanging element. The structure resembled that of Terry Riley's *In C* in that one player kept the pulse all the way while the others shifted around it. And the lyrics were another kind of game: They was a bit "meta," a record about cutting a record, specifically about Masterdisk, the mastering lab helmed by Bob Ludwig that Don Dixon had pointed out to me years ago and that I tried to use exclusively in those first years. We started with the first nine digits of their actual phone number—(212) 541-502[2]—and a fragment of their address at the time and continued with references to other mastering details: "pre-groove echo," "cut it hot . . . cut it slow" (a technique of cutting a vinyl record at half-speed to improve the top end). "Jill," of course, was the receptionist's name, although it was also a tip of the hat to Jill Christiansen, who worked with NRBQ at the time. And "slightly disheveled" described my usual state when arriving for Masterdisk sessions after typically being up all the previous night finishing a last-minute mix.

So we had a dissonant, never-ending guitar loop built around a major-second interval, a herky-jerky kick-drum pattern, fluctuating meters, a most obscure and totally nerdy subject matter, and me as the unsteady lead singer. What could go wrong? Somehow this was the song that Scott had to offer as evidence to convince the label he was the right producer. I don't know how we made this choice, but we ended up back at Power Station putting tubular bells on every other accent and incorporating a solo that consisted of the piano and guitar both playing chromatic scales up and down, starting on the same note but then proceeding in opposite directions. Certainly the most unlikely of all these elements was the addition of what we called a "rap" at the end, where I pretend to call and actually speak to this Jill, only to be put on hold. (There was little rap music at that time; by "rap," we might have been thinking more of fifties rockers like the Big Bopper.) Finally, we were friends with a band called the Bush Tetras, and their "Too Many Creeps" was a downtown anthem, yet they had been getting some bad reviews. So we added in the exhortation "don't beat around the bush" line as a kind of secret message to show our solidarity with them. And to put the icing on the meta-cake, we mastered it at Masterdisk, bringing an even wider grin to Ludwig's ever-smiling face in the process.

> *Five four one, five oh two—what is the number?*
> *Sixteen, West Sixty—what street is the street?*

There is a girl on the fourth or fifth floor
Buzz at reception, slightly disheveled

Ask for Jill, ask for Jill
She'll run, she'll hide
When you try to confide
What you feel inside, what you feel inside

Now that the building Jack built is for sale
Now that Jonah has swallowed the whale
Don't stand still, ask for Jill

Cut it hot, cut it up, cut it clean, cut it slow
When she walks in: pre-groove echo (echo)

And you know, it all kind of worked in the end. It's a "devil in the details" song. Like a drinking duck toy, it hardly ever lets up. Coming back to it now, it strikes me as sounding like a forgotten track from *West Side Story*; maybe it's all the tubular bells? The folks at the label rightly felt it was a bit odd, but they were impressed with its sound, as well as that of the groovy little surf instrumental "pH Factor," which we cut live in the spectacular cedar-cathedral room of Power Station A, with Peter nailing the guitar solo, which sounded a bit like "Slaughter on Tenth Avenue," and then running over to the Ace Tone organ, guitar still strapped to his back, just in time to play a bridge melody on it. And Litt got the thumbs-up to produce the dB's second album, which was to be called *Repercussion*.

Jukebox
The More You Look, the More You See

"Cool," Pylon, *Gyrate*, DB Records, 1980

I was standing inside a phone booth surrounded by grazing sheep, outside a bed and breakfast in Wales ... or was it Scotland? ... That spring of 1981, on my first UK tour, the destinations were already blending together. On the other end of the line, back in the US of A, was Danny Beard, a record-store owner in Athens, Georgia, which was a then-vital "rock town" that had spawned R.E.M., the B-52's, ... and a band proclaimed by some of those same folks to be the "best band in America": Pylon. The dB's had gained some understanding of the Athens scene when we played a show there in 1979 in Pylon's rehearsal space turned club, a room on the second floor of a building on the main downtown drag. It was called the 40 Watt Club because (we were proudly told) there was one forty-watt lightbulb dangling down from the ceiling and a forty-watt receiver as the jukebox. (A club under that name has persisted, in different locations, for decades, now with probably 40,000 watts under the hood.) Although the club had been packed for our show, at the end of the night the shoebox at the door held perhaps less than forty dollars. We asked the designated doorman, a local legend named Ort the Record Dog (the nom de vinyl of William Orten Carlton), "What gives?" He explained, exasperated at my lack of comprehension, "Chris, these people don't have any money!"—he had let almost everyone in for free. And the town was full of freedom in many other ways: The combination of a temperate climate and a cutting-edge art school had encouraged the bloom of a delicious bohemia.

In the early 1980s, Pylon had put out a minimalist dance-rock record on Beard's in-house store label, DB Records (no relation). Called "Cool," it had insistent, bass-line-fueled grooves supporting almost Pentecostal-hypnotic declarations by Vanessa Briscoe, who insisted that "everything" is cool. An album, *Gyrate*, followed later that year, which earned the band a cover of *New York Rocker* magazine, and the tunes permeated every inch of the Manhattan club scene. At some point I had casually mentioned to Danny that

Pylon (left to right: Michael Lachowski, Curtis Crowe, Vanessa Briscoe Hay, Randy Bewley); photo by Michael Lachowski

I would be glad to work with them in the studio if it ever came up. Now he was spending big bucks on an overseas phone call to say that, when I returned from tour, I had the job if I wanted it.

I wasn't sure I did. I had loved Pylon's last record. But I suspected, correctly as it turned out, that their knowledge of the vocabulary of music was, like their music itself, very minimal, and I thought that perhaps we would have trouble communicating. Also, they were rising icons, and sophomore records are always treacherous. It was a lot to shoulder. On the flip side, they were great—it was that simple; I said yes. A few months later, in the summer of 1982, after a trial run at Mitch Easter's new Winston-based Drive-In Studios that resulted in a twelve-inch disk called "Beep/Altitude" and featured Warner Bros.' Roadrunner on the cover, I found myself in Athens doing preproduction with the band. I asked Gene Holder to coproduce the Pylon album with me, as we complemented each other well. Yes, they were a bit green; I'm not sure if they even knew the names of all the notes. Since they were mostly visual artists (painters) now in musicians' clothing, we set up a big classroom greenboard and drew Venn diagrams with chalk; backed by this visual aid, the song structures and arrangements coalesced. The band members had a great work ethic, they loved what they were doing, and we had a ball together. During the late seventies, summertime Athens was an effervescing, walkable town, much like Chapel Hill but with the UGA art-school element seeming to add a glint to everyone's eye. That fall, we finished the album back at Mitch's Drive-In Studios, which was located in a garage attached to his parents' new house. In retrospect, I think the record, called *Chomp*, at times became slightly overcomplicated with so many cooks and so much preparation, but it has a lot of charm.

The material was written in a style that was becoming more and more popular: *rehearsal-room collaboration*, where songs were derived from jamming, starting often with a repeated bass and drum groove over which a guitarist could vamp licks and chords until something clicked. Cassettes of this could be given to a singer, who would try to find words and a melody after the fact, perhaps out of an unrelated notebook of earlier lyrical musings. This compositional style was somewhat gestated by the abundance of affordable cassette recorders, especially the popular Sony Professional Walkman, the iPod of its day. This kind of collaboration was totally alien to the all-at-once auteur songwriting I had been raised on; it was far from the Gershwins or Goffin-King and Doc Pomus in the Brill Building, but it made for a lot of happy accidents and selective dissonance, which I liked. Unfortunately, it is hard to avoid eventually being boxed into a corner when you don't know the building blocks of music, when you are relying on happy accidents; it is hard to evolve and easy to repeat yourself without being aware of it.

Pylon's sound included the use of "wrong-note bass," an obstinate, intentional conflict between the bottom note and the chords above it, which was a technique I knew from early twentieth-century Impressionism. The dub style of reggae, a mixing engineer's playpen with elements abruptly dissolving into echo or flipping to unreal proportions, was also an influence here. And the unexpected dissonances and consequent resolutions were energizing and exciting on the dance floor.

A favorite exponent of this style of songwriting was England's Gang of Four, whose guitarist, Andy Gill, spewed out remarkable clusters of musical agitprop, sometimes followed by several bars of surprising silence, while the singer, Jon King, recited what seemed to be Marxist critiques. This combination of electric dissonance and politics had been heard earlier — for example, in works by the English band Henry Cow, an accomplished musical Marxist commune featuring guitarist/violist Fred Frith. They were named after Henry Cowell, an associate of Charles Ives who composed, among other works, piano pieces where masses of keys were played at once with long planks of wood. But unlike Henry Cow's music, the Gang of Four's records were danceable. King's lyrical anger and indignation were matched point-to-point by Gill's guitar abuse, their albums were magnificent polemics, and their supercharged live shows in New York clubs were highly influential for all the new rock bands touring the CBGB-derived circuit, as well as, later, for Nirvana and other nineties Seattle bands. These jam-generated tunes were one step further down the path on the search for the new.

"Cool" was the 45 that had announced Pylon to the world in early 1980. It blew up all over New York — not on radio, but then no one in the scene was listening much to radio. It was the clubs that mattered, Hurrah, the Mudd Club, Danceteria, Tier 3. In the new midnight Top Forty of clubland, "Cool" ruled. (And continued to rule when it was used, surprisingly, in a Lexus commercial in 2016. It was hard to imagine any of the band at the wheel of that high-end car, but I hope they got a fee that put a bit of gas in their tanks.) The verse lyrics reveal their kinship with the visual arts: It's "watch," not "hear."

> *Pure form, Real gone,*
> *Like wild, Good vibes*
> *There are these forms I like to watch,*
> *There are these shapes which talk to me*
> *I like forms, and forms like me*
> *The more you look, the more you see*

Jukebox

We've Got Your Sons' Blood on Our Hands

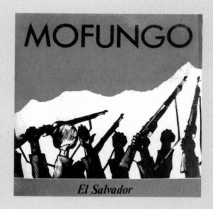

"El Salvador," Mofungo, Rough Trade Records, 1981

Named after an alternative spelling for a Puerto Rican dish that features fried pickled plantains, Mofungo was a politically attuned, socialist-inclined band that included, at that time, drummer Jeff McGovern and guitarists Willie Klein and Robert Sietsema (who doubled on bass). The band grew out of a musical/social network that included Blinding Headache, with polyrhythmic drummer Rick Brown, and, later, Information, with Chris Nelson (one-time graphics maven at *New York Rocker*), Phil Dray (now an independent historian and the author of *At the Hands of Persons Unknown: The Lynching of Black America*), and Brown. (I assumed later that Robert also contributed the band name, as he was to go on to be a famous foodie journalist, first for the *Village Voice* and more recently for Eater.com, who specializes in pointing out ethnic delicacies that, for example, might perhaps be found only under a certain Queens railroad trestle on alternate Tuesdays when an elderly Ukrainian woman wheels her hand truck there for a few hours at dusk. I was wrong here, however; I've since learned that he credits Dray with choosing the name.) For several years, the musically apolitical dB's shared a sixth-floor rehearsal room with Mofungo at 584 Eighth Avenue, and we enjoyed them greatly.

This was in a fabled edifice known simply as the Music Building, and other tenants included Madonna, They Might Be Giants, the Fleshtones, the Ramones, and producer/drummer Fred Maher (originally from Material, who helmed Lou Reed's *New York* and Matthew Sweet's *Girlfriend*). It was hard to predict who you might see wandering the halls. One day, Andy Warhol and his retinue walked in to our space, stared, and then walked out, without explanation. Television and the Patti Smith Group also were in residence at various times. With the windows open in the summertime (no air conditioning), the collective cacophony was often astonishing. But even on those rare occasions when the rest of the inhabitants fell silent, Mofungo was capable of quite a cacophony all on their lonesome.

Sometimes the density of their ideas made for difficult first listening, but the intentions behind their 1981 single "El Salvador" were clear as a bell; it expressed their rage over US support of the Salvadoran junta in the civil war that killed over 75,000 in the 1980s. It starts with a sonic *rrawwwah* realization of that rage, a distorted electric guitar whose strings are being slowly scraped up in pitch against the sharp edge of a cymbal on which McGovern is simultaneously playing a roll. It follows that with the kind of droning, anthemic anger that electric guitars can express so well. It was recorded at Public Access Synthesizer Studio (PASS) at 16 West Twenty-Second Street, on a machine that (judging by the high-end flutter) had dirty heads. They squeezed in a Lower East Side sax section, a synthesizer, and some harmonies as well. I mixed it at 39th Street Studios, near the rehearsal space. I might have also helped bring it to the attention of my friend Geoff Travis, at his Rough Trade Records in London, even then a bastion of open-minded expression. And it was rightly proclaimed by the *Village Voice*'s Robert Christgau to be the "political song of the year." Protest music has often been critically associated with the acoustic-guitar strains of Dylan's "Blowin' in the Wind" and "Death of Emmett Till," but "El Salvador" makes it easy to see why Dylan went electric – there's nothing like grabbing an electric guitar and some drumsticks and shouting your mind.

> We've got your sons' blood on our hands
> As your people cry, we can't hear their cries in this land.

14 Your Ballerina Curls

Run back to your mo - ther, tell her all___ the cruel things that I did. It comes as no sur- prise___ to her,___ I was ne-ver smooth e-nough for her kid. A

HOW DOES ONE WRITE A SONG? I REMEMBER SEVENTIES ads for Prell shampoo that showed a pearl floating through the amorphous goop. And I used to think songwriting was like that: You had to have something loose inside you, something rattling around, and you shook it up and then followed it around and took dictation.

Cliché-lovers command, "Write what you know"—as in, "those who *know* history are doomed to repeat it . . . and repeat it" (thanks to inventive guitarist Henry Kaiser for this observation). But it is good advice. The *New Musical Express* once cited a quip I have always adored: Producer Nick Lowe, after recording a blistering Telecaster take probably by Billy Bremner, turned to the guitarist and said, "I see you've read my pamphlet on

Photo by Gail Goers

guitar playing; perhaps now you'd like to buy the complete set?"
I thought about this over the years, guffawing every time, and
then set about actually writing an introductory pamphlet for all
the first-timers I was producing, laying out what it was *really*
like to make a record. Wishing someone had warned me! Then I
pulled a Pete Seeger and set it to song instead.

"Tape Op Blues"

The engineer sits in his cocoon,
he's set up mics all around the room
The producer reaches for a smoke,
the tape op tells another joke,
and I stand at the microphone,
out of time, and all alone
and wonder what they're saying about me

Two months ago, we were all friends,

we couldn't wait till we'd begin
The A&R man would come around,
we'd think of ways to put him down

I got a new guitar, wood from Peru—
the other eighteen just won't do
We picked the place where we'd record:
an indoor swimming pool, a diving board
But now I stand at the microphone,
out of reach, and all alone
and wonder what they're saying about me

The first few weeks went swimmingly,
we fired the drummer, and drank coffee
The basic tracks went like a knife through butter
(and we congratulated one another)
Friends came by, we made them play
on our busman's holiday
Titles for the record flew, like
"Chicken Feathers," "Into Glue"
Now I stand at the microphone,
out of time, and all alone,
and wonder what they're saying about me

Each track was played so many times,
we'd cringe before we even heard the rhymes
Each note we'd placed so carefully
was out of time . . . and out of key
"We've got to think of something fast,"
the producer said, from behind the glass,
"now what would the Ramones have done?"
(I thought about what kind of gun.)
As I stand at the microphone,
its burning deck, and all alone,
and wonder what they're saying about me,
I wonder what they're saying . . . about me.

Some of the lingo of this lyric harks back to an earlier, pre-Internet time, when there were astronomically fewer people making records and yet astronomically more records being sold, so budgets were larger (thus the mention of the "swimming pool" attached to the studio, although this is hyperbole; it would have been a hot tub at best, unless you were in the superelite). And technology was much more difficult, computers pretty much being reserved for corporations and spaceflight; recording required not only someone to bark orders (the producer) and someone else to move knobs and sliders (the engineer) but also someone to sit at the back and switch the reel-to-reel tape machine on and off: the *tape op*[erator]. The tape op was near the bottom of the pecking order and was supposed to keep silent and be invisible to the process—which seemed often to mean, au contraire, a stream of sardonic, sotto voce bon mots issuing from the back of the room. The term *A&R man*, which designates the person at the record label charged with finding musical talent and then liaising with it during the creative process, has also mostly gone by the wayside. Although oft reviled, true A&R people, who had both musical smarts and keen instincts about commerce, played a big part in creating many of the great major-label records from decades past. They were like the spymasters who stay at headquarters and maintain perspective on the agents, who are often confused by the ever-shifting landscape in the field. My best experiences as a record producer have been when I had strong, intuitive A&R along for the ride.

The dB's never did "fire the drummer"—Will Rigby's feel was in many ways the most essential element of the band's sound—but that became a trope of later major-label record production; it was often the first thing out of a producer's mouth when the stakes were high. And there were historical precedents: George Martin, who attempted to replace Ringo on early Beatles sessions; Hal Blaine and Jim Gordon in LA, who subbed stealthily on singles for the Byrds; and countless others.

Of course, the saddest part of "these times today" is the widespread closure of the big rooms, though fortunately, some persist:

Hoboken's Water Music remains, Kernersville's Fidelitorium is constantly booked, and as I write this, the former Power Station, which had become Avatar, has now been purchased by Berklee College of Music as the new location of their New York campus but will remain a recording resource in some fashion. In general, however, excellent musicians working in large groups are no longer allowed to react to one another in real time but instead must add their parts one by one, a devolution if there ever was one. Laptop records have made for some great listening experiences, but these do not usually involve ensemble performances.

Specifics have thus dated my "pamphlet" somewhat, but the paranoia and alienation so often attendant on the process of group creativity appear secure. (I thankfully now view this from a distance.) Let me know if you'd like to buy the whole set!

————

It was now 1981, over three years after the Kossacks had ended, and I was fully ensconced in my quartet of fellow Tar Heels, playing guitar and trying to chart a course. As a band, the dB's had recently turned pro, meaning we had fully embraced poverty. The first album had been released overseas but not in the United States. Peter still had an occasional job at the hip record store Musical Maze; he had the résumé for it, since he had been our hometown spins clerk in high school—"Where It's Been Reznick's for Records for Years" had been the Winston store's proud claim. When we could, Rigby and I worked at the Spring Street Bar, a painter and gallery-owner hangout in Soho, serving endless wine spritzers to gallery owner Mary Boone and Long Island ice teas and chocolate cake to car-wreck sculptor John Chamberlain's underage kids. I remember once offering the dessert menu there to fellow CBGB denizen Chris Frantz, now graduated to celebrity status as the drummer for Talking Heads, who refused it by comically singing, in imitation of the Who's Roger Daltrey, that he was watching his "Teenage Waistline." The price of new fame. All the art world paraded through that bar, perhaps because of the owner's willingness to take paintings as payment for bar tabs. But the prime weekend shifts, when the good money was made, were off limits, because we would be gigging in some tiny corner of Tribeca, Boston, or Philly. Gene still occasionally dealt rare guitars to the likes of the Who, George Harrison, and ZZ Top, but now away from his Southern connections, he was finding these gems hard to come by, and nationwide, the supply of sixty-five-dollar sunburst Les Pauls languishing under sofas or yellowing in yard sales had finally been about depleted. We nourished ourselves the best we could on the excitement of new songs and atrocious reheated pizzas from a Sbarro pizzeria across from the Music Building, there below the Port Authority bus terminal. We were centered in the garment district, which helped us save on cab fare: Discarded rolling bins used to move T-shirts were always good for wheeling drum cases and guitar amps twenty blocks down the sidewalks to gigs.

A young "outsider" composer named Glenn Branca had made a huge impact locally with his massed guitar orchestras, starting in 1980 with *Lesson No. 1*. These early works of his reminded me a bit of more subdued compositions by George Crumb, whom I had met in college; I had attended performances of his prepared piano pieces, where the instrument was sometimes played with mallets, like a marimba or a hammer dulcimer, or "prepared" with bits of foil or rubber. And Henry Cowell's technique of banging on piano keys with blocks of wood also loomed large in the back of my mind. But Glenn was swinging mallets on our own dear electric guitars, where previously Led Zeppelin's Jimmy Page had only stroked the strings with violin bows on occasion. It was a gargantuan sound, and I wanted that for the dB's. For "Happenstance," a simple breakup song of mine, we arranged the rhythms in this way to match the anger of the lyric, with all guitar strings pulsing on the eighths and the bass generally staying away from the chords' roots, and I tried playing my guitar with the side of a drumstick instead of with a guitar pick. It wasn't quite there, though (Branca sometimes had fifty guitarists onstage, and we had only three), so we arranged for Rigby to

Roger Hannay playing the piano with mallets; courtesy of Wilson Library, University of North Carolina

add drum accents that, via studio switching devices called noise gates, would make the guitars accent strongly in tandem every time he hit. Rigby was in effect able to play the already-recorded multiple layers of guitars by remote control.

Another planned element of the song came from travels outside of the city. I remember the echoed "think" in the chorus as coming not from the Aretha song but from the SLIPPERY WHEN WET signs on the highway then. When it was *not* wet, these signs would be flipped on their hinges, folding in half, and turn into a sign saying just THINK—and I loved that reminder, in its all-encompassing vagueness. As we banged away that summer, I wanted more signs, ones that said BREATHE and LIVE. We were counting down the weeks until the creation of our second album would commence.

Stands for deciBels had been made guerrilla-style, in dribs and drabs of studio time, by begging favors, saving quarters, and cutting corners. We had even mixed some songs at Easter's Drive-In Studios while it was under construction, trying to mentally dial out the sound of drills whirring as the control room window was being secured inches from our noses.

But for the second album, *Repercussion,* we traded our publishing rights for a real budget with a real producer in real studios, although the UK label had insisted that we come across the pond, where they could keep an eye on us . . . and the money. It was still a New York event for us, though; we rehearsed and wrote diligently for hot summer months with the windows open in our wreck of a rehearsal room on Eighth Avenue, accompanied by the roar of the city, working with Litt, trying to create something that would make us proud. None of the budget went to us for Manhattan living expenses, of course, so we were still scrambling to make ends meet, and the pressure started to fray our nerves.

There was artistic confusion, too. We felt hugely sympatico with the "New Guard," digging ESG and the Bush Tetras, playing club shows and drinking too much in after-hours clubs like Mudd with No Wave musique-concrète rebels such as DNA and daredevil Lydia Lunch, but we had learned our songwriting chops by studying the best of the old (Kinks, Chicago blues, MC5), and our boots were now planted on both sides of a widening fissure. The aboveground press struggled to categorize and commercialize it all; battle lines were being drawn between two flags, New Wave and punk. In the trenches, among the downtown musicians, neither of these boxes seemed remotely appealing. We talked more of what was exciting, what was groundbreaking, innovative. What was cool.

A "power pop" box on a press questionnaire might have been attractive to us North Carolinians for about a minute back in 1975, but that felt like eons earlier. By the early eighties, power-pop practitioners seemed to us to be overly reverent of the past, with slight chips on their shoulders, a British gear fetish, and hair dryers at the ready. We had moved our sympathies to the other side of the aisle. We were too scruffy, too "disheveled," and our tastes were too catholic. Some of the dB's tracks could undoubtedly fit in that power-pop box, but for every one that did, another would be busy punching holes in the paper.

In July 1981 we relocated to London, to the Who's relatively luxurious studio, Ramport, to make the record. And it felt like our luck was changing: We had the producer we wanted, and the studio's centerpiece, its audio console, itself supported this theory of changing fortunes. It was one of the deluxe Neve models we loved, the Rolls Royces of recording. Legend has it that the very devout workers of the Neve factory would gather to pray over each model before it left on a truck. This one had been a custom order, the Who having famously specified that the front edge of the 8088 model be covered in fifteen feet of *seamless* leather. No amount of prayers, however, had succeeded in sourcing a single cow that big.

As we got down to work, we were dismayed to find that this particular Neve was a scratchy, flawed device, often crackling and spitting at our touch during the recording and forcing us to redo overdubs. Years later I was recording at Bearsville Sound Studios, in upstate New York, when the very same console arrived, purchased when Ramport closed. I was sure that Albert Grossman, the owner and possible target of Dylan's "Dear Landlord," had bought a very expensive lemon. I watched from the side as Todd Rundgren, head engineer George Cowan, and the staff opened it up, only to find it was full of hashish. The English engineers' smoke of preference was tobacco and hash, and they would roll the cigs on the faders; over the years this had added up to a blizzard of particles. A little vacuuming, and both the hash and the crackles disappeared. If only we had known . . .

The trip to England also meant that we had left girlfriends behind at a time when a transatlantic call might be five bucks a minute. With the added distraction of English "femmes fatales" (i.e., the women who worked in offices near us), emotions were stretched like guitar strings. Peter's girlfriend traveled to London for a few days during the sessions, but if anything, this escalated the tension. I was still blue over an unrequited love, followed quickly by an unlikely Blighty infatuation, and contracting pneumonia in the second week didn't help matters, especially for a singer. New York is a coffee town, but the ubiquitous whistling English tea kettles seemed the perfect metaphor for our overheated situation. Although I had been the de facto producer for the first album (Alan Betrock, who shares the credit with the band, specialized in saying the right thing at the right time but wasn't a constant presence), I now experienced some growing pains in that direction as well. With the able assistance of Gene Holder, Scott Litt, whom I had more or less handpicked as a producer, took the record in perhaps a better, more musical direction than I would have done, but his approach differed from mine quite a bit; it was more visceral and close-up, less romantic and mopey and wide-angle/orchestral.

Of course, we had fun at first, inmates in a new asylum, with baseball in Hyde Park and my new facial affectation earning me the nickname Soul Patch from the cute cashier at the Chinese takeaway. And the occasional transatlantic call from Carly Simon, who had helped with a few of the lines on "Ask for Jill" and was still friends with Scott, was a bright spot. As was the Keystone Kops arrival of the Rumour Brass (aka the Rumour Horns), who, after first arriving at the completely wrong studio, added their clarion call to the amazing kitchen-sink arrangement of "Living a Lie." But I became more and more withdrawn, alienated, with ginseng-and-honey concoctions draining my sleep . . .

We were all bunched together in a damp London basement flat, and the mold and mildew pretty much shut down my fragile lungs, so I didn't sing "Happenstance" until we had moved to George Martin's AIR Studios for mixing, where we shared the hallways with the then hit band Adam and the Ants (with our old friend from EMS in Putney, producer Chris Hughes, on drums and in face paint) and Paul and Linda McCartney, sometimes with sixties chart-topper Lulu but never with bodyguards (despite John Lennon's murder the previous year). McCartney was working on "Ebony and Ivory" at the time and seemed very curious about the activity in our room; he and Linda would come in every morning to say, "How's it going, dB's?" We'd usually say nothing, both too tired and too gobsmacked, I guess. And this ennui continued all that week. I clearly remember Mac and me standing by the soda machine around midnight, him wanting to chat, very friendly, and me being unable to converse with him, both intimidated (although really he seemed like just a fellow musician) and feeling some kind of ill-defined peer-pressure obligation to wave a punk flag and not Engage the Old Guard. I still feel guilty about this—how stupid, throwing away the chance to learn something, anything, in conversation with such a pioneer. (I did have some nice conversations with the very patrician George Martin, and I wasn't so reserved around their engineer, Geoff Emerick, with whom I had several revealing chats about Chris Bell's obsessive mixing . . . and mixing . . . and remixing sessions with him for "I Am the Cosmos.")

Despite my midnight rudeness, McCartney's team loaned me his own Neumann U47 tube vocal mic, with a pop filter like a shield from the days of King Arthur's knights, so that I could sing "Happenstance" into it on the very last day of the recording sessions. This was totally awesome; it was hard not to think about the fact that the soundtrack to my sixties had also moved the mic's capsule. In fact, the connection went deeper: I discovered only recently that the crickets on the sound-effects tape we took from the EMI closet and added to the song were the *same* crickets as those used on *Abbey Road*—it was like the Beatles themselves did a cameo for us . . . except it was their fellow insects instead.[10]

Although the band focused mostly on the sound of "Happenstance," including layers later threaded in by Scott Litt, its words have given this song life as a bizarro Mother's Day spin for radio DJs everywhere. I guess there is a shortage of rock songs that put down the *mater*.

> *Run back to your mother, tell her all the cruel things that I did*
> *It comes as no surprise to her, I was never smooth enough for*
> *her kid*

A mother knows what's best, she said, a mother knows
   what's good
So run back to your mother, she always said you would

Happenstance we fell into the off-the-cuff, vitriolic remark
All I ever wanted was to make you so damn happy
But a mother knows what's best she said, a mother knows
   what's right
So run back to your mother, out of mind, out of sight

Think for yourself, think it through, don't let her live for you
Think for yourself, think of me, we could be so happy
Think for yourself, think for yourself, think for yourself—
you'll come back to me

When it happened, as it happened, it was the worst thing
   I've ever felt
One day, in your cul-de-sac, you'll realize what it meant
A mother knows what's best she said, your ballerina curls
So run back to your mother like a good little girl . . .

When I hear this song now, my head fills with vivid images from
that time: of drinking Pimm's Cups at Wimbledon during the
epic final match between Björn Borg and John McEnroe; of
the cookies on a silver platter carted in each morning at AIR
by our ever-cheerful tape op, a young woman named Renate
Blauel (who afterward surprised us by becoming Elton John's
wife, although only for a short time). But my strongest memory is
of the very last night of mixing, as the antibiotics finally kicked in
and some parts of my voice returned—down to the wire, finally
singing the miserable and self-pityingly desperate "Happenstance" alone in the room. Watching the control-room crowd
through the window. *Wondering what they were saying about me.*

15

She Took the Soda Pop

Dan-ny went home 'n' killed him-self last night,   she'd ta-ken ev-'ry-thing, she'd ta-ken

1.   ev-'ry- thing   2. ev-'ry-thing She took his cash,   she took his checks___   She took

"**A**MPLIFIER" IS THE MOST WELL-KNOWN OF ANY SONG by the dB's, but in many ways, it's also the least characteristic of the band's early sound. With the help of a contagious rhythm, the jolly song describes someone who has nothing left, who has reached the end of his rope. It was literally written in the streets and reflects the New York we were experiencing; sometimes it seemed like all we had in the world, the only consistency, was the motley collection of oddball Vox, Marshall, and Rickenbacker amplifiers in our rehearsal space. I was there for the rehearsal and recording (and I appear, uncredited, on the version included on the band's third full-length release, Bearsville Records' *Like This*), but it's all Peter Holsapple's writing, so

I went "to the horse's mouth" for the origin of this one. Here's what Peter wrote about it:

> Sometimes the best songs come to you when a pencil and paper are unavailable, and this was one of those times. . . . I wrote "Amplifier" during a walk alone at dusk, to my East Village apartment from rehearsal at the Music Building . . . My gait down Broadway inspired the initial kernel of song, then it got sideswiped by Bo Diddley's beat. The refrain just fell out over those descending chords, although at first it was Johnny going home and not Danny (renamed for Danny Amis, our Minneapolitan friend from the Overtones). The laundry list came later but not by much, and I had the song pretty much finished by the time I reached Second Street. . . . As soon as I got the arrangement locked in, the band learned and began playing it almost immediately. . . . All the product of a brisk stride downtown![11]

"Amplifier" is based on a "3-2" clave beat, a rhythm central to Latin American music, especially Afro-Cuban material. Bo Diddley introduced this groove, sometimes called by the mnemonic "shave-and-a-haircut," to fifties rock and claimed it for his own with signature songs such as "Hey! Bo Diddley" and "Mona." Buddy Holly ran with it for his "Not Fade Away" (1957), and the Who continued with their 1968 hit, "Magic Bus." Tom Petty and the Heartbreakers used it for their second single, "American Girl." Bow Wow Wow charted the same year as the dB's release with a cover of the Strangeloves' clave-beat 1965 hit, "I Want Candy," claiming to take the original version's rhythm back to its Burundi roots—although their drummer, Dave Barbarossa, who also played with Adam and the Ants, later insisted that this was just his take on the Latin and reggae rhythms he had heard while growing up. So the dB's were in good company.

So much of rock music is unsyncopated 4/4 that it was great to have other patterns to choose from in a set, including this one and those of our "Storm Warning" and "Happenstance." "Storm

Warning" has just the 3-2 clave rhythm's strong first phrase, though without Bo Diddley's accents, and leaves off the second phrase, the "two bits"; the core rhythm for "Happenstance" could be rendered mnemonically as "just a haircut—no shave, please." In this same spirit, the band's live shows often included a performance of the Beatles "Tomorrow Never Knows," whose long, loopy groove's accents could conceivably be summed up as a period-correct mnemonic "don't try to cut m'hair."

> *Danny went home and killed himself last night*
> *She'd taken everything, she'd taken everything . . .*
>
> *She took his cash, she took his checks*
> *She took the soda pop, there was nothing left*
> *She took the love letters out of his desk*
>
> *She took his car, she took his bike*
> *She took everything she thought he liked*
> *And what she couldn't take, she found a way to break*
> *She left his amplifier*
>
> *And an amplifier's just wood and wire*
> *And wire and wood don't do any good when*
> *Your heart is blazing like a wildfire*
> *And all you've got to show for it's an amplifier*

16
Wine in Plastic Cups

Wine___ in plas-tic cups, lis - tening to the wind

I___ will tell you ev -'ry-thing, where do I be - gin?

O N MARCH 23, 1980, A TORNADO TOUCHED DOWN,
briefly, on Central Park. I was watching high up from
a window with a friend, looking for signs of imminent
destruction, drinking a highbrow wine from a disposable plastic
cup . . . and thinking of lines of a Television song: "I love disaster, and I love what comes after." Ours had been a whirlwind
romance, so fast that you could question whether it had touched
down to the ground at all or instead had simply spun around
in the ether, all dust particles and stripped ions. But we sat, in
the aftermath, and watched. Sometimes a new love seems to
open a window through which can be glimpsed a rowboat on a
Magritte ocean of possibility, a way to escape to a transformed,

New York Rocker *masthead, with the dB's; photo by Laura Levine; courtesy of Andy Schwartz*

hitherto unsuspected country. But windows are made only for glimpses—they are barriers, not doors.

The clubhouse for "Our Set" at this time was the fabled *New York Rocker* magazine offices, at 166 Fifth Avenue. Alan Betrock, my friend and inspirational neighbor in that first year, had started the mag in the first days of CBGB and then sold it to Andy Schwartz, a delightful, energetic whip-cracker (and rockabilly guitarist) who whittled down the staff to talented, essential contributors able to think for themselves, including writers Byron Coley, Ira Kaplan, Michael Hill, Richard Grabel, and Glenn Morrow; photographer Laura Levine; and graphic designers Chris Nelson (from Information, later of Mofungo and the Scene Is Now) and Elizabeth Van Itallie (who later became a close friend and designed several of my album jackets). Standards were as high as the pay was low. On evenings when no deadline loomed, musicians could pull amps and drums from the corner and rehearse or even record on the ever-present TEAC four-track; the dB's made a record's worth of demos at those offices, released later as the bulk of *Ride the Wild Tom-Tom*, which also includes a forty-five-second commercial (never aired) for the mag that proclaims, "I keep up with rock 'n' roll, I read *New York . . . Rocker*." But there was nothing better than dropping by *Rocker* on nights they went to press, when the esprit de corps intensified into the wee hours and the chanting and stomping from the Gnostic church next door reached a matching fever pitch.

Laura Levine's birthday party at New York Rocker magazine office. Left (left to right): Ira Kaplan, Laura Levine, and Georgia Hubley. Photo courtesy of Laura Levine. Below (left to right): Michael Paumgardhen, Randy Gunn, Will Rigby (vocals), and Peter Holsapple (vocals), with Georgia Hubley (drums), Ira Kaplan (guitar), and Bob Singerman (trombone). Photo by Laura Levine.

I had never seen art layouts for publication before, and there were no computers involved then; it was fascinating to see how glue and type were turned into a printed page. I especially liked the screens, the halftone dot patterns, and the way a percentage of information could be removed from a photograph, often quite coarsely, yet our brains would interpolate, would fill in the blanks, to see something like the photo's original subject. How much could be removed before the image was no longer the image? How far could you stretch imagination? (Later, working at the Pace art gallery one summer on a Chuck Close exhibit, prepping the room for this by repainting an already gray wall from a can of official "Chuck Close Gray," I had more time to ponder this pointillism writ large.)

So the title of "From a Window to a Screen" shows how I was trying to create a similar lyrical dot pattern, to remove most of the information from the events, to use just a few phrases yet still convey the sadness and sense of resignation I felt at the end of the affair. (Although there was a play on "window" and "wind-oh" in there, too, somewhere.)[12] I sometimes felt that I myself had become a shadow, with only a halftone percentage left. Vaporized.

I wrote "Window to a Screen" in one fell swoop, in an apartment on East Eleventh Street. I presented it to the dB's at a rehearsal for *Repercussion*, and we ran it down a few times, but I didn't think it got much of a warm reception, and we were trying out a number of new things that day. I had pretty much discarded it and was on the way to forgetting it altogether when Will, who often functioned as our foursome's unofficial aesthetic arbiter, brought it up a few days later and said he thought we should give it another chance. This time it clicked.

> *Wine in plastic cups, listening to the wind*
> *I will tell you everything, where do I begin?*
> *Some would say we were friends: I won't*
> *Make that mistake again, I won't*
> *Make that mistake again*

Careless at the start, cautious at the end
Ives was on the stereo, I remember when
Some would say, "What happened?"
I won't make that mistake again,
I won't make that mistake again

And Charles Ives's music was a soundtrack that summer. I believe I was thinking about *Central Park in the Dark* as we stared into the night across Fifth Avenue, but his *Unanswered Question* sounded about right, too. Later, in the studio, I had to fight a bit to get the disjunctive melodic quotation from "Shall We Gather at the River?" laid on top of the dB's song in that Ivesian way, but I'm glad it's there.

17 The Distance That Surrounds Us

... and I___ could scarce-ly be- lieve we were tal-king in___ the kit - chen Oh, the

way you looked right_ threw me_ oh-oh, oh_____

WE WERE BLINKERED GROWING UP IN WINSTON-Salem; our peer-group fascination with pop and rock guitar music had left little room for most of the other arts. By the early late 1980s, artistic life in Manhattan revolved around Soho, Noho, and Tribeca, where real estate and rentals were cheap and the visual arts were everywhere. The photographic notion of wide versus narrow focus, or *depth of field*, was a revelation to me. It was a metaphor for the quality of attention: "To see the world in a grain of sand." With music, I was slowly learning to mentally sweep through frequency ranges and timbres, to zone in on the tambourine or the baritone sax and then switch to the organ or the kick drum—the spectrum of sound coming in my ears was unchanging; only my inner focus was shifting.

Instead of listening to the radio, I took to playing rolls on a single ride cymbal for hours, moving around to different spots on the shiny metal surface, and listening to the amazing changes in timbre and pitch that would rise up out of the undulating *swoosh* and *rrrrar*, until it seemed unclear whether the sound was coming from outside or in.

I was also touring, not only in the United States, but also in Europe: first that UK club tour, in 1981, then another, opening for Dave Edmunds starting in March 1982. So there were hours, on trains or in vans, staring out the window at the world's kaleidoscope: French poppies, English rain. The world was suddenly both bigger and smaller. And stranger. I recall a night in Copenhagen, midnight in the basement of a small bed and breakfast, sitting at a card table with the band and a group of Dutch sailors, emptying bottle after bottle of high-octane aquavit. The fighting that eventually broke out among the sailors looked to be choreographed in slow motion as a ghostly femme fatale, wearing white gossamer, wandered silently around and around the room, smiling cryptically while unflappably dodging the smashed chairs and flying bottles. I awakened the next morning with this hallucination still on my mind. It was not until I reached the lobby for checkout and saw her again that I realized it really had been Nico, late of the Velvet Underground, who had been floating through the wreckage.

"Depth of Field" was my first song where it all came together, where the flanging sound and the glacial tempo matched the lyrics like a "handshake drug" (to use Jeff Tweedy's term). It was written in 1980 and intended for the dB's *Repercussion* record. I finally had a song I could be proud of. I had always tried to fit a lot into each tune, but now I felt as if I had an infinite amount of time. Why hurry? "Yes, I know you like the fast songs, you dig the complicated lines . . . but it's so simple, it's so straight: forevermore, in a figure eight" (a symbol for infinity). The tempo was very slow, as if taking place on a planet with a greater gravitational pull, as if it took more effort to lift the hand for the downstrokes, as if you had to have real intent behind every gesture. The super slo-mo lava flow of "I Am the Cosmos" had seeped into all our pores as precedent. I remember being in Holland for the first time, on one of these same tours, and thinking about a line from Elvis Costello's "New Amsterdam," "till I speak double Dutch to a real double duchess"; now, in shunning such gobbledygook, I wanted instead to have it be "Dutch to Dutch"—speaking to each other in the same language.

> *. . . and I could scarcely believe*
> *we were talking in the kitchen.*
> *Oh, the way you looked right threw me . . .*
> *Now we have depth of field*
> *What was once concealed*
> *Is out in the open,*
> *with no holds barred,*
> *And nothing else so real*
> *as our depth of field*

First lines—of books, songs, romance—are hard. Back in London, I had been enlisted by Carly Simon and Scott Litt in a brief attempt to write a song that contained nothing but famous first lines; I think Simon suggested the first line be "Call me Ishmael," from *Moby Dick*. Somehow this had morphed into the line about Jonah in "Ask for Jill." Here, however, I wanted to skip the problematic first line entirely, to start in the middle of the action. So it starts, "*and* I could scarcely believe . . ."

"Depth of Field" is a love song, but it was inspired by the beginning instead of the end—it was rapture, the joy of feeling time expand to the point where every second could last indefinitely.

———

It was also a bellwether for the end of my tenure in the band I had started. When it got bumped from the song list for *Repercussion*, replaced by another glacial-tempo song, Peter's impeccable "Nothing Is Wrong," I realized, without rancor, that I needed a new situation. It was not easy to decide to leave the group; we had been through a lot together in those few years and were finally starting to get some attention. But I had not even argued against the song's exclusion in the final stages, though it cut me to the quick. I didn't think I could win the battle. Ultimately, Peter and I were writing too many songs to restrict ourselves to just five or six apiece per vinyl album, with two years in between. If the longer length of CDs or the current streaming options had existed then, things might have been different. But those were the facts at the time. As a writer, I found it discouraging to bring in what I considered my best work and have it be set aside and unheard—although it was no one's fault. It was economics. In those days, each song cost, on average, at least $2,000 for recording, overdubbing, mixing, and mastering; records thus had to trumpet the most immediately catchy and upbeat material, ideally with a crisp backbeat and playful kick drum, so that discotheques could use them to further dehydrate the dancers and drive them back to the bar, where the money was made.

Looking back, I see that I must have sometimes frustrated my bandmates with my general restless impulse to get under the hood and move gears around, with respect to both the music and the production; at a certain point, any sensible band just wants to get in the car, give it the gas, and arrive at the destination. In addition, my inner metronome is unquestionably *slowwww*, and slow songs drag on a young, energized group's set list: "Yes, I know you like the fast songs . . ."

Still, that time of banding together to create those first two records was a special one for all of us. And it was not a tabloid breakup; we might have smashed glass for the microphones at times, but we were still Southern gentlemen, shy of confrontation, when the tape wasn't rolling. And you have to keep this in mind: We had played together in many high school bands, some lasting only a few months; others, less than that. We were used to change. For us, then, the dB's practically held the record for longevity at that point. This is not to say that it didn't hurt to leave; no high school band experience had been nearly as

Before a benefit concert, February 1985, at Reynolds High School, Winston-Salem, North Carolina (left to right: Chris Stamey, Ted Lyons, Will Rigby, Mitch Easter, Faye Hunter, Peter Holsapple, and Gene Holder); author archives

transformative as those five years, with those three friends. It wasn't easy, either, for me to be the one to raise my hand and ask for the hall pass on the sad afternoon when we met to acknowledge that the split was for the best. But it didn't seem to come as a surprise to the rest.

Peter, Will, and Gene (now on guitar) continued the band, touring with various others, most regularly with New Orleans bassist Jeff Beninato, making outstanding recordings together, including *Like This* and *The Sound of Music*, until finally dissolving the unit in 1988.[13]

Jukebox

Don't Push Me, 'Cause I'm Close to the Edge

"The Message," Grandmaster Flash and the Furious Five, Sugar Hill Records, 1982

In 1980 Kurtis Blow's record "The Breaks" blew up. A very early rapping record, its six and a half minutes contain multiple "breakdowns" and feature, for the first time, an unbelievable amount of low end. The way I heard the story, Masterdisk's Bob Ludwig let his young assistant take over the booking, as it wasn't a high-profile major-label session. Howie Weinberg had perhaps not done a lot of solo mastering at that point. He fired up the tape, worked on the sonics for a bit, and then asked Kurtis what he thought. Kurtis simply replied, "More bass." Howie pumped it up a bit. Kurtis reviewed. Once again, "More bass." This went on and on. One assumes that the more senior Ludwig might have stayed his hand had he been behind the desk, but it was probably harder for Howie, just starting out, to deny a client's direct request. The track ended up with just about the *most bass ever*; a new standard for massive low end was set, and soon all the rappers wanted Weinberg and his "more bass" mastering. (Apologies, especially to Howie, if this third-hand tale isn't precisely the way it went down, but I like the story.)

It was a later record, however – 1982's "The Message," by Grandmaster Flash – that took the volatility of New York's powder keg to the next level. (I assume he took his first name from the Ampex 456 Grand Master, the preferred brand of high-output analog tape that was everywhere in the studios of the day.) It captured that summer's claustrophobic, pressure-cooker vibe in New York, which has always been a pedestrian's town. Whether or not you have a budget for taxis or chauffeurs, you're going to end up walking, or squeezing into a crowded subway car; at some point, it's the only way to get to most places fast enough. You're in the hive, bumping into strangers, dodging, jaywalking. This is, in fact, one of the best things about living there, especially in the downtown areas away from the greatest population density. You run into friends on the street seemingly much

New York Rocker *cover with Tina Weymouth (of Talking Heads) and Grandmaster Flash; photo by Laura Levine; cover courtesy of Andy Schwartz*

more often than the odds would predict. But there were times then when it also seems like one of the worst things. During the latter half of the seventies, a new national policy of deinstitutionalization begun in California under its then governor, Ronald Reagan, led New York State to release over 80,000 mental patients. Over half of these ended up in New York City, with the Bowery becoming a ground zero for disturbed, homeless, abandoned men and women.

This was not yet the town that it is now, where Times Square is a brightly lit Disney playground. It was the city where, on October 30, 1975, the *Daily News*'s headline read FORD TO CITY: DROP DEAD as the president categorically dashed any hope of federal aid in avoiding the hovering prospect of municipal bankruptcy. In those years, there was a general sense that the rest of the country had turned its back, abandoning the weird, edgy East Coast conclave of immigrants to its fate. So when "Don't push me, 'cause I'm close to the edge" started blasting out of midtown speakers from all the shops, it was as if someone was reading the minds of the passersby in a city where fight-or-flight reflexes were already pretty much permanently engaged. "The Message" was one of the first DJ-created records that wasn't just about boasting and partying; it indeed had a message. The sound was great, too, but it wasn't only about DJ tricks this time: The MC was front and center, a real lead singer, driving the record. It was released on the Sugar Hill label, the place to be then, which in 1979 had filled its coffers with the genre-defining Top Forty smash "Rapper's Delight" by appropriating the bassline and other elements from Chic's "Good Times." And "The Message" hit in both the R&B and the pop charts, showing that this kind of music could have significant mainstream popular appeal.

> Broken glass everywhere
> People pissin' on the stairs, you know they just don't care
> I can't take the smell, can't take the noise
> Got no money to move out, I guess I got no choice
> Rats in the front room, roaches in the back
> Junkies in the alley with a baseball bat

18

The Air Is
Full of Air

Oh_ ye - ah . . . So beau-ti-ful in re- pose___

(Oh_ ye -ah) Out-side it's snow-ing on the chim-ney smoke___

"WHY CAN'T WE LIVE TOGETHER?," A PLEA FOR WORLD peace, had reached number 3 on the *Billboard* chart of February 10, 1973. It was made by Timmy Thomas, a Memphis session musician then recently relocated to Miami, from only a Lowrey organ (the same brand Garth Hudson used in the Band) and an early, chunky, and cheesy Roland drum machine, plus his very soulful vocal performance. That was it. I loved its sparse, spooky sound and its simplicity. A case of opposites attract: I was a guy with maximalist tendencies who was regularly drawn in by *minimalism*.

———

I had been introduced to the concept of minimalism in music

during my first semester of college. Roger Hannay, the head of the UNC music composition department and a brilliant man who had studied with Howard Hanson and Aaron Copland, had asked us to write a "minimalist" piece for our principal instrument and to come to class prepared to play it. Not knowing the minimalist tradition at all, I wrote something that had no connection with its aesthetic, a kind of funky pentatonic score for my electric bass (the scale's five notes being the "minimal" part). This score included an instruction to cut the high string with scissors at a certain point for the *kerrang* it would make, a technique evocative of Gustav Metzger's oh-so-sixties Auto-Destructive Art movement (and British band the Who). Surely, I thought, this simple special effect was going to seem old hat to these jaded comp-class modernists in the days when a contemporary piece might consist of the single instruction: "Pour milk into a piano and amplify." I played it for the class, scissors at the ready, but hesitated to cut the string, instead just describing this to all—bass strings were really expensive to someone on a freshman's budget. Nevertheless, I become known for a while in the halls of the music department as "crazy string-cutter guy." Roger, however, pointed me in the direction of the library, and there I went, to discover a different kind of New York music.

———

Minimalism originated in the Soho and Tribeca downtown scene in the early sixties and was originally called the New York Hypnotic School. Although by definition its key requirement was merely that a work have a restricted palette—whether of pitch, rhythm, timbre, or any other musical element—in practice minimalist music often moved very slowly, with looped phrases or other static, repetitive textures. La Monte Young would set up drones with oscillators, perhaps a perfect fifth apart, and let them play without interruption for extended periods (sometimes months) in his living loft. His Theatre of Eternal Music ensemble (later called the Dream Syndicate) included a young composer named John Cale, who was to bring some of this experience to his viola drones with Lou Reed in that seminal New York band they helmed, the Velvet Underground. One piece by Young reputedly consisted of twelve-bar blues changes played over the course of a whole year, one bar to each of the twelve months; the chord changes apparently became significant physiological events for the people living in the building—ah, that ascension after four straight months on the tonic, the abdominal catharsis of going from the I to the IV.

Another member of this New York set, a composer named Terry Riley, had a kind of game piece (a composition with game-like text instructions, perhaps for connecting modules or fragments, resulting in performances that are structurally different each time) called *In C*, which the UNC student New Music Ensemble was to play a few months after the class on minimalism. The score offers a sequence of fifty-three short phrases, the same for each player. These can be repeated several times, and entrances can be staggered; the musicians have lots of options over the hour or so that this piece typically takes—even the instrumentation is unspecified. Riley had initially conceived the composition to be arhythmic, but as he was finishing it, another minimalist, Steve Reich, suggested what would become its unifying pulse: constant eighth-note Cs, to be played on a piano or other pitched percussion instrument (preferably, according to the score, by "a beautiful girl"). *In C* is quite lovely and became a gateway to early minimalism, as it was essentially very tonal and thus not a particularly demanding listening experience. (There was, however, a recent performance, on March 30, 2017, at Zankel Hall in the Carnegie Hall complex, that resurrected the original, sans Reich's pulse addition, as part of a month-long series curated by Reich himself. I don't know if the beautiful girl spec'ed in the score was given another task.)

Reich had created a piece that spoke more to me, one that involved the reel-to-reel tape recorders I loved. *It's Gonna Rain* (1965) used as source material an outdoor recording of a Pentecostal preacher describing the end of the world. He proclaims, "It's gonna rain for forty days and forty nights," and Reich loops the first three words on two different tape recorders, starts them together, and then lets them drift out of synch, like this:

> *It's gonna rain it's gonna rain it's gonna rain it's gonna rain it's gonna rain . . .*
> *It's gonna rain   it's gonna rain   it's gonna rain   it's gonna rain   it's gonna rain . . .*

Other variations follow, but listening to the whole piece for all seventeen-plus minutes is a very powerful experience. Devastating.

———

The true hypnotic flavor of the minimalist aesthetic might have been missing from my foolish "cut the bass string" piece, but it was clearly a factor in two songs of mine from 1982, both on my first solo record, *It's a Wonderful Life*.[14] The title track has a lyric that consists of only those four words repeated many times in melodic variations over a single repeated bass note, with the electric guitar in a purpose-built tuning (low to high, F–A–C–G–B–E) and punctuation from a keyboard chord triggered by a tom-tom. Somewhere between hypnotism and positivism, it was written by notating taped improvisations with Carol Whaley, at that time an aspiring drummer, playing the groove. The recording features just a duo performance by Ted Lyons, with tones triggered from his drums, and myself singing and playing guitar. It didn't end there, however. I made a nice twelve-inch remix where I added Henry Cow's Fred Frith on viola. Then I tried a totally different arrangement, this one on acoustic guitar and sans vocal but with orchestration and other melodies, which appears on some editions of the *Christmas Time* collection. I've since rejiggered it as a successful John Zorn–like game piece, first performed at the Hopscotch Music Festival in Raleigh, North Carolina, with some players from New Music Raleigh in 2014; in this version, a small chamber ensemble uses hand signals to pass around fragments of the melody.

The album's other minimalist composition, however, has a full lyric. "Oh Yeah" is *musically* minimalist, though, with four major chords (A, E, G, D) repeated over a droning root (A). The recording sounds very Tinkertoy to me now, since the keyboards are all triggered by similar drum hits courtesy of Lyons, a great player whom I managed to convince to become a bit of a windup monkey as the only authorized operator of a peculiar, antique studio contraption I dubbed the Groovegate System. It was a bit of a Betamax failure to the computer sequencers' VHS-like triumph, but it had seemed like a good idea at the time . . . Let me explain.

A clever archeologist might one day theorize that the unlikely and unwieldy contraption that was the Groovegate System had been created by a follower of Rube Goldberg. I wanted to get that Timmy Thomas sound live, but with a real drummer. I didn't have many options for this back then, however; the explosion of affordable sampling technology was years away, and most computers still filled entire floors of office buildings. So I created a hookup where individual drums—a rack tom, say, or a mounted kick drum—would flip switches on a noise-gate strip and thus unmute sustained pitches on a keyboard. It was all as primitive as could be: We used metal fishing weights from a hardware store to continuously depress plastic keys on the Ace Tone organ, and I had found a professor at Princeton University who could rewire the keys of a fifty-dollar Casio to sustain infinitely. The weights made the organ notes sustain, but the noise gates allowed the signals to pass through and be audible only when a drum was smacked and only for as long as the drum's tone sustained at a preset level. The fishing weights had to be lifted quickly and moved to other keys between drum hits when we wanted different notes, which thankfully wasn't all that often in this drone- and ostinato-based music.

This meant that a skilled drummer (which is where Ted came in) could be free with tempo, playing rhythms more nuanced than any lockstep computer sequences, and the sounds would follow him exactly. If he sped up or slowed down, so would the organ tones. To make the device even more unlikely of success, the raised, mounted bass drum (in the style of the Velvets' Mo Tucker) left Ted with a free right foot (it would normally have operated a kick-drum pedal). This foot became the bassist, tap dancing over a 1.5-octave pedal keyboard synthesizer (similar to a pipe organ's pedal set) that would be heard only when the mounted bass drum was hit. He was thus continually dancing up and down the scale with that foot, playing funky bass lines, while balancing on his left—a visually captivating spectacle. Ted, a free-thinker and fellow innovator, was the only person I could ever convince to work the gizmo, which made him a brother in arms (legs?) to the rare individuals who can play those custom instruments made out of airplane fuselages that outsider composer Harry Partch created for his forty-three-note-scale compositions. (Partch was already a trained composer when, in 1930, at the age of twenty-nine, he burned all his previous works because of their disdained European influence and set out on a hobo's life, riding the rails and writing radical and intensely idiosyncratic new works for customized instruments.)

I liked the Groovegate because it allowed the two of us to sound something like a full band. And it helped us stay rhythmically tight; we had no middleman, since the drummer was also

Track sheet for "Get a Job" from the Wonderful Life *album, illustrated by Peter Holsapple; author archives*

the bassist. Having concocted and become saddled with this absurdity, I then wrote songs and arrangements for "Groovegate and guitar" that tried to justify it. And we toured the country for a while, playing clubs, adding another player or two; alumni included Rick Brown and Phil Dray, percussionist Jay Johnson, and Captain Speed alumnus Mike Greer.

On one such tour, I reconnected with Alex Chilton in New Orleans. He had been sequestered there, staying away from the music racket completely, working as a dishwasher in a restaurant, and avoiding alcohol—as he put it, "I don't drink gasoline anymore." He described how, after he had been pontificating on some subject to a fellow restaurant worker, the guy had turned to him and said, in a tone dripping with sarcasm, "Yeah, Alex, you're right . . . and the whole rest of the world is wrong." Never one to lack the strength of his own convictions, Alex then told me, smiling, "And you know, I think that guy knew what he was talking about!" It was good to see him doing so well and being so unchanged. New Orleans seemed to fit him in a way that New York and Memphis no longer did, and he was to remain a resident there for the rest of his life.

After these forays out into clubland with the contraption, we retired to Easter's Drive-In Studios to document it all. Even when nothing in a song really called for the concept, as was the case with the aforementioned "Depth of Field," we would still include some Groovegate in the mix. The album *It's a Wonderful Life* mostly comprises these round pegs in square holes. After this, the Groovegate System joined Betamax and Edsel in the museum of the dodo bird (more specifically, the back of my storage closet).

There is a real song hidden in "Oh Yeah," despite the rinkydink realization, and it found favor in the Athens, Georgia, camp, including the R.E.M. folks, who, as I recall, especially liked the Lewis Carroll non sequitur exuberance of "the air is full of air . . . the air is full of yeah!" When I play the piece now, it's much more traditional—no noise gates—but still quite minimal, just four chords over a drone note. And, I have to say, it's often quite lovely.

Oh yeah . . . So beautiful in repose
Outside it's snowing on the chimney smoke
I walk out as if to catch my breath, full of thirst,
You as beautiful as water, as invisible as water is . . .

Oh yeah . . . I brush your hair, you draped in your
grandmother's quilt
And me in my father's guileless conviction
What a pair of fools we are! We want a World's fair,
and a long, long Tunnel of Love

The air is full of air . . . the air is full of yeah!

19 Like a Party Balloon on the Strand

So long to all the lies___ It's been so___ long, but here is ___ good - bye

And for once___ in your life, tell me_ the truth___ here at the end___

EW YORK'S APPEAL STEMMED IN PART, ESPECIALLY FOR
a musician from the hinterlands, from a simple fact: It
was where the studios were. (This echoes the reply that
Willie Sutton supposedly gave when asked why he robbed banks:
"Because that's where the money is." Given how expensive studio time was back then, the parallel is even more apropos.) Oh,
we had a few audio caves when we were growing up in North
Carolina—Reflection in Charlotte, Crescent City in Greensboro—but the Manhattan places were the ones where the music
flowed out into the culture. And in the late seventies, no place
was more full of wizards than was Power Station, at 441 West
Fifty-Third Street.

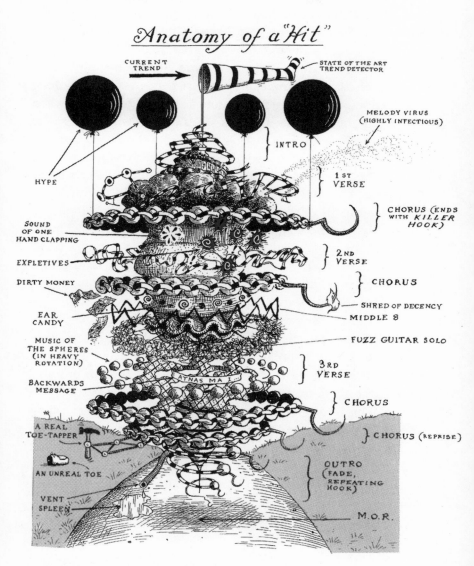

Illustration by Peter Blegvad; used by permission of Peter Blegvad

It was a huge contrast to go from watching pop hitmakers Hall and Oates recording at Power Station in the daylight to seeing the B-52's or Richard Hell and the Voidoids raising Cain in the ultrahip, anything-goes Mudd Club, at 77 White Street in Tribeca, during the wee hours. I was fascinated by the secret handshakes, the studio noise gates and sidechain compression and Fairchilds and LinnDrum piezo triggers—really, everything involved in making modern pop music sound great—but when it came to the music itself, I was still a downtown guy, a spy in the house of loud, trying to learn the ways of the enemy in order to flip them to the advantage of the downtown revolution.

Why put up with the long hours, bad food, frayed tempers, and lack of sunlight in the studio? NRBQ mentor and Chic engineer Bill "Bear" Scheniman used to say that it was simple: "That's where the magic lives." Songs like the Drifters' "Spanish Harlem" were filled with the sound of *rooms*, but hearing is a more mysterious sense than vision. When listening to a recording, you have to "hear around corners," to imagine the room that the notes are bouncing off of. All sorts of factors are involved in reproducing this: the types of microphones, their positions, the way the signals are processed, left-right assignments in the stereo image—all these let producers paint not only with combinations of pitch, timbre, and rhythm but also with careful amounts of both real and artificial reverberation effects. This results in a sensory dislocation: Your eyes are seeing the wallpaper in your living room, but your ears are hearing a space in London or Los Angeles, or perhaps a room that exists only in dreams. If you listen hard enough, your real room falls away, and you find yourself in the other. It's a bit like *Being John Malkovich*; you are hearing an idealized version of what the artist might have heard. I liked many aspects of the producer's job, including that of coming to a project with an outside perspective, sussing it out, clearing out perhaps only a few impediments to a creative space and (ideally) then watching a musician's art suddenly flower to fill it. But that alchemy—of finding a sound, a room, a combination of tones, a space that can fill and fascinate and transport the imagination—remains an essential attraction for me.

Two ears, two speakers: stereo, it all made sense. Phil Spector had done marvelous things with mono room sounds in the early sixties, sonically implying vast spaces, but mono was a constricted palette. The seventies had often flirted with ways to use four sound sources, with *quadraphonics*, a way of making a recording seem more three-dimensional. But where do you put the speakers? They would end up under bookcases, or facing the wrong way, with some accidentally wired with flipped polarity so the centered sounds canceled out. I myself liked stereo, which really presents the ear (and brain) with *three* sources of information from sum and difference: the left channel, the right channel, and the ghost center image of sounds mutual to both. I'm not saying that quad sound had no real pluses, however. Musician and producer Al Kooper once told me that he had bought a four-poster bed in the late sixties, and when quad first came in, he had hung a speaker on each post. At the end of a date evening, after the requisite "Hey, why don't you come up to my place for a drink?," Al could say, "Lie here on the bed with me for just a minute and listen to this quad stuff, it'll blow your mind!" and then hope that nature would take its course.

In an era overrun with brittle, low-res digital reverb units, one of the many innovations at Power Station was the use of their elevator shaft as a natural reverb chamber whose depth of sound could be adjusted by moving the elevator car. Of course, this made for more stair traffic than was ideal; when the shaft was being used in a mix, the car could no longer budge from the designated position. The cathedral-like Studio A doubled as a great reverb chamber as well, with speakers on the floor sending sounds out to adjustable mics way up at the tippy top. Another innovation was the secret so-called Bruce Springsteen fader, which was rigged from the final volume-control slider at the far right of the board. Springsteen would sing as he felt it, and that would be the vocal take, *done*, even if there were a few blemishes, a few places where the pitch fell shy of the mark. But he had moved into a realm where repeated radio play might make these flaws much more noticed, so the wizards addressed this by wiring the slider so that it controlled a primitive Eventide 910 harmonizer. Using this setup (discussed only in hushed terms), and years before Autotune invaded the airwaves, the engineers could miraculously push a given syllable up or down, back to pitch, and keep the Boss on the right path. I'm not sure that even Bruce knew about the stealth use of this magic wand. (To be fair, I doubt it was used much, since the 910 was a pretty glitchy device.) To the best of my knowledge, though, this was the beginning of the audio cosmetician industry that still rules the day here in the next century.

There has been a lot written about perceived sonic differences between yesteryear's analog and today's digital recording techniques. But one thing that has been overlooked is the difference in smell. Tubes get hot and burn off dust, and different brands of consoles smell different once electricity is flowing; the Neve in Power Station's Studio A smelled a lot different from the SSL console in Studio C. The tape matters, too; as analog tape rolls by the capstans and guide wheels, it sheds small amounts of its metallic oxide and binding; most pro engineers could tell by nose alone whether the tape spinning around was 3M/Scotch, Ampex, or Agfa.

Much later, around 2005, after digital had largely taken over, Mitch, whose Fidelitorium studio still offered analog, quipped in an interview that he still used tape partly because he needed the smell to "activate his reptile brain" during sessions. And we were off to the races! Don Dixon, Mitch, and myself conspired over email to address this posthaste. We knew there was a market for lava lamps in control rooms, as these added a useful visual distraction during a mix, and we thought we could come up with something that would do the same for odor. I named this device the Reptile Brain Activator, and long technical discussions ensued among the RBA think tank. We settled on a design with one 5X4G tube sticking out of the top of a small gray chassis with a mesh holder above it for ground-up squares of two-inch multitrack analog tape. The tube heats up, and it becomes an oxide- and plastic-incense burner.

Adding a further wrinkle to our marketing concept, we remembered how hotel chambermaids from the fifties would take the sheets Elvis Presley had slept on, cut them into small squares, and sell each square for ten bucks. We decided we would take short slices from outtake reels of famous clients (I believe I suggested that first R.E.M. album, for starters) and offer these, pulverized, as gourmet upgrades, perhaps $100 a slice. The actual smell of recorded fame in your home studio! It went as far as one actual prototype, constructed kindly for us by Steve Carr at the boutique (and highly recommended) Carr Amplifiers, which sits in my studio to this day. Unfortunately, it just wasn't as smelly as it needed to be, and we lost the window of time for further R&D on it. Life moved on. (In the end, Dear Reader, no actual R.E.M. tapes were harmed; there is no need to alert PETA ["People for the Ethical Treatment of Analog"].) Perhaps someone reading this can improve on the idea and take it to market. But I digress; now back to the late seventies . . .

Chic's guitarist Nile Rodgers and bassist Bernard Edwards, both excellent players, took up residence at Power Station for their productions, as did a young Bob Clearmountain, who had recently retired from playing bass in a band called the Bats. It was a time when punk rock was filling the newspapers but disco was filling the coffers. CBGB and a discotheque called Studio 54 were both packing them in, but it was the latter where the cash was piling up. One late night, after being turned away from an overcrowded "Studio," Nile and Bernard instead returned to Power Station and recorded a song they wrote on the spot. The rest was history; "Le Freak," with its distinctively crisp, briskly strummed guitar chording and sparse, choked bass, was a worldwide smash, the first of many for Chic, and they never had trouble getting into that dance hall again.

Talking Heads were flag bearers of a second wave of CBGB bands, art students from the Rhode Island School of Design with Ban-Lon shirts and a dislocated, deceptive normalcy who had opened shows for Television (as a trio) and then signed a major-label deal with Sire in 1976. Tony Bongiovi, who had created Power Station, produced the first Talking Heads record in a tough-love fashion. Rumor even had it that certain of Tina Weymouth's bass parts were secretly replayed by session guys after the band had left for the day—a story that was most shocking to me back then, as I was a big Tina fan and an advocate of band integrity as well, but similar to whispers I later heard about some of Aerosmith's drum tracks in the nineties.

After all that time he had spent at Motown, Tony was said to be able to mix anything in just two hours, and he had a lot of mixing rules that helped things go quickly—for example, reportedly he would immediately reach over to cut off any violas, without even listening to them, because, he said, "No one wants to hear that." Indeed, a catchphrase from that era, although not necessarily reflective of his work, was, "Squash it and hose it [i.e., compress it and put reverb on it] and let's get the hell outta here." He would even sometimes let others record the lead vocals (a most crucial stage) while he watched *Airplane!* for the hundredth time, as he reportedly found the singing part kind of boring. Even though diametrically opposed to such philosophies, I was very fond of the guy, who was quite a character; I was impressed when he walked out the door during an Aerosmith session and whispered to me, "Chris, it's like working in a museum of natural history!"—this being just a few months before Aerosmith allied with Run-DMC for the remake of "Walk This Way" and thus became rockosauruses reborn.

One day Tony hired his nephew, John Bongiovi, as a custodian, but John would also spend some quality time on the couch in the lobby, buttonholing session guys drifting by to ask whether they would play on his demos. I'm not sure about the details of their falling out, but one day John wasn't around, and the next (or so it seemed), he was Jon Bon Jovi, rock superstar. And then it was suddenly David Bowie on a couch instead, watching TV hour after hour in the kitchen nook as Nile Rodgers crafted the swing brass for him on his blockbuster *Let's Dance* record, just one of many hits that came out of that studio in that era. (I was to think of Bowie on that couch years later. I was working with the exciting yet cerebrally inclined Le Tigre on several great records, when charismatic band member Kathleen Hanna explained to me, "We're not one of those bands that gets up and jumps around with guitars, we're one of those bands that sits on the couch.")

Of all the Power Station anecdotes, the one I have dined out on the most was related to me by Scheniman, another mainstay of the era and, in 1975, the bus driver for the Rolling Thunder Dylan supergroup tour, his qualification reportedly having been his ability to drive the bus with one hand and keep a tipsy Roger McGuinn from toppling over with the other. Bill described a generic-disco mixing session for some producers associated with MCA, a label often mentioned in conjunction with the mob at that time. Tony came in unnoticed to the back of the room as the mix was really coming together, listened for a few seconds, and then predicted loudly, "It's a hit!" The two producers turned a whiter shade of pale and then dove for the floor, cowering under the console to avoid what they thought was an imminent assassination attempt.

And to this day, whenever someone in the studio with me gets excited and exclaims, "It's a hit," I have an impulse to run for cover.

While in England, the dB's and Scott had become friends with the Soft Boys, especially Kimberley Rew, the "Richard Lloyd" lyrical guitarist to Robyn Hitchcock's "Tom Verlaine" stylings. The Soft Boys were probably the band I felt the most kinship with at that time; their *Underwater Moonlight* was a brilliant disk. And we had seen one of Kimberley's first bar gigs with the USO band he had gotten to back him, the Waves (not yet "Katrina and . . ."), who were stationed in London when not entertaining the troops elsewhere in Europe. (Gene, Mitch, Peter, and Will had also cut a single with Rew, called "My Baby Does Her Hairdo Long.") A few years later, then, in 1986, it was only natural for Rew to ask Litt to help craft a song as a single. It was pretty much a one-day thing, though, because of the Waves' small budget and Power Station's high hourly price tag: cutting drums, brass, vocal, and mixing as the sun came up. They walked out the next morning with the finished "Walking on Sunshine," and it became a constant on the airwaves and in TV commercials ever after and a part of the studio's continuing hitmaker tradition. That same night, in another room, the *band* Power Station was finishing "Some Like It Hot," which went on to become a smash as well and somewhat of an ode to the studio's mixing style, with one of the most take-no-prisoners, artificially reverbed snare sounds ever. It was, however, somewhat ironic that the sound of the band named after the studio didn't reflect the natural acoustic sound of that great cathedral-ceilinged room at all.

And speaking of being "a spy": I sometimes enlisted Litt for nighttime reconnaissance missions, like the evening he and I took turns, song by song, mixing 8 Eyed Spy's album, with Lydia Lunch singing lead, at 39th Street Music. She wasn't in town for this, but she later seemed quite pleased with the record, except for the cool presampling stutter edits Scott cleverly razor-bladed out of the tape on their Captain Beefheart cover: "I'm crazy 'bout the boy from Diddy Wah-Wah Diddy Wah-Wah Diddy-Diddy Wah" or some such. She complained, with a laugh, "You made me sound like Betty Boop!"

Easter had earlier tried to join the legion of New York studio owners. In 1978 he had found a very cheap building just north of the World Trade Center, and for a few years he and Faye Hunter had lived in this huge, empty space while trying to find their way through a maze of municipal permits and associated bribes. They had interesting company: Their neighbors included a band called the Plasmatics, whose lead singer, Wendy O. Williams, would chainsaw instruments and sledgehammer TV sets onstage. But civic regulations eventually proved to be too much, and the couple repaired to Ken and Lib Easter's new house in the country outside Winston-Salem, converting its twenty-foot-square finished garage space into the tiny Drive-In Studios. Surprisingly, they now found the studio success they had sought in New York. R.E.M. came there to record their first influential releases, followed by the Bongos and then a long line of indie acts. The space was small, but because there were no nearby houses, they could place amps outside, under the carport, effectively giving the studio an additional sound booth as big as all outdoors.

In 1981 Easter formed Let's Active with Hunter and Chapel Hill drummer Sara Romweber. The band signed with I.R.S. Records and in 1983 had an early success with an EP, *Afoot*. They had recorded the tracks at Drive-In, but they mixed some of the record, including the intoxicating singles "Room with a View" and "Every Word Means No," with Litt in New York at Power Station.

One of my favorite New York studio experiences occurred in 1980 when I was invited to be a fly on the wall at a recording session with B. B. King, who was to contribute overdubs on *Torch*, a standards record that Mike Mainieri was producing for

Left to right: Chris, Sara Romweber, Pat Irwin, Faye Hunter (the Raybeats), and Mitch Easter (standing), in Winston-Salem, North Carolina; Easter archives

Carly Simon. During my high school years, I had spent much of the summer of 1969 sequestered at my grandparents' stone cottage in the Blue Ridge Mountains with King's *Live at the Regal,* one of only three records I brought with me (the others being Dylan's *Nashville Skyline* and the first Led Zeppelin release). The bluesman had also played Winston-Salem around that time and knocked all our young socks off. B.B. arrived that day and was very humble and polite, and when he started to play, he was . . . kind of lost, flat and sometimes out of key. *Hmm.* The next take, more of the same. Nervous looks all round in the control room. But the third was transcendent, as was the fourth, and maybe there was another, equally amazing run at it. It was spooky, his going from zero to 100 mph like that. I left knowing I had experienced the presence of a truly master musician. (In the end, I think his solo was replaced by a sax played by David Sanborn. Ah, shoe biz.)

———

When it came to mixing my own songs, I could afford Power Station only intermittently, but in 1986 I had a melancholy finger-picked folk ballad called "27 Years in a Single Day" that everyone around me felt enthusiastic about, and the label sprang for both the studio and staff engineer Garry Rindfuss to do the mixing. The song would be an "answer record," a release that would reply to another. For example, a strange, almost Bollywoodesque disco hit by Anita Ward called "Ring My Bell" had been all over the international airwaves in 1979, and an answer record, "Let Me Ring Your Bell Again," by Frederick Knight (who also wrote "Ring My Bell"), scored some significant play as well. Lynn Blakey, who would later play in Tres Chicas, had been, while a college DJ at WQFS 90.9 FM, the subject of the Replacements' 1985 song "Left of the Dial." At this point, though, she was in a Greensboro-based band called the Broken Crayons, which started performing a song reportedly about *me,* "27 Years of the Blues." I thought this called for a similar reply of some kind.[15]

I wasn't so long out of music school that I had forgotten

Bach's clandestine spelling out of his own name, musically, in some of his works, using the notes B♭, A, C, and B; stemming from medieval usage, early German musical notation used the letter *B* for the note B♭ and *H* for the note B♮. (Schumann and Schoenberg continued this tradition in their own compositions years later, with the same four notes, as homage to Bach.) So with this in mind, I schemed a chorus where the melody begins by emphasizing the second of the tonic A-major chord (a note B on "*se*-ven"), followed by the seventh of the following E minor (an F♯ on "*years*"), thus musically spelling out "2, 7," the two numbers that are in the first word of my song's title.

Jukebox

Calling Out, in Transit

"Radio Free Europe," R.E.M., Hib-Tone Records, seven-inch vinyl, 1981

The members of the North Carolina Girls' Club gave first warning. The informal group, comprising Carol Whaley, Nancy Heidel, Myra Holder (Gene's wife), Holly George (the editor of Rolling Stone Press and later, as Holly George-Warren, author of a comprehensive Chilton biography), and occasional member Faye Hunter, had begun to hold women-only meetings at various members' Manhattan apartments, and in the summer of 1981 they were all besotted by the first seven-inch single by R.E.M., which Easter had produced at Drive-In. They were moved by it in ways that hadn't seemed accessible to the likes of DNA or Teenage Jesus and the Jerks. The CBGB pinball machine was flashing again.

"Radio Free Europe" evidenced a kind of fast, melodic guitar pop largely absent from the indie bins at the back of the college-town record stores in those years. For one thing, the guitar tone was clear and plain, not distorted, partly because of the lower-output pickups on the guitar Peter Buck had chosen, a Rickenbacker (also the instrument of choice for the early Beatles). This clarity let richer, "extended" chords come out effectively: Distortion adds so much harmonic richness to each note that more complex interval combinations get overwhelmed and turn to sonic mush. A clear tone works better.

The song's prechorus section features a progression of F♯, A, and B chords played as arpeggios (i.e., one note at a time). The high strings, E and B, are allowed to ring freely as drones, however, creating both ninth chords (on the A) and eleventh chords (on the F♯ and B, respectively). This chiming, ringing effect, reminiscent of the sound of an electric twelve-string, wasn't new to the era. I asked Buck about it recently, via email, and he replied: "Using open B and E strings on the guitar while playing up the neck . . . [is] a great trick, giving the player the ability to add melody, harmony, or dissonance to a song. It's also easy! . . . [It] would seem to be a Southern thing. I first heard it on the first two Big Star albums. We had all recently seen the dB's, and that innovation was certainly in their bag of tricks also" (e.g., "Black and White," "If and When").

Letting some open strings ring against chords played as arpeggios is a great way to make three or four musicians sound much bigger onstage. Much as "wrong" (or nonchord) bass notes under a triad can open up a song harmonically, simply fingering a chord and then, while keeping your fingers in the same position, moving your hand to "wrong" frets while letting open strings vibrate was to remain a fertile source of new material for not only several of R.E.M.'s future tunes but for those of a host of bands that followed. Buck adds: "'Radio Free Europe' was a collaboration between the four members of R.E.M., with Mike, Bill, and I working on the chord structure. We wrote a lot of songs around that time with a similar guitar voicing — 'Sitting Still,' 'Gardening at Night.' . . . The list is kind of endless. . . . In fact, I wrote and recorded a song using those open strings just two days ago!" And the song's arrangement also stood out because of what was *not* included: There was no guitar solo, something that was to remain a regular R.E.M. feature — or lack of feature.

Mike Mills's bass lines on the record also distinguished the record from its contemporaries. Mills plays the song in guitar range, with a bright tone, sometimes filling the role of a rhythm guitar with his constant eighth notes in the verse and then, in other sections, playing melodic lines that ride on top of Bill Berry's rollicking drumming. It was perhaps more like something you might have heard from Chris Squire, bassist for seventies prog-rock heroes Yes, far from the more common style of boring, low-string lockstep with the kick drum. And on this song, the verse melody seems to have come from the bass line.

Do any of these ingredients explain why the record became the talk of the town? No. They do not suffice. The clincher was a strange twist on commerciality: The melody that their singer, Michael Stipe, had devised made you want to sing along, but you just *couldn't make out the words he was singing*. Much as with the Kingsmen's "Louie, Louie" in an earlier era, everyone who heard the record had a different take on what the lyric might be. This lent a quality of abstraction to the music, and the mystery pulled the listener closer to the speakers. "Oh, I almost got it, let's play it again." It let the listener dream into the music. Although, to be fair, sometimes the words were enunciated clearly enough, but they didn't make expected, literal connections. You could actually make them out, but you didn't believe you were hearing them correctly.

In 1984, this appealing abstraction was taken to another level, as far as English-speaking audiences were concerned, with the rock-dance "99 Luftballons," by Berlin's Nena, which had been released in Europe in 1982 but took a while to get to the United States. It became a chart-topper despite, or perhaps because of, its being entirely sung in German. I was part of its fan club, enjoying it greatly just as vocalese; it was nice not to have the words get in the way. And like "Radio Free Europe," Nena's disk started with an amorphous synth intro. (When Nena released an English-translation version, some of the appeal of the track drained away, at least for me.)

There was a North Carolina backstory to "Radio Free Europe." In Chapel Hill in the mid-seventies, Peter Holsapple had been casual friends with a clerk at Schoolkids Records named Jefferson Holt.

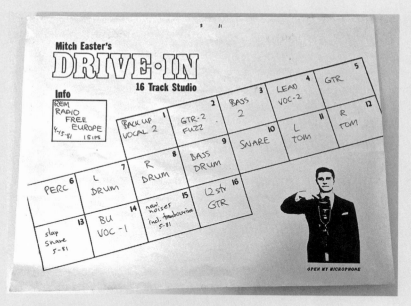

Original analog-tape track sheet for "Radio Free Europe"; Easter archives

When R.E.M. played one of their first out-of-town gigs, at the Station in Carrboro (a town adjacent to Chapel Hill) on July 18–20, 1980, Holt, the son of state representative B. Holt, was there, and he thought he saw something great, something in the classic tradition of the Who, in the rawness and freshness of their presentation. Shortly thereafter, he was in the van as the band's new manager.

R.E.M. had experienced recording in a studio only once before, in Georgia. The session was not a wholly successful one, but they had seen what "Rock Lobster" had done for fellow Athens band the B-52's, when another local record store guy, Danny Beard, had pressed up some copies on his indie label, DB Records. So Jefferson reached out to Peter Holsapple (now in New York) for studio advice, and although Peter had yet to hear what the band sounded like, he suggested that Mitch, recently returned to Winston from lower Manhattan, could do a great job in his new Winston-Salem studio.

Mitch recalls: "There was that sense back then that a lot of studios were not hip to the new sounds, and were too expensive. I was trying to position myself for exactly the kind of scene those guys were in. As in, sort of 'pro' but not really respecting the mainstream standards or approaches." I asked him about the sometimes indecipherable words to the song, and he recalled, "Michael had a lyric sheet, but he chose to sing right in this corner where he couldn't be seen, so I can't be sure! But I did find some lyrics from that session in his writing on the back of a track sheet."

Holt and the band made four hundred cassette copies of the Drive-In recordings (which included two other songs, "Sitting Still" and "White Tornado") and mailed them out to everyone they could think of, finding a taker in the tiny indie label Hib-Tone. And the record blew up. By the end of 1981, *The New York Times* had included it in its list of the years' ten best singles, even though it had no major-label involvement and primarily just word-of-mouth publicity. More important, it found a great home at what was beginning to be a major force in creating music careers: college radio. It was as if universities

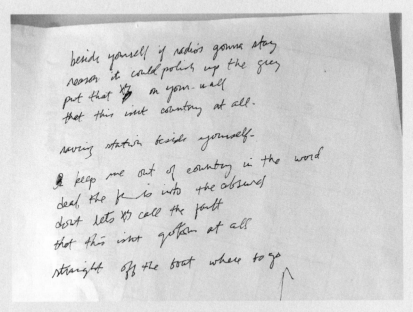

Original lyric sheet for "Radio Free Europe," used at the session for the Hib-Tone single; Easter archives

had been harboring an audience who had been waiting for years to hear a band that was neither their parents' boring jammers nor the window-smashing, gobbing UK punk crew. R.E.M., who were not ashamed of their literacy and romanticism and whose cover graphics connected with university art-department tropes, became this band, an answer to these music fans' prayers.

It didn't hurt that people who were drawn to see them live because of the mysterious single left thrilled by the charismatic, energetic, straight-ahead presentation and by Stipe's forceful, passionate singing — even if they were often still not sure what the words were. The band made converts at each new show. Mitch recalls: "I do remember seeing them for the first time, in Athens, when they opened for XTC. People were going crazy for them, and singing along to songs that were not available as recordings. I had never seen anything like that, and it was a glorious sight! I think when I met them they had been together for about a year, and it seemed like they had serious fans everywhere they had been." But even live, there was a sense that you had to lean in close to make sense of it all; there was still an appealing mystery enshrouded in the electric rhythms. We all wanted to break the code, to be a part of whatever the secret society was about.

Something that stood out was that they did this without relocating to a metropolis. They stayed put in Athens and in some ways remade it in their own image; they became ambassadors for the South, putting kudzu on their record sleeves and including works by local, eccentric folk artists, such as Howard Finster and Reuben Aaron Miller, on their covers and in their videos. Instead of hiring a big New York firm, they added Athens lawyer Bertis Downs to their enclave. Not only did they not leave; other bands from around the country relocated to Athens because of the band's mystique, perhaps hoping there was something in the water that would let them find recognition as well. (Not that R.E.M. were strangers to Manhattan; my first conversation with any of them took place there, with the urbane and personable Mike Mills, just the two of us alone at the bar one afternoon — at CBGB, natch.) Just a few years before, it had not been possible for the members of the dB's or Easter and

R.E.M. at the Rat (Boston), 1984; photo by Laura Levine

Hunter to gain headway in the South with music that was in many ways similar. But by 1981, a new infrastructure was in place, with adventurous nightclubs supported by those local college radio stations, and it welcomed R.E.M. with open arms. They became that generation's Beatles, a foursome whose whole exceeded the sum of the parts, with Holt in those days serving as their Brian Epstein (and Peter Holsapple, a bit later, as their Billy Preston). A band that was magic, one you could believe in, one you could trust.

20   Never a Time

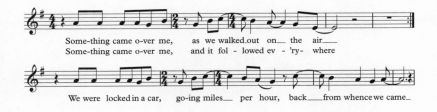

Some-thing came o-ver me,   as we walked out on the air___
Some-thing came o-ver me,   and it fol - lowed ev - 'ry- where

We were locked in a car,   go-ing miles___ per hour, back___from whence we came_

MANHATTAN'S MAGNETIC PULL HAD DRAWN MUSICIANS from all quarters during the late seventies, and as the dust settled on these wide-eyed immigrants, alliances started to form. Anton Fier, late of Cleveland, was a baby-faced clerk, alongside John Zorn, at Soho Music Gallery, at 26 Wooster Street. He first showed up on my map when, in 1978, he was recruited to play drums with an Ork act, the Feelies. He also moved in the experimental jazz circles associated with Bill Laswell and the Material gang, and he had a deep knowledge of all kinds of music. We would end up in a corner at parties talking passionately about Miles Davis or King Sunny Adé as drunken chaos escalated around us. Sometime around 1981, Geoff Travis, who ran the hip UK label Rough Trade, had enticed Anton to England to play drums with the Raincoats; the dB's were there, too, so our time in Britain overlapped a bit. When Laswell helped create the huge hit "Rockit" for jazz icon Herbie Hancock in 1983, Fier got hired to join Hancock's world tour, essentially replicating Michael Beinhorn's frenetic drum-machine patterns on the record. He came back a touring veteran, and as you would expect from a year of playing essentially drum rudiments every night, his technique was precise and monstrous.

Anton was aesthetically confident, a born leader, and an astute judge of other players' abilities. We had briefly tried to form a band together a bit earlier. He and mutual friend Arto Lindsay were writing songs together, and they asked me to join as a bassist (and perhaps a musical translator), but the record deal fell through the day before we were to fly to Canada to record. The only live show that came from this lineup occurred at the Peppermint Lounge, on a bill with another group that was performing one of Zorn's game pieces. I played vaguely

Anton Fier; photo by Laura Levine

bossa-nova guitar voicings to harmonize some of Arto's melodies as he sang liltingly in Portuguese.

In 1984 a motley crew soon coalesced around Fier. Its members included Jody Harris (an agile, Steve Cropperish guitarist from the Raybeats and Contortions), entrancing downtown chanteuse Syd Straw, and a marvelously inventive fellow named Peter Blegvad. Peter's dad, Erik, was an illustrator who included *Bed-Knob and Broomstick* and *Mud Pies and Other Recipes* among his work, and Peter had the knack as well, drawing backgrounds for Charles Schultz's syndicated *Peanuts* cartoons in a vast, derelict loft near Wall Street (and later creating his own amazing *Leviathan* weekly strip for the London *Independent*). But Peter was a songwriter, skilled poet, and enthusiastic guitarist to boot, erudite and whimsical, and he had returned to the United States after time in the seventies among the UK Henry Cow/ Fred Frith enclave of jazz-influenced avant-gardists. Kind and thoughtful, he always sported a twinkle in his eye. I admired his dedication to a lifelong art project called "Imagined, Observed, Remembered"; using no visual aids, he would draw something from his imagination, and then he would look at the object or a photo of it and draw it a second time, followed by a third version drawn only from memory, after some months had gone by. Taken together, these became a kind of map showing how his mind worked. Brilliant, really. The combination of Blegvad and Fier provided me a valuable continuing education, and I was eager to learn more, so that year, when they asked me to come to Paris to play Peter's witty songs, I leapt at the chance.

I fell hard into the "American in Paris" mystique, hanging out at Shakespeare and Company, walking everywhere, perching in front of Notre-Dame and trying to mentally dial back the centuries to the time when the landscape was still wilderness. John Greaves, from Henry Cow, was on bass, and Peter's brother, Kristoffer, sang harmonies and played guitar as well. We would rehearse in the mornings, after *café-calva* (coffee and Calvados), and then take a lunch break for more drinks; well-fueled afternoon rehearsals would explode. But the evenings were mostly free. I would sit with a candle and a bottle of Côtes du Rhône in our hotel "garret" and work on songs late into the night. In particular, I was trying to finish a new tune, one with an ascending riff I had modeled after something on John McLaughlin's first Mahavishnu Orchestra album. I wrote verse after verse in a disassociated dream-diary style that I thought was of a piece with writers ranging from Nerval to Robbe-Grillet, although of course it was really nothing of the sort. A few years earlier, Blakey and I had been to a lecture Robbe-Grillet gave at UNC-Greensboro, at which he showed his film *La belle captive*, and afterward he explained that the varied interior and exterior scenes were all shot in the same small interior room. Although this was cleverly disguised in the film, the approach created a uniformly surreal, dream-state substrate for all the action, which included several scenes of travel by motorcycle and car. It was from this half-remembered movie that I appropriated the quick-cut driving motif of my song. The little high-strummed, raked-arpeggio quarter-note crescendo that comes at the end of the "ah" choruses probably has something to do with Ravi Shankar's groundbreaking *Festival from India* double album that was often on my turntable in the sixties, and the faster melody that book-ends the improvisatory section is also most likely a child of this.

Something came over me, as we walked out on the air
Something came over me, and it followed everywhere
We were locked in a car, going miles per hour,
back from whence we came
Something came over me, in the driving rain,
in the driving rain

And we could watch from the roof, as the water fell in line
We could see through the air like it was invisibly fine
We could see through our skin as the bones, enraptured,
elongate entwined
We could see through the air in the naked light,
in the naked light

There was never a time when we felt so good inside
There was never a time when we could not even cry[16]
I should hold up the moon to illuminate, eliminate it all
Maybe that's what we did, maybe you recall:
I took off your shoes

I first called it "The Swing," as the gentle back-and-forth sway of its between-the-lines IV–V motif was based on memories of courting on Southern verandas, usually accompanied by mint juleps. Then I had the idea that by titling it "Something Came Over Me," after its first line, I could use the song itself as a kind of magical-thinking incantation, something that could transport both me and the listener each time it was heard. Legal pads full of scrawled, disjointed imagery piled up on the wobbly Parisian table alongside empty wine bottles, and although I had doubts each morning when I reviewed my efforts, by the time the night arrived, I would be back at it. Blegvad was in the room down the hall in that Paris hotel, and perhaps I hoped that mere proximity would help me soak up some of his finesse.

In the end, those epic legal pads didn't survive the trip back to New York, and I think it's just as well. I was able to remember a few of the lyrics, however, more than enough to frame a troubadour-style song whose improvisatory "transportation" bridge section often made any performance a lengthy one. It's not my best song if viewed from a technical perspective, as it's a bit of a hodge-podge, but it has become a signature song for me: It continues to be strangely affecting in performance. I've recorded it three times without being very happy with any of these; all three miss the impact of its best live performances. And I'm okay with this. Perhaps it's a creature that should live only in the wild. I've sometimes tried to retire it from sets, but I find it hard to stay away from the song's imagined incantatory power; by the time I sing the first lines, I can usually see through the back of the theater, walls melting away, and I'm in that hotel room again, in love, lost, enchanted, desolate, seeing Paris for the first time.

It was around this time that I started to think of producing as something I would like to do more. It helped that Water Music Studios opened their doors to me for my projects and were supportive of my efforts. In addition, the staff early on recognized the value of the older equipment that I liked: The studio's tools included an API console, Ampex tape machines, and Universal Audio outboard gear. I worked there on a single with Yo La Tengo and a solo album by Myra Holder, among others, and started to find my confidence.

As a creative process, producing differs greatly from songwriting, and there are all kinds of approaches. As a producer, though, I have always focused on both the nitty-gritty of the songwriting, ideally working with song structure and arrangements *before* entering the studio, and on the singing, making sure that the vocal tracks are as effective as they can be and that nothing upstages the vocals. And of course, I also understand how it feels to be an artist—the psychology, and sometimes the temporary psychosis, of being on the other side of the mic—and I always try to help alleviate any anxiety. Producing is a great job. It's quite an honor to "join" a band or pact with a songwriter for an intense period of creativity; it's very rewarding to make a positive difference in the music, sometimes by adding very little, but just enough. Then, too, the short-term nature of the relationship is a plus. At the end of making a record, you don't have to sit in a van for thirteen hours, day after day, as you travel through the Midwest. You just go home. Most of my time in New York was taken up with my own music, though, and only when I returned to North Carolina, in the nineties, did my production career really start.

Jukebox

Backseat for a Bed

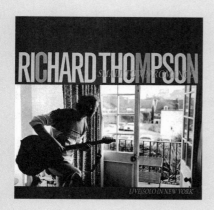

"Small Town Romance," *Small Town Romance*, **Richard Thompson, Hannibal Records, 1984**

The Paris adventure with Blegvad had renewed my fascination with the troubadour songwriting tradition, but my interest in it did not begin there. A songwriter named Townes Van Zandt had made an indelible impression on me when he played at Wake Forest University's Wait Chapel back in 1968. The folksinger, fresh off his first album, *For the Sake of the Song*, was on tour with his Poppy Records bandmates the Mandrake Memorial, a Philly group that used the Rock-Si-Chord organ and an early guitar-triggered oscillator box played by future *Guitar Player* magazine columnist Craig Anderton. It was a bizarre pairing, the wild, trippy quartet sounds of Mandrake followed by this stick-straight folksinger, up on stage all by himself. His relative normalcy that year, in the aftermath of the Summer of

Love, really stood out, and I loved his songs and attitude and the way he filled the room with music by himself, with just a few carefully chosen words and some basic cowboy chords on his guitar. But what I remember most, I'm afraid, were his blue jeans, which shockingly were not bell-bottoms! I had never seen unflared jeans on a performer before; it was a different time.

Singer-songwriters were far rarer birds in the sixties; in the wake of the Beatles and the Stones, it was all electric-guitar groups. Most answered the call to plug in and cash in. When I saw these few remaining stalwart folkies in concert with their wooden boxes, they were often ignored, incomprehensible in the boomy venues, just someone a promoter had put on to fill time economically and keep the stage clear before the headliner took command of it. But when they were good, there was a real power there, and courage as well, for it isn't easy to stand alone on a stage with just the simplest of tools, one acoustic guitar and one voice.

Following punk's first explosion, troubadours influenced by it began to emerge. Billy Bragg, a fan of the Clash, was a good example, playing the same venues as the bands but unaccompanied. Chilton would sometimes play Loudon Wainwright's "Motel Blues," just voice and guitar, and Loudon's catalogue was consistently outstanding. Bruce Springsteen's gloomy 1982 *Nebraska*, recorded on a cassette that lived in his back pocket for some time before being pressed into a record, was an influential return to the folk approach. (In 1987, Holsapple, opening shows for R.E.M. as a solo act, was to find a more energetic approach, dubbing his the "No Nebraska Tour.") Suzanne Vega was then on New York stages such as the Bottom Line singing "Tom's Diner."

Starting in November 1983, the venerable Gerde's Folk City club, at 130 W. Third Street, began offering a series called Music for Dozens. The scene of Bob Dylan's first professional gig and host to a generation of Village folkies, the club had lost some traction over the decades. In hopes of reviving it, the management let rock writers Michael Hill and Ira Kaplan book Wednesday nights under that banner, thus forming a bridge between the downtown rock scene and the folk tradition. Across this bridge walked one of the finest songwriters

I've ever heard, Richard Thompson. Beware: He can break your heart with a single well-turned phrase, then lift it right back up with a miraculously deft twist of his fingers on the strings.

Thompson's first established band was Fairport Convention, which offered a plugged-in take on traditional British music. We often had their records on our turntables in high school; Holsapple was especially taken with the style. And Peter had turned me on to the first Thompson solo disk, *Henry the Human Fly*. So we were already familiar with Richard Thompson's guitar prowess before heading north. I had also seen Richard and Linda Thompson's electric band in New York, including one of the last concerts, where the palpable tension between the divorcing couple seemed to push Thompson to places in his guitar playing I had never before heard anyone go. Up to that point, the two Television guitarists and Roy Buchanan had been the most transporting in-concert guitar improvisers I had seen. (I had yet to see Jeff Beck but was saving him a spot on that roster.) Thompson joined the short list on that night with Linda, perhaps vying for the top spot. Jaw-dropping, spellbinding, transfixing: These words did not suffice.

I think it was his guitar firepower that initially made his songwriting somewhat "hidden in plain view" for me. So I'm grateful that Kaplan and Hill's Music for Dozens framed Thompson in a different way, one that shone a light on his amazing tunes by themselves. The live concert disk from Folk City, *Small Town Romance*, although not a perfect recording, leaves no questions about his skills as a classic solo acoustic troubadour. In just a few words, the title song conveys the aching sadness of a romance withering under the assault of an unsympathetic community, with Thompson's melody hitting a melancholy diminished fifth on every chorus. It is just about a perfect song. And it was one that hit home: In a city of millions, the circles we traveled in then still numbered only in the dozens; our romances in that small group were as revealed and gossiped about as the one in his song.

Small town romance, back seat for a bed
Nothings must be whispered, rumors must be fed

Small town romance, everyone knows your mind
They peep from faded curtains, they read your valentines

Oh, you got to get away, oh you got to get away,
Oh, you got to get away: oh, they can't stand love in a small town

21

Anyone Who
Had to Laugh

Oc - ca - sion-al glan ces a - cross_ a room, as if__there were no one else there

Oc - ca - sion-ly, ca-sual-ly peck_a cheek, as if__ to say you_ could still care

I SPENT 1984–1985 MOSTLY TOURING WITH LYONS IN groups of various configurations, both under my name and as sidemen for singer Marti Jones, who was touring in support of her Don Dixon–produced *Unsophisticated Time* disk on A&M. Sometimes these tours included two adroit keys players from Queens, Cathy Harrington and Mary Mac, who also played together in a synth-dance duo, Venus Two. Although our aesthetics didn't always mesh, I was grateful for the duo's dedication to performing my songs in those years, and we usually had a great time touring together. I also joined Yo La Tengo onstage for the first time in the fall of 1985; I would play guitar (and once bass) with them intermittently for the next two years. The year closed with the release of *Christmas Time* on the Twin/Tone subsidiary Coyote Records, a collection of holiday tunes suggested by Gene Holder. The disk includes Ted's brilliant absurdist piece "The Only Law that Santa Claus Understood," which evokes Ennio Morricone's spaghetti Western soundtracks, and reunited the original dB's lineup for its title number. "Christmas Time" (the song) was recorded using some time at Bearsville studios that New Orleans native Jimmy Ford, the current manager of the dB's, had swapped for the band's uncredited appearance as models in a Miller Beer print ad. Will, Gene, and I stepped into each others' rhythms easily at the session, like they were comfortable shoes, and quickly recorded the percolating track, which combines a staccato, rockabilly verse feel, Beach Boys harmonic suspensions, and chorus chords with those unfretted "jangling" top guitar strings again ringing out. For the lyric "time stands still," Will created a drum break that nodded toward the Move's "Do Ya," with multiple drum overdubs, some sounding *shwoop schwoop* because the tape was running backward while he played some of the layers. (Peter Holsapple was traveling in France and couldn't fly in for this date; he added his parts later, at Water Music.)

After we had finished the basic track at Bearsville that night, the photographer's crew and the Madison Avenue cats descended and carefully lined up Will and Gene as well as some preselected friends—including the four Wygals, Janet, Doug, Jeff, and Trish; A&M's Julie Panebianco; Winston-Salem guitarist Eric Peterson; engineers Mark McKenna and Ken Lonas; and Amy Rigby (Will's wife)—for a deep shot through the control room out through the playing space. I was surprised to be asked to be in the shoot, as I was no longer in the dB's, and at first I refused, not having been a party to the agreement. In fact, I think I walked out. But I had benefited from the gratis studio time, and as I recall, threats were made to pull the plug on the whole thing; it was all or nothing. So, under duress, I acquiesced. And thus I became a national poster boy for beer. The result: an ad showing me standing at the front next to Amy with a Miller

On a bill with Let's Active and the dB's during the "Who's on First?" tour, at the Dream Palace in New Orleans during Mardi Gras; photo by Carol Whaley

Miller Beer ad at Bearsville Studios (left to right: foreground, Chris, Will Rigby (drumsticks), Amy Rigby; at console, Eric Peterson, Gene Holder, Mark McKenna, Ken Lonas; in studio: Julie Panebianco, Janet Wygal, unidentified, Sky Daniels, Jeff Beninato, Jeff Wygal, Doug Wygal); author archives

in my hand, the only plus being that my cranium seemed to be translucent (I had turned my head quickly while the shot was taken). I did love that aspect of it; during that period, I felt translucent, ghosted, on most days.

I did not drink Miller, but no one mentioned that when the shot became a two-page centerfold in *Rolling Stone* and *Spin*.

———

It was fun to be part of a band again, even if just for a minute. But my real activity continued to be a solitary, interior one. Oh, that delicious feeling of having a song brewing. It was like nothing else. I would leave my apartment in the blinding, treeless sunshine of a Hoboken morning, get the bus into Port Authority on the west side of Manhattan, grab a cup of coffee at Le Bon Pain, and stride across midtown to wherever that day called me, all the while standing stock still in that parallel dimension of songwriting as the melody and lyrics percolated up and around my consciousness. This dualism would continue throughout the day and into the next as I peered sideways into creativity's realm, picking through the thousand musical and lyrical options until reducing the song down to its most sparse and necessary components. Each time, there was that certainty that *this* song was going to be the best one ever. And it was secret knowledge: I might be surrounded by dozens in a subway car, or talking to a sales clerk in a bookstore, or doing an interview at the record label, but I was the only one who knew that, simultaneously, this music was being born. Drunk on this strange, subtle elixir, I would imagine I knew how it must feel to be a secret agent assigned to a mission in a foreign land, as I maintained my façade of normal activity, all the while impatiently counting the minutes until I could return to a private space and transcribe or record this encrypted "message in a bottle" that had been fermenting, then formulate a way to float it out into the world. There was also the excitement of anticipation, the delusion of inevitable triumph, as my ego would balloon and I would imagine the hero's ticker-tape parade one day—hearing back from my peers, accepting congratulations from all sides at having finally written *the* song, the single tune that would crystallize all I had tried for in the hundreds that came before it. Each such creative adventure was backlit by such new hope.

Sometimes these bottled messages were dashed on the rocks, never recorded or performed, their inadequacies glaringly apparent after the process was complete. Sometimes sober reflection would be necessary to reshape them after the unquestioning state of first-draft creation had passed. But the more I wrote, the more I tried to keep the original "first thought, best thought" construction intact. Sometimes, after returning to the mundane, workaday world, I didn't fully understand what I'd written, but if it had an affective power, I was more and more inclined to let it be.

I was always trying, throughout these years, to find new places to go in my songs and to incorporate a more exact, detailed kind of lyric writing under influences such as Thompson and Blegvad.

When a song is cloaked in loud guitars and smashed cymbals, as so many of mine had been, it's often better to have a Rorschach approach to the lyrics. Signpost phrases that emerge from such a wall of sound can point in the intended direction, but if listeners can use their own imaginations to fill in a few of the blanks in the obscured parts, they can become participants in the experience. It's the interactive aspect, the "Louie Louie" effect again, which was present even in the previous decade's song most apt to trigger my own flashing pinball-machine lights, Big Star's "September Gurls." Many of the lyrics of my recordings up to this point had worked in this way.

With a moody new song in the summer of 1986, though, I realized that I had hit a turning point, a pivot away from this vagueness. "Occasional Shivers," a traditional thirty-two-bar torch song with a jazzy progression, has nothing in common with the prevailing trends of its day. It is, however, very much a companion piece to the earlier "From a Window to a Screen." In fact, the play on "like" at the end—"I hear you like the wind," meaning both "I hear you softly but always, like I hear the breeze" and "word on the street has it that you are most fond of the wind"—makes this connection directly; specifically, it ties to the other song's second line, "listening to the wind." (Further evidence of the connection: The melody of both songs descends from the same first note, a middle C [as written in the original keys; "Window," however, was moved up a step, to A-flat from G, for the dB's recording], against a somewhat dissonant, unexpected kick-off harmonization. In "Window," the C is a flat ninth rubbing against a B⁷ chord; for "Shivers," it's the seventh of a Dᵒ chord.)

(Although "Occasional Shivers" was like nothing else I was writing then, it became a bridge to material I have been writing in recent years: I now see this song as a kind of foreshadowing for my 2015 return to the style of the Great American Songbook, a development stimulated by finally finding myself with a piano in the house again. Ironically, I rarely wrote in this very New York mode when I actually lived there, but a piano is not something you can slip into a backpack if you are enjoying the peripatetic life of a working musician, and back then I knew only a few of the jazzier chords on guitar.)

———————

I grew up thinking that vinyl singles were a sort of magical creature, as if a positive charge on one side and a negative on the other would let them sit and vibrate on the shelf like little yin/yang batteries. So having a flip side that contrasted with the main song was a great thing to do. "Occasional Shivers" was written specifically to be the B-side of a 1986 green-vinyl seven-inch 45, a remix of the overwhelmingly cheerful "Christmas Time." And I knew that the rosy picture that the A-side painted didn't cover all the bases, that sadness and reflection were always peeking around the corner of the holidays. I wanted to address the flip side of December.

Frank Sinatra famously avoided Hoboken after escaping from it, but according to legend he would occasionally still repair to a bar, perhaps a mob hangout, directly across from the original Water Music Studios. We would see the limos line up, sitting in wait for hours. It was easy, working late nights at the studio, to look out and imagine Ol' Blue Eyes sitting down there alone, holding a glass of whiskey in the "wee small hours of the morning." The other image I had in my head was the bar at Chumley's, the former Manhattan speakeasy. "Occasional Shivers" was a "one more for the road" song for the "darkness before the dawn."

> *Occasional glances across a room, as if there were no one else there*
> *Occasionally, casually peck a cheek, as if to say you could still care*
> *Though that was long ago, years or days, I forget,*
> *I must admit, when I'm near you, I still feel . . . occasional shivers*

Perhaps you remember the bitter taste, perhaps you recall
  with a smile
Perhaps you envision the rapt embrace, the tentative kiss
  of a child
Funny how the chance remark bears a sting, and yet
I don't regret, when I'm near you, I still feel . . . occasional
  shivers

Anyone who had to laugh should hear what we've become:
We've come undone, though I hear you, like the wind:
Occasional shivers, occasional shivers, occasional shivers . . .

To get a most lonely sound, an audio equivalent of looking at the world as warped through a glass of Scotch on the rocks, I concocted a novel recording scheme for the song, essentially playing as a live band all by myself. I recorded all the backing tracks in advance, one by one, on a portable eight-track, half-inch Otari tape recorder while wearing headphones in the office of Water Music, while a metal band was recording in the big room. Then I moved the tape machine to the studio proper and set up eight little guitar amplifiers, spaced around the floor where musicians might have been, one each for the organ, tambourine, bass, and so on. By standing in front of the amps and balancing the levels realistically, I was able to sing and play guitar backed by my "robo band" and record it all with just one stereo microphone, *wham bam*, like a Sinatra-and-orchestra session in the old days. Because the amps were spread around the room, the overlapping sounds created an amazingly believable sonic picture without any added artificial reverb, yet I could rely on "the players" to get it right every take. I did one take in this case, and that was it, recorded onto two tracks in one go (well, I did a second take but didn't use it). It got a realistic ambient, melancholy sound, everything phase-coherent, as if the listener were standing in the room with me, the amps hissing and crackling like a phalanx of fireplaces.

I sometimes wish I had made all my later records this way.

The Whole World's Dirt

You were loo - kin' for a rea - son—

to run in cir - cles on the week - end—

HAD MADE ONE INDIE SOLO ALBUM, *It's a Wonderful Life* (1983), and one EP, *Instant Excitement* (1984), while publicly still considered a member of the dB's; the band's management felt that to officially announce my departure might complicate the record deal in the works with Albert Grossman. And there was a sense of freedom in this: I was still under the umbrella of my old gang and didn't really need to have the "anything to declare?" manifesto of traveling under my own artistic passport. But by the time of my second record, *It's Alright* (last of the initial-*I* trilogy), I felt more of a need to figure out who I really was as a recording artist.

In trying to strike a balance on the dB's records, we had often selected those of my songs that contrasted with Peter Holsapple's often more immediate tunes. Peter had a knack for grabbing you right out of the gate, a talent made doubly clear from his very first demo session as a solo artist, around 1974; he had gotten a clerical job at the university and had celebrated by coming over to the studio at Mitch's Chapel Hill house to record "Now I've Got My Name on the Door"—a still unreleased potential hit and the start of many declarative earworm missives. Peter was also a versatile guitarist, whereas at that point I was a bassist who had strapped on a guitar a few years earlier out of necessity; I arranged my songs without specific guitar voicings and then played leads to fill in the holes. Peter, like Chilton, wrote rhythm guitar parts that were integral to his songs, tightly connected to the melodies.

But now, without Peter to share the songwriting, both the exoteric and esoteric were up to me; it was now *my* name on the door. This notion of striving for balance in song selection, as I had done when picking the two complementary sides of Chris Bell's single, remained important to me and was to be a guiding principle as I produced records for others in later years. Working out of both Water Music and the Twin/Tone house studio, Nicollet, in Minneapolis, I reached out to a wider circle of friends, including Alex (who sang harmonies on the title song and "The Seduction," saying about the latter, "We sound just like Simon and Garfunkel"), Fier and Lyons on drums, Richard Lloyd (for his dead-on rhythm guitar; I still played the solos), and Hoboken denizens cellist Jane Scarpantoni and Joe Jackson bassist Graham Maby.

On one of my trips to Nicollet, as I was sitting in the coffeehouse across the street on a brilliantly sunny morning and trying to finish up some lyrics, I was surprised to see Chris Mars, the Replacements' drummer, walk in to the adjacent offices of Twin/Tone, getting a big smile from the receptionist in the window. The Replacements had recorded several albums for this hometown label, starting with 1981's *Sorry Ma, Forgot to Take Out the Trash*, before moving to the big leagues at Seymour

Stein's Sire Records, and these older records were still a big part of the smaller label's cash flow. The band's leading light, Paul Westerberg, was developing into one of the best songwriters of his generation, with emotional depth and a real gift—almost in the old-school country music tradition—for the slightly twisted, unexpected couplet. As I knew, the band's relations with Paul Stark, Twin/Tone's boss, had been strained for a while, so a few minutes later, when a grinning Mars walked out with an armful of reel-to-reel master tapes and, after giving a friendly wave to the receptionist, strolled down the street, I assumed that all had been resolved. But later that day, the word went around: The 'Mats had boldly stolen their old master tapes and thrown them off a bridge into the river. (Most of these turned out to be just backup copies, although the masters for the *Tim* demos that Chilton had produced apparently did drown.) Finally taking out the trash: a dramatic gesture, indeed.

Marshall Crenshaw had been part of our karass (as Kurt Vonnegut would say) for some years now. Like the dB's, he had been under Alan Betrock's wing at first, although he had quickly graduated to Warner Bros. under Karin Berg's watchful eye. Crenshaw was a triple-threat talent, a great singer, guitarist, *and* songwriter, and although a New Yorker now, he stood apart from the CBGB diaspora, unabashedly loving fifties rock and roll, a punk only in the sense that Eddie Cochran was one. A native of Detroit, perhaps where he derived his joking eighties motto, "If you can't be good, be loud!" (although he was pretty much always good), he had been a seasoned pro since playing John in *Beatlemania* (with another mutual friend, Los Angeles guitar ace Rob Laufer, as George). Working with Litt and U2 producer Steve Lillywhite at Power Station, he had created one of my favorite recorded "pinball" moments: his amazingly elongated vocal phrasing at the start of the choruses to a song called "Whenever You're On My Mind." At one point we worked together on a couple of my songs, "Cara Lee" and the now lost "When We Talk about Our Love," at Bearsville Studios with Bill Scheniman.

Marshall Crenshaw; photo by Deborah Feingold.

"Cara Lee" had been written in a two-bit hotel across from the Greyhound bus station in Nashville, Tennessee, fertile soil indeed. Maybe a little bit of Hank Williams was in the air, but I think it was more Roger Miller's "King of the Road." The song is the lament of a lonely musician on a backwoods tour—nothing new about that. (The line "the whole world's dirt" always makes me smile, though; it sounds so bitter, but I was thinking of the New York Earth Room, a sculpture by Walter De Maria that consists of a gallery space in Soho at 141 Wooster that is simply filled with mud.) Working in the "Peggy Sue" tradition, I borrowed the first names of my girlfriend, Carol Lee Whaley, although this was a writer's device and not a biography. In keeping with the Tennessee vibe and the apologetic sentiment, I thought of it as a mournful pedal-steel number. When I brought it back to New York, Marshall had added an insistent four-to-the-bar kick drum, and we upped the tempo, which I kind of dug. But that version (never released) was left in the dust once I started playing the song with my band, which included the exciting drumming of James Brown fan Lyons, who kicked the pace up even higher.

It's Alright was overall a very downbeat record, which maybe reflected the mood of the musical times, the fallout after the supernova of the punk explosion. Much like the sad years after 1967 and the Summer of Love, the mid-eighties seemed to have a sense of "Now what?" in the air. I cut "Cara Lee" again to match that, going back to the original vibe, a slower, more stately tempo, with Anton Fier on drums. But Marshall came back to the studio and added the same buoyant vocal harmonies he had sung on the earlier version. I liked the resulting track fine, but for that record, I focused my attention more on the marching-band sound of "Incredible Happiness" and the guitar tones of the title tune, which I considered an important song.

And then reality knocked. I submitted the album to the Hoboken indie label Coyote, run by the kindly Steve Fallon, of Maxwell's. Steve, both a compassionate host and an arbiter of talent, had started a record label with Bill Ryan, the proprietor of Pier Platters, Hoboken's hip record store. My old friend Glenn Morrow, late of *New York Rocker* and not yet at his own Bar/None Records, had signed on as A&R and label manager. Glenn basically gave me an "emperor has no clothes" speech, telling me in no uncertain terms that the record needed a single and that "Cara Lee" could have been this except for its too-stately tempo.[17]

Although Morrow urged me to just go back to an earlier, faster take, I instead went "old-school" and gave myself the same advice I had cheekily given Chris Bell for his "I Am the Cosmos": "Speed it up!" I had learned from the Beatles and Big Star that running the tape a bit faster was often a bit better. (Sadly, I took this a step too far when mastering the first dB's record at EMI in England with George "Porky" Peckham, who had mastered the Beatles European issues previously; I blame coffee, not Porky, for my having made that record almost Chipmunky at times.)

I ran the "Cara Lee" tape faster . . . then a bit more . . . then a *lot* faster, up almost a semitone, from G major to A-flat. The sadness peeled off, and it became a chipper rockin' singalong, with a chirpy Stratocaster intro and that sudden Beach Boys thirteenth chord rising up at the end of the bridge. I owe Glenn a lot for having been bold enough to speak out here; he was totally right (it was better art), and it really reinforced my appreciation of good A&R input.

———

"Cara Lee" went from Nashville lament to Marshall's dance groove to live rockabilly to stately processional to artificially sped-up cheerful; in the business world, the last version went from Coyote to distribution through the bigger indie label Twin/Tone, which had been started by engineer Paul Stark after Stark had put some money in the bank from a very nonindie rock hit: "Funkytown," by Lipps, Inc. And then it went all the way to A&M Records, a genuine million-selling major label, although one started also as an indie, back in 1962, with Herb Alpert's garage recording of "The Lonely Bull." A&M was at that point run by Beach Boys associate David Anderle, once known as Los Angeles's "Mayor of Hip," who heard my record once via ace (and dear friend) Karen Glauber and signed it on the spot, his only (and very savvy) complaint being, "Why does this album have so much *drum*?" (Hey, it was the eighties; there was always too much "drum.")

The final stop on its journey was the requisite silly video for MTV (with Ted Lyons as the drummer and childhood friend Faye Hunter playing the bassist) and a faux coffee-cake promo container for the cassette that said "Nobody doesn't like Cara Lee" in imitation of the Sara Lee bakery slogan. There was never an attendant windfall, but I got to hang out in Los Angeles with the delightful Glauber at the former Charlie Chaplin studios at La Brea and Sunset that A&M inhabited, hearing stories about label mates Sting and the then-unknown Sheryl Crow (Karen always knows all the stories) and watching Richard Carpenter park his red MGB sportster on the way to sad, daily sessions for records without his sister, Karen, that I don't think ever saw the light of day—all of this a strange evolution, and one I lay at the feet of "Cara Lee."

23 Newspapers Collect on the Street

She thought she meant— what she said   when they were mer-ri-ly wed

But in the cold— mor-nin' light,   what she saw she did- n't like

N THE FALL OF 1984, BACK FROM PARIS AFTER THE BLEG-
vad adventure, I continued studio work on my own songs and
made some contributions to Freedy Johnston's *Can You Fly*,
but I was pulled more and more into Anton Fier's orbit. Influenced by jazz composer Carla Bley's 1971 superstar project *Escalator Over the Hill*, he had conceived of a "curated band" called
the Golden Palominos. With guitars by Fred Frith associate (and
aluminum-fortune heir) Henry Kaiser and myself and bass by
Bill Laswell, we recorded a deluxe remake of "Omaha," a Moby
Grape folk-rock tune from the sixties about nuclear catastrophe.
Anton and Steve Fallon had made a mad road trip to an R.E.M.
gig and convinced Michael Stipe to sing deconstructed lyrics on

the track; I sang some, too, and served as an assistant, standing in the room hammering out the right pitches on the piano to cue Michael each time he had to sing.

The single turned out beautifully, and Anton started work on a full album in this style (really the second Golden Palominos record, but it was the first to penetrate the marketplace), with contributions from Carla Bley; Cream bassist Jack Bruce, who played on *Escalator* and whose *Harmony Row* solo album had made him one of my heroes; John Lydon (aka Johnny Rotten); and best of all, Richard Thompson. New Yorkers Blegvad, Straw, and Harris were still involved, as was ace singer Lisa Herman. Carla, sporting her distinctive fiber-optics 'do, seemed bemused by it all and was soon replaced on Hammond B-3 by the amazing Bernie Worrell, a childhood prodigy with a degree in classical piano performance from Juilliard who nonetheless was famous for simple, funky synth-bass lines with George Clinton and

The Golden Palominos at Daytona Beach (left to right: Anton Fier, Peter Blegvad, Jody Harris, Chris, Lisa Herman, Bernie Worrell, Michael Stipe, Syd Straw); courtesy of Peter Blegvad

synth squiggles for the Talking Heads' hit "Burning Down the House." We would record high above Radio City Music Hall, in Plaza Sound, a studio with peepholes down to the Rockettes' high jinks.

Stipe continued working on the Palominos record as well, and I began to really appreciate his work process; far from the perception of him in some quarters as a vague lyricist, he was actually very careful with language. He turned me on to writer Shelby Foote and the Black Mountain poets, and he would show me his notebooks and explain how lines connected and intersected. We were fellow Southerners in that cosmopolitan collective, and I was glad of his company. I also liked his photographs; he would take a roll of exposed film, run it back to the beginning, and take another set of pictures, getting double exposures that were blessed by synchronicity much of the time.

After the Golden Palominos *Visions of Excess* came out, early in 1985, touring commenced, and it was often "mad dogs and Englishmen" all over again. The bands I had been in were mostly four-piece ensembles, but this was a rock orchestra, and Anton was a visionary on a mission, sometimes seemingly summoning his idols Jim Gordon and John Bonham. Indeed, we would play Led Zeppelin numbers for encores, the redoubtable Syd Straw serving as our own Robert Plant. Years earlier, in a more innocent time, it had been Anton and myself at the back of parties talking while chaos reigned. Now Michael and I would be carrying on civil conversations while Rome burned around us. On several occasions I was glad that our upscale hotels all seemed to have wheelchairs at the ready, as locomotion was sometimes a problem for some band members. When we traveled by bus, Jack Bruce kept us all enthralled with stories in the darkness. I remember a cautionary tale Jack, a former addict, told late one night as we rocketed through the oblivion of the Midwest. He had been shooting heroin in a bathroom, he said, but was in too much of a hurry to wait for it to cool. He shot the hot stuff and then watched in the mirror as his capillaries reacted. He saw his face crinkle and wrinkle, à la *Dorian Gray*, in only a few seconds, melting forever into that of an old man. (I later confirmed this change by comparing pictures before, during, and after Cream.) He claimed that this happened as well to a model friend, but on only one side of her face; in some ways, this was even more frightening to us, huddled around the Greyhound campfire that night.

I had cut my teeth on Cream's *Disraeli Gears*, so it was amazing to play bass while Jack played guitar(!) and sang such glorious songs as "Deserted Cities of the Heart" and "I Feel Free" backed by Anton's precise accents. I made it a point to work up every detail of Bruce's original bass lines, only to have him gently chastise me sometimes for overplaying. I had to laugh, although his point was that they were just songs, not museum pieces. (I would play guitar when Jack played bass, and that, too, was a treat.)

Apart from Anton's beautiful and often heroic drumming, Bernie Worrell's playing was probably the musical marvel of the tour. What a musician! He could pull silver shards of sound out of the B-3 and then flip on a dime and spit out yellow and orange flames that sounded as if they had come from the exhaust of the vintage purple Dodge Charger he drove around Manhattan. His on-the-spot, ever-changing orchestrations of the songs were an inspiration to us all. Afterward, relaxing back in the hotel, he would tell us "kids" tales about the Funkadelic days and then chill out with his teeth in a glass beside him. We felt like we were getting a glimpse into an earlier time, when giants walked the earth.

One early gig was on January 8, 1986, at the Metro, a cavernous disco in Boston. Most folks drove up the night before, but I had to fly up in the early morning because of a session conflict. Reading *The New York Times* on the plane, I spied an amazing front-page story, the supposed discovery of *hypercharge,* a weak "fifth force" that resists gravity and varies according to atomic structure.

HINTS OF 5TH FORCE IN UNIVERSE CHALLENGE GALILEO'S FINDINGS

A new analysis of early 20th-century experiments has produced results challenging both the findings of Galileo that all falling bodies accelerate at the same rate and a fundamental element of Einstein's general theory of relativity.

This has led physicists to suspect that there may be a fifth, heretofore unidentified force at work in the universe.

Scientists said the new study, published in the Jan. 6 issue of *Physical Review Letters,* could have a profound influence on thinking in physics and cosmology if the results can be substantiated by further experiments. . . . [I]n the new thinking, gravity is not the only force at work; there is also presumably something called hypercharge, which acts on objects of different compositions so that they accelerate at slightly different rates.[18]

If this (later debunked) theory had proved correct, it would have meant that, in a perfect vacuum, a feather might hit the ground *before* a stone instead of at the same time. Arriving at the venue in the nick of time, I eagerly showed this to Michael, and we both marveled. He asked to keep the article, as he said he was working on a song that this would fit into perfectly.

When R.E.M. released "Fall on Me" the next year, their first aboveground radio smash, it became clear which song he was talking about:

> *There's a problem, feathers, iron*
> *Bargain buildings, weights and pulleys*
> *Feathers hit the ground*
> *Before the weight can leave the air*
> *. . . Fall on me*

And I had another example of the specificity and craft behind his lyrics, which became apparent if you had access to what lay behind them.

One night with the Palominos stands out in my memory. We were playing the Felt Forum in the Madison Square Garden complex over Penn Station, on July 14, with Bob Dylan appearing in the large space. Before the show, the promoter told us that everyone in the common backstage area was strictly obligated to follow a specific rider in Bob's contract: If he had the hood of his sweatshirt down and off his head, it was fine to talk to him. If he had the hood up, however, no one could say a solitary word to him; he had to be left absolutely alone unless he himself initiated the conversation. We were good soldiers and promised to keep our lips together, and indeed, a bit later, Dylan walked into the backstage green room under his careworn gray hood, looked over the deli platters, and ambled up and down the hall that connected all the spaces. It wasn't easy to stand silent, however, and for a moment I wondered whether someone in his management office had played a trick on him long ago and he was unaware why he was being regularly shunned backstage at all his concerts over the years. Perhaps Syd Straw had arrived too late to get the instruction, or perhaps she just thought it silly, but after Dylan had made a few jaunts up and down the hall, she marched right up to him and, with her characteristically disarming grin, asked, "Hey Bob, how's it going?" He smiled warmly, although I don't think they had ever met before, and the two chatted for a good while, he still behooded, and had a grand ol' time until he had to head to the stage. So much for being a good soldier.

The desire to be isolated from society before a concert may be close to universal among performers. I have certainly felt that way. The idea of small talk with strangers can cast a large shadow, especially at that point in a tour when exhaustion is all you can remember. But most of us don't have the clout to enforce isolation. My favorite (although unverified) story of an artist who didn't want to mingle is one about Prince that I've heard from several people. During one European tour, he was never seen backstage before any of the shows. Right before the lights went up, however, a small motorized forklift with a large wooden crate on it would trundle down the backstage aisle and bump against the edge of the stage. The crate would be raised to stage level, one side of it would swing open, and Prince, in full regalia, would walk out of the box and play the show. At the end of the concert, he would walk back into the crate and close the flap, after which the forklift would lower it and roll on through the exit and up to a waiting car—with the star having made no contact whatsoever with anyone who wasn't on the stage during the show.

The whole crazy Palominos crew toured America in the spring of 1986, though Bruce and Fier spent the band's two days off by flying to Europe, where they performed, under Bruce's name, in Austria and Hungary. It was an intense and sometimes volatile group of characters, but at our best, we created real fire on stage—and comedy too, at times; playing at the Coach House in San Juan Capistrano, California, on March 25, the night after that mad dash to Europe, Anton passed out at the drums, exhausted, facedown on the snare, at the end of the show. We still needed to play the encore, so Michael led those of us still standing into Bill Withers's "Ain't No Sunshine" and, singing all the while, danced around Fier with a container of baby powder, dusting the drummer's unconscious figure with the cornstarch snow as the audience sang along. A lovely sight.

Then we were off to Europe in July for a short tour that included the extremely prestigious Montreux Jazz Festival. We were housed for several days in the *Last Year at Marienbad* ambiance of the Montreux Palace hotel on Lake Geneva, with Miles Davis strutting around the lobby surrounded by bodyguards, and we all made a road trip to the Musée de L'Art Brut, full of folk and outsider art, which made Michael very happy. Then came July 19, our night to appear. VSOP, a quintet that included bassist Ron Carter and Anton's old boss Herbie Hancock, was also on the bill and played an extremely immaculate, focused, and sober set. Unfortunately, Herbie afterward proved to be a "hail-fellow-well-met" sort, buying us round after round at the backstage bar, and the Palominos were not ones to hesitate in this regard. We stumbled on as headliners at maybe two in the morning. Now multiple cups to the wind, Jack decided that he was not going to go on stage unless he was allowed an unaccompanied bass solo, but in the end, he was persuaded to play the set without this. We opened with a Little Feat song, "I've Been the One," and ended with three great Bruce tunes: "Weird of Hermiston," "The Consul at Sunset," and, from Cream, "Deserted Cities of the Heart." Michael and I (and singer/pianist Lisa Herman) were still pretty much in compos mentis, but sadly, I do not remember this prestigious and much-anticipated show as being our shining moment.

We left the stage and straggled to the vans as dawn broke, and an hour later we were on a train to Milan, sans sleep, to play that afternoon on a soccer field, where we shared a triple bill with George Benson and the astonishing John McLaughlin, joined that day by David Sanborn. We thought we were going down a storm; Jack was singing, and the whole audience seemed to be chanting "*Bruce, Bruce.*" But it became clear as we persevered that they were *not* on our side; later I found out that the sound we heard was the way one boos in Italy.

Back in Paris at the end of the tour, after a midnight gig at Bataclan that involved chairs smashed backstage over a fee disagreement and, memorably, a sound engineer mixing from inside a plastic DJ box where he could hear essentially nothing, we said our good-byes. Anton and Syd headed off to Amsterdam, but most of the gang dashed out the next morning to make their flights back to the United States. (I myself was to head to London to visit the Blegvads.) Unfortunately, the tour manager hadn't realized that Paris has *two* international airports; they all went to the wrong one and missed the flights. The tickets were trash, and all involved were stranded in Paris for several days, with no resources except shoe leather and no money for the ever-increasing hotel bill, let alone flights back to the States. The local record company had turned against us several days back and were refusing help. I postponed my departure and hung out with the rest as a gesture of esprit de corps, and I remember this as the most fun part of the tour: walking all over town, pooling our loose change to buy bread and wine and feed pay phones (in this pre–cell phone era, long-distance calls were a nightmare), bonding over our predicament as lost Americans. Glory days.

A second Golden Palominos record, *Blast of Silence*, followed in 1986, with Fier, Harris, and Blegvad doing most of the writing. I was peripherally involved, but I was contracted to make a second album of my own, *Fireworks*, for A&M, and it was all I could think about. I was determined to make a leap forward with this one, and I worked on it every waking moment. The R.E.M. camp influenced Michael to jump ship, sadly; of course, his first loyalties rightly lay not with the Palominos but in Georgia, where that band was now beginning to work with Scott Litt, whom I had enthusiastically recommended to Stipe on that train to Italy. (They had met a new level of success with Don Gehman and "Fall on Me," but his methods fell wide of the band's aesthetic; they found an inspired match in Litt and continued with him for many chart-topping records.) The great melodies and lyrics Michael had written for the Palominos were replaced by ones devised by various other singers, including Don Dixon and Matthew Sweet—the band's modus operandi was to create instrumental tracks and then have the singers write the words and most of the melodies later to suit their individual styles. (One of Michael's unused Palominos lyrics became R.E.M.'s "Finest Work Song.") When it came time to confirm for a Palominos tour, I was still in the middle of my record.

Matthew Sweet was an old acquaintance. I had been a hired guitar on a 1985 Don Dixon–produced album with his bass-and-drums duo, the Buzz of Delight, which got him signed to CBS as a solo artist (although sadly, they then put the Dixon record on a shelf, wanting just Matthew as a solo act). He had covered my song "Ask for Jill" as well, using a binaural head mic that sat on a mannequin head.

In addition, he was already a guest singer on the new Golden Palominos disk, and we all had recently backed him on his own songs, with Litt producing at Power Station. A singer and guitarist, Matthew had a secret "uncool" Nebraskan past: He was

Chris with Matthew Sweet, both "asking for Jill" in Grand Central; photo by Carol Whaley

also an accomplished jazz-fusion bassist. For the Buzz sessions, he had excelled on a modified bass of his own invention, an instrument Don Dixon had christened the Bagbone (with the top two strings pitched an octave above normal, in the guitar range). I suggested to Anton that he get Matthew to replace me on bass, along with new guitar recruit Richard Lloyd, with whom Anton and I had been cutting tracks for *Fireworks*. And I stayed behind to work with Jim Rondinelli, Sweet's engineer on a then-unreleased album called *Girlfriend*, on a brand-new song called "The Newlyweds."

I had been writing mostly obscured, shouted confessionals up to that point, but the Kinks were a big favorite, and I loved how their leader, Ray Davies, would write with great sympathy about things he had only observed or imagined.[19] Although not yet married, I had dear friends who had tried and failed to make marriage work. It seemed deeply sad, even from a distance, that this great adventure would end so often, so casually, and often just shortly after it had begun, with one of the partners perhaps calculatedly thinking, "*Hmm*, I can do better. I can upgrade." Yuppies were on the rise in Manhattan, and there was an exposed ruthlessness loose on Wall Street, where I sometimes worked with Rick Brown as a temp for a merciless ambulance-chasing law firm. "The Newlyweds," a simple, understated folk song with minimal accompaniment, was not typical of my writing (more like John Prine or Townes Van Zandt perhaps), but it remains one of my favorites. I like the way it escalates from narrative to despair, the way the muted guitar part mirrors the shut-down emotions of the guy who finds himself left behind, dropped from a height, a stone, not a feather.

> *She thought she meant what she said*
> *when they were merrily wed*
> *But in the cold mirrored light,*
> *what she saw, she didn't like*
>
> *"I can do better than him"*
> *She thought it over and there and then*
> *walked out on her old life,*
> *walked out on being his wife*
>
> *Newspapers collect on the walk,*
> *the neighborhood starts to wonder*
> *There're phone calls he didn't make,*
> *billed from a Midwestern state*
>
> *And I ask him how he feels,*
> *and he says, "Nuthin' much"*
> *Does he ever think of her?*
> *"No, hardly never"*
>
> *But it's the little things that hurt him still,*
> *the little things that are hard;*
> *and he can't get over the little things*

He goes in to places they might have gone,
if it had lasted a little longer
There he does the things they would do,
but gets bored after a week or two

There's a woman who works in the front—
he always liked her
But in the back of his mind
there's something he can't define

And it's the little things that hurt him still,
the little things that are hard;
and he can't get over the little things

What good is a ring?
It's just a circle, it makes no sound
What good is anything?

And it's the little things that hurt him still,
the little things that are hard
and he can't get over the little things, no
he can't get over the little things, no
he can't get over the way she held his world up
. . . and let it drop.

24   I Want to Break Your Heart

I wan-na break your heart,   see what you real-ly are

and may-be when I'm through   well, you can break mine, too!

SOMETIMES THE SONGS THAT FALL SHY OF THE MARK are the ones you remember most fondly: the failures, the prodigal sons. Sometimes you never find an exact turn of phrase, the perfect chord, yet the songs march out the door nonetheless, into the world, only to return later as *what ifs*, to haunt and taunt. And sometimes, if the chorus sounds right and the drummer hits his marks, a multitude of sins can be forgiven.

"I want to break your heart, see what you really are" is how it starts. What I *meant* by this was that I wanted to break the code, to get beyond the surface, to find the essence. It was the spy thing, again—the same as in the basement lab at Nokomis Court or the hotel in Paris—the idea that there was another layer to it all, hidden behind the fabric, something that could be deciphered, laid bare, if only the right cord was pulled, if only the curtain could be raised.

Then all would be revealed, a layer found in the overlap between two people, two lovers, to be discovered in those silent moments together when time stops. It was Rimbaud's "Je est un autre" rejiggered as "We are an other." If I could uncover who held the ragged other half of the torn picture postcard, then together we could find the key; we could see around corners. We could find a place to stand, a place for our lever with which to move the world. We could put together that lie detector—or dare we call it a truth detector?

We could find the story that had been waiting there for us, always, behind the painting.

"Hi, Don Quixote, good to see you again," you think, despairing of such unabashed romanticism. "It's been a while."

I was haunted when I came to New York in 1977. You can see it in my eyes, in pictures from that time. Some come to the metropolis to find their fortune; others, to find themselves. Singing "The Summer Sun," I was like Robert Heinlein's cat in the sci-fi classic *The Door into Summer*, perpetually wandering from door to door, always thinking that the next one would be the right one: I wanted to swing it open and find something *outside* myself, to discover what lay beyond the often wintery backdrop of day-to-day existence. I had been looking for this all my life, sometimes glimpsing rays of light. But by the end of the eighties, I was growing weary of turning those doorknobs and finding only the cold.

I knew what I meant. But when "I Want to Break Your Heart" was included on a record called *Mavericks*, which went on to become one of the most beloved collections I've been associated with, I quickly realized that my interpretation of the lyrics—and by default, the song itself—was fatally flawed. It seemed that all the women in my life took it as a kind of legal warning label on a Stamey-shaped pill bottle! I spent a lot of time explaining my take on the lyric to them, with varying degrees of success. So, yes, a blemished effort, but still a favorite. I do think that if you listen to the passionate, sincere sweep of the chorus, its vocal harmonies and power-chord strings, you can understand where I was coming from. But I'm getting ahead of our story . . .

———

As a Southerner and erstwhile New Yorker, I'll admit it: I had always been a bit phobic about Los Angeles. The early eighties punk scene even put up an East-West rivalry, as per Fear's sneering single "New York's Alright If You Like Saxophones." From that general era, a few bands from Los Angeles stood out—Peter Case's Plimsouls, the Go-Go's, the Dream Syndicate, and the Bangles—but that was about it, for me. And the city's smog was rough on my lungs. But I had enjoyed my time with A&M Records, and Gary Stewart's gang at Rhino Records were always a blast. The more I visited the city in the early nineties, the more I found to like.

Just as Manhattan had earlier tilted us toward Hoboken, by the end of the decade, many of my friends were rolling down an incline to the West. Syd Straw, the charismatic and witty singer from the Palominos, was often out there, Matthew Sweet lived in the hills, and Benmont Tench had been in Los Angeles for over a decade. Scott Litt had married a Southerner, Anne Patteson, and they were spending most of their time there now. Former Hobokenite Karen Glauber had graduated from A&M to helm LA-based industry mainstay *Hits* magazine, all the while staying loyal to her original musical passions, which included later finding a place of honor in her living room for Verlaine's anodized-pickguard Jazzmaster guitar from the *Marquee Moon* sessions. There was a Southern California community now swirling around Peter Holsapple, all good musicians and singers, some of whom played with him and Susan Cowsill (from the family band from the sixties whose hits included "The Rain, the Park & Other Things," "Hair," and "Indian Lake") in the free-floating, harmony-heavy Continental Drifters. Others, such as committed music fans Dave Jenkins and Paul Rock, facilitated memorable shows at venues such as McCabe's Guitar Shop.[20]

For me and my fellow Southerners, New York had always been the shining city on the hill. But Los Angeles was the other bright American beacon, another destination city for artists. Even the jazz-era songwriters I loved who seemed so much of a piece with Manhattan had often spent some time picking up Hollywood's big-screen paychecks. And I think I might have ended up there myself, after Manhattan, if things had turned out differently. For example . . .

I didn't care so much about the movie-star sightings at Trader Joe's or Ben Frank's, and dining next to Fabio at the health-food joint the Source didn't raise my blood pressure, but one morning in 1990, when I was apartment-sitting for Straw, I was left slack-jawed at unexpectedly connecting with a Mississippi-born legend. This fellow Southerner, too, had briefly made a stand in Manhattan, a decade before I had, but he had ended up in Los Angeles at the end of his adolescence. They say "never meet your heroes," but once again—as had been the case with Chilton, Bruce, Davies, and McCartney—such an encounter exceeded my most grandiose expectations. Curtains were blowing in the breeze that morning, birds sang Disney-like themes in the trees, and I picked up the ringing phone beside the bed and heard dulcet, deep-South inflections saying "Hi, it's Van Dyke Parks."

I hope you already know all about the man. If not, a warning: His CV reads like a composite from that of several different lifetimes. Best known for having collaborated with Brian Wilson on a once-lost Beach Boys record, *Smile*, Van Dyke was a child prodigy, singing with the Met and acting in movies with Grace Kelly at age ten, then studying music at the Carnegie Institute of Technology before moving to Los Angeles in 1963. He found a place in the city's record industry—playing folk music; successfully pitching his brother's song, "Something Stupid," to Frank Sinatra; arranging "The Bare Necessities" (*The Jungle Book*); and then, after *Smile*, creating a ground-breaking, through-composed, somewhat Ivesian ode to American music, *Song Cycle* (1967). In 1970 Parks became the head of Warner Bros.' new music video–promotion department, an industry first, which set the stage for MTV's audiovisual revolution a decade later. And he has continued to do landmark work on high-profile recordings and films of all stripes.

We chatted for a while that morning, as I basked in the glow of his ready wit, and he told me he liked my work (which surprised me) and suggested we should do something together—which did happen, although not for a few decades.[21]

I started to think: Damn. I'm on the phone talking to *Van . . . Dyke . . . Parks*. I'm in California, in the warmth of the sun; back home, New York is an icicle. Life is good here.

————

I found even more to like there on the Opposite Coast: Peter Holsapple and I, long out of touch, had reconnected during some of my visits to Los Angeles late in the decade. He was living there with his wife, bassist Ilene Markell, between tours as a sideman with R.E.M.

We discovered that we really enjoyed working together now that we were away from the sometimes hothouse vines of our old band. Our mutual admiration for the Everly Brothers was the key, not only the church-correct voice leading of their harmony parts but also the sincerity and joy of their music. I think we were influenced as well by the Lovin' Spoonful's canon and the contemporaneous, cool first duo-vocal record by the Williams Brothers, smooth singer Andy Williams's nephews Andrew and David. In 1990 I hired Peter as a multi-instrumentalist for a Peter Blegvad record, *King Strut*, that I had produced in London for BMG, and a grand time was had by all. We had enjoyed working with some great English talents as well during the sessions, including Andy Partridge of XTC; B. J. Cole, a first-call pedal steel player who toured with John Cale; Danny Thompson, acoustic bassist with Richard Thompson, Tim Buckley, and Nick Drake; and Pino Palladino, electric bassist with John Mayer, the Who, and Paul Simon. (It was also on this London trip that I met an expatriate Tar Heel named Diane Long, who was teaching an exciting new kind of yoga there and who became my teacher all through the next decade. But that's a different story.)

A year later, in 1991, Peter visited me in Hoboken, where I now lived with Carol at 921 Washington Street, conveniently just one block from Maxwell's. And he and I began work on material for a possible duo project.

Peter brought a beautifully sad tune, "She Was the One," about finding and then losing a soulmate. It was a three-handkerchief tearjerker in the best possible way, and a shoo-in for the list. I offset this with a cheerful-sounding song, "Geometry," about friendship in times of need, and we arranged it as a harmony-vocal number. As a refresher course in how such harmonies could work in masterful hands, we worked up a song by the Byrds' Gene Clark, "Here Without You." The record started to take shape. There was an openness about this new collaboration with Peter, even an innocence. We were each enthusiastic about each other's contributions and, in a kind of feedback loop, each expression of enthusiasm would spur us to write the next song in hopes of engendering more such peer praise.

This receptiveness to naïveté soon found a theme song, although it was a repurposed *trunk song*—to use the Broadway term for a song written for one purpose but used for another. Peter had produced *Groovy Neighborhood*, the first studio album by a band called Pianosaurus, at Water Music in 1987. Alex Garvin, Steve Dansiger, and Bianca "Flystrip" Miller performed all their music exclusively on toy instruments. For their sophomore album, *Back to School*, Peter, still producing, also contributed a song, "The Child in You," which was pretty much a perfect fit for them. This record was never released, however, the tapes reputedly having been grabbed by Garvin when he left the band under perhaps distressing circumstances, and the recording has never been heard by anyone outside the band. Peter's song, however, remained. It was an excellent one, very innocent in a John Sebastian, Lovin' Spoonful kind of way, even when played on instruments that were not plastic miniatures. And so we added it to the roster.

Chris and Peter at Bearsville singing on Mavericks; *photo by Carol Whaley*

   The Everly Brothers records were fueled not only by sibling harmonies but also by barnstorming acoustic guitars. This flavor informed my "Lovers Rock" tune, a rapidly strummed traditional-sounding folk ballad about a couple who go up to a "lovers leap" on the edge of their town, looking for the same kind of transfiguration that I had sought in "I Want to Break Your Heart." During the sixties, I would summer with my grandparents near Blowing Rock, North Carolina. Some trick of the winds there caused objects thrown off a high cliff there to ascend instead of fall, and this was in my mind when I had my beleaguered couple finally make a leap of faith off the rock and float off into heaven's ether. Perhaps I was also thinking of Bobbie Gentry's "Ode to Billie Joe," a smash hit in 1967, which describes something mysterious being thrown off the Tallahatchie Bridge, followed by a suicide off it as well, as Southern townspeople continue matter-of-factly eating their black-eyed peas and pie.
   We didn't want to make a strictly retro record, however. Peter expanded the rhythmic vocabulary with the big percussive sound

of "I Know You Will" and the harmonic context with the jazzy "Taken," both unashamed declarations of affection. I went the other direction, as per my long-running tendency to try to balance our records together, with a country-styled waltzing lament, "You Haven't Got the Right (to Treat Me Wrong)." And I put the wolf among the sheep with the overdriven fuzz guitars of the aforementioned "I Want to Break Your Heart." The final piece of the puzzle seemed to be "Anymore," a dream of a Peter tune in 5/4 that I thought shared some of the abstraction of the music he had performed on stages with R.E.M. and also some of the ethereal quality of my favorite dB's song, "Moving in Your Sleep." It seemed like we were done, like we had a record. But wait . . .

I had asked Peter to bring along his box of discarded demos. While digging through it early one morning, I found a few verses of a supercool bluesy-funky organ tune on the end of a cassette. When he woke up, I sang him an idea for an abrupt chorus I had written, one that restated his "I hear an angel" line from the verses, and he liked it. Back in high school, Peter and I had worked up "Sloop John B," Brian Wilson's arrangement of the traditional Bahamian folksong, included in Carl Sandburg's *The American Songbag*, which was a hit for the Beach Boys, and I recalled those times fondly. So we added in the flavor of its somewhat angular bass line and traded off lead vocal lines just as the Beach Boys would trade off lead singers. Then we tossed in a big, shimmery Guild acoustic twelve-string excessively compressed by engineer Bill Scheniman with a Urie 1176, a sound that we already were using on our cover of "Here Without You." We didn't know that "Angels" was destined to become a small pop-underground single of sorts, with attendant MTV video by director Phil Morrison. Or that it would lead to an international tour the next year. But we did know that it sounded like a single to *us* in the living room that morning.

We were both tickled with this cowrite, yet we then sadly went back to writing *separately*, for the most part. Go figure. It's just hard for two people to be in the room together at the exact moment when the Prell pearl starts rattling the cage of one of them.

The next move was to stroll down the street and demo a few of the songs at Water Music, with Ilene on electric bass, Dave Schramm (frequently seen with Yo La Tengo) on guitar, and ace engineer Scheniman behind the board. We sent these off to Gary Stewart, then at Rhino Records' new RNA label. He was charmed and immediately offered to release the tracks "as is," done deal, but we were more ambitious for the project than that. He agreed to underwrite a full-production record, and so we began.

Peter and I created some of the basic tracks in the apartment on Washington Street, but for the most part we worked at Water Music and used Ilene as a third band member, along with our Hoboken hit squad of Schramm, James McMillan, Jane Scarpantoni, and Alan Bezozi. It was a great boon when we added percussionist and drummer Michael Blair, who had performed with Tom Waits, Elvis Costello, Lou Reed, and even Harry Partch and who Peter knew from R.E.M. sessions. We recorded all over that studio, in the kitchen, in the hallway, and (shades of Power Station) in the elevator shaft, getting complaints from the neighbors, who asked if we were "chasing feedback around the room, trying to capture it in a bag." (We were not, but we might have done so if we had thought of it first.) Then we were off to Bearsville, to mix with the skilled hands and warm heart of George Cowan, and finally to master with longtime ally Greg Calbi at Sterling Sound. Still sparking off the theme song of "The Child in You," we used Carol Whaley's documentary photographs to create a CD booklet that was a kind of children's illustrated guide to our process.

It was the strangest recording experience I had ever had: Everything went right, our colleagues were consistently amazing, and there was a persistent joy to the whole proceeding. As much as I had loved playing with Will Rigby and Gene Holder, it felt complete now to be a duo. It was easy to think, once we had the finished record in hand and were making our plans for touring, that a bright new day was imminent. But as Peter sings in "She Was the One," I should have known . . .

25 All Around You
Now the Stars
Are Falling Down

there is no-thin' in___ the world___ could make me change my mind,

___ you take a-way the world, and when you leave, you leave a part of you be-hind

RECENTLY TOOK A CPR COURSE—BETTER LATE THAN NEVER, right? As part of the video instruction, they showed a CGI version of a comatose man and then zoomed in on an interior view of his heart, which is beating irregularly at high speed, fluttering wildly, and jumping in his chest, but no blood circulates. Then an arriving rescuer uses a defibrillator to shock the heart, momentarily stopping it. This bolt of lightning administered by a benevolent stranger appearing out of the blue lets the heart start beating again, lets it find a slow, regular, confident rhythm. And life resumes anew.

I was that guy with the fluttering heart, at the start of the nineties in New York.

Astute readers may have observed that many songwriters

devote their efforts almost exclusively to a recurring subject: that evergreen four-letter word, *love*. My catalog was no different. For every "Cycles Per Second" or "Espionage," there were ten songs like "Cara Lee" or "Depth of Field." You might rightly think that, since it's possible to get a medical or law degree in three or four years, I should have been an expert in the subject after a decade of study. But despite having pried the topic apart in many ways, having looked at it from many angles, I had repeatedly failed to get it right.

I've been trying to tell the story of my *songs* here, but it's hard to completely separate their story from mine. My longest relationship in New York had been with Carol Whaley, the very bright, passionate, highly skilled photographer who had moved to New York from North Carolina only two years after I did. And it's fair to say that we'd been through the romantic wars together, side by side. We were kids, emotionally, when we starting dating, and perhaps our immaturity then shadowed our many attempts throughout the eighties to find balance as we rode that roller coaster of a decade together. We were not unique in this: It was a turbulent time for all my friends, most of whom had married and divorced at least once by then.

Carol and I were still trying to figure it out between us when something strange and unexpected happened to me. I know it's a cliché. I know you have every reason to be suspicious. But the plain fact of the matter is this: I fell in love. At a glance. Undeniably, completely. It was so basic and fundamental a change, both in myself and in Dana Shumake, the young woman I met at a friend's place one summer night while visiting my parents in Winston-Salem, that even now, thinking back, it surprises and astounds me. She and I were initially slow to react to this; we barely said a word to each other at that first meeting, although, as the saying goes, our eyes spoke volumes. I returned to New York; she, to Chapel Hill. It took several years of occasional lunches, increasingly frequent letters and phone calls, and Carolina visits to realize that this profound, shared event was not going to let go of us. Nor did we wish it to.

Writing songs at Bearsville Studios; photo by Carol Whaley

I realized that I had one more song to write for *Mavericks*.

We demoed "Close Your Eyes," and then I wrote out all the tempo changes, the places the demo organically sped up or slowed down. After putting down a guide metronome track with those tempi, we rerecorded it carefully and elaborately, with Michael Blair playing drums and lots of cool orchestral percussion. I was thinking about the sound of a comforting Beach Boys song I loved a lot, "Don't Talk (Put Your Head on My Shoulder)." In the end, though, after much work, we played the two back to back, and the demo recording was better, even if rougher. So that's what we used on the record. We "flew in" Gene Holder's guitar solo from the second version, even though the tempo between the two versions was sufficiently different that the guitar overdub is out of time. (Sorry, Gene; it was the last day or so of mixing, and I should have gotten this tighter, but we, too, were "out of time." Then again, your solo floats beautifully.) The glockenspiel at the end is supposed to evoke the sound of tiny falling stars as seen through closed eyes. But you knew that.

Songs are not only a way that we writers talk to the world. They are also a way that we talk to ourselves, sometimes saying things that our conscious minds are not ready to admit. When I wrote "Close Your Eyes" as my final song for the record with Peter, it was not yet certain that Dana and I would be together, that I would move to Chapel Hill in 1992 to be with her, that we would raise a family together in a hundred-year-old house in the woods just south of town, that we would share a life. But some part of me had faith, some part of me knew, and giving voice to this, in this song, helped carry me through the complicated, bittersweet detangling of my Manhattan life with Carol after returning from the *Mavericks* tour, and into the subsequent joyful embrace of my new one with Dana. It had been an incredible journey in New York, one that had begun with that morning phone call from Chilton as I sat in palatial Alwyn Court staring out at the skyscrapers and the Park and the future, but, as the song says, I was waking up "in another country" now. It was time for me to return home.

And you're a part of me;
at the heart of me
there's always been an element
no one could see

But I've started to
believe in you,
when you say that
"Now there's nothing we can't do,
if you want to be
A part of me"

And you wake up in another country;
All around you now the stars are falling down . . .
. . . in your dreams . . .

Afterword

I AM WRITING THIS NOW FROM CHAPEL HILL, NORTH CARO-
lina, the town where I was born, the town I left for New York
back in 1977, and the town I returned to in 1992. The town
where I married Dana a year later, where our daughter, Julia,
was born, in 1999. James Taylor grew up right through the woods
behind my back door; Elizabeth Cotten wrote "Freight Train"
across from the tracks where coal trains still travel several times
a week. I feel like I belong here; my heart is at rest here.

But in a sense, I feel native to Manhattan as well; it is, as
always, a "moveable famine." My mind expanded there so much
and so fast that I still find New York in its every nook and cranny.
I like knowing that the city is always little more than an hour's
plane ride away, that I can pop up there for an afternoon if I
have the shekels and the inclination, do a quick recording session, drop by the Strand bookstore or the Pearl River Mart, and
then be back here in time for some late-night banana pudding

at Crook's Corner on Franklin Street. As much as I love and savor North Carolina in all its uniqueness and splendor, there are times, reading the *New Yorker* in bed late at night, when I feel like I'm living in a borough that's just beyond Brooklyn.

Manhattan is native to me in yet another sense, however: The songs of Gatsby's jazz age, the Great American Songbook, played by my father on the family Steinway baby grand, are among the strongest memories I have of my childhood. I used to repair to that living-room Steinway for hours, pushing the keys together to make combinations I liked. My dad could read piano music, and so sheet music, not records, provided the popular songs we heard in our household. That piano was the first deluxe purchase my parents ever made, and it no doubt severely strained their budget for quite a while. World War II songs such as "I'll Be Home for Christmas" and "I'll Be Seeing You" ached with the melancholy of wartime separations. *Oklahoma, Annie Get Your Gun,* and other musicals were an evening's entertainment at the

The family piano; author archives

community theater. Radio was mainly for news; filling my ears were mostly the Great American Songbook tunes, along with Mendelssohn, Schubert, and Chopin.

From the twenties until the early sixties, Manhattan was ground zero for excellence in songwriting. Broadway was filled with memorable melodies whose witty, often polysyllabic lyrics rewarded close examination, the music and words coming from a veritable rogue's gallery that included Harold Arlen, Irving Berlin, Leonard Bernstein, Jerome Kern, George and Ira Gershwin, Johnny Mercer, Cole Porter, Richard Rodgers, and Harry Warren. This was the music my father played and sang for us of an evening. I would watch the *Thin Man* movies, set in thirties New York, and imagine that each of those songwriters lived the life William Powell portrayed. A new tune by Porter or Berlin, arriving as notes on paper, was an event. And rightly so: A competitive standard of excellence was evolving, one that used the expanding harmonic language of jazz—the extended chords, the flat-fifth, ninth, eleventh, and thirteenth intervals— and jazz itself had internalized rich new combinations of tones from Impressionism, as well as slightly flatted, bent intervals from the blues.

Leonard Bernstein's energetic, fluid score for *West Side Story*, initially heard on Broadway in 1957 and then more widely in the 1961 film, was in many ways both the crowning achievement of this era and its last hurrah. It was soon to be washed away, first by Elvis Presley and company's blues-based rock-and-roll revolution and then by the Beatles' adaptation of this, although the latter added to the blues forms a persistent taste of the British music-hall harmonies and more chromatic melodies, the added-sixth chords and interior modulations, that bassist McCartney's father had exposed his son to as a child. New York adapted, and Tin Pan Alley gave way to the so-called Brill Building writers, both at that building itself, at 1619 Broadway, and also in a companion site, Aldon Music, at 1650 Broadway. By the start of the sixties, these buildings housed the hives of small rooms with pianos and pads of paper, where a new generation of songwriting teams daily huddled to absorb the rollicking new music, now based on the electric guitar, and churn out a novel soundtrack for adolescent America, creating yet another rogue's gallery: Carole King and Gerry Goffin, Barry Mann and Cynthia Weil, Ellie Greenwich and Jeff Barry, Doc Pomus and Mort Shuman, Jerry Leiber and Mike Stoller. . . . And the older, more elaborate forms and harmonic approaches faded away.

In 2105, when the piano of my childhood found its way back to me in Chapel Hill, I discovered a kind of magic inside it. Perhaps you know this clichéd country songwriter's exhortation: "I got this old guitar the other day; I think there are some good tunes hidden innit." I myself saw that as, on the whole, just one more good reason to avoid moving to Nashville. (Later I learned to love that town, however!) Guitars don't have songs carved into them, I thought. They are merely slide rules, tools to verify what is going on in a songwriter's inner ear. But the piano indeed seemed to have grooves worn into it.

My melodies had always incorporated a wide range of intervals, but the accompaniment had generally stayed as cowboy chords. On piano now, it was all different: The Great American Songbook harmonic vocabulary just fit. I started to whittle out songs for a New York of the thirties, forties, and fifties, one I had not directly experienced but had learned about at my father's knee, a dreamscape of gin gimlets, tuxes, and mink coats, chivalry and Cary Grant's Romance with a capital R. And just as four- and five-note chords became de rigueur, so did multisyllabic words and more sophisticated rhyme schemes. My personal New York had been full of strum and Drang. But now, south of the five boroughs' borders, I spend hours at the keyboard exploring this new vocabulary, taking a few earlier songs—such as "Occasional Shivers," "I Want You, I Need You, I Tell You," even "Driving" (Sneakers)—as the road once less traveled but now rejoined, full throttle.

My artistic heroes have tended to be restless souls, people who are always trying to take it further. To make the pinball lights flash ever brighter. Picasso, Joyce, Schoenberg, Gershwin,

Stravinsky . . . I've never been overly fond of rock stars, but I love musicians. Alex Chilton constantly evolved as a player, going from Beatles voicings to blues and folk and then to *Real Book* jazz and baroque. Marshall Crenshaw had no incentive to resume guitar lessons after many great, successful records, but he did, returning to the fray with a greatly expanded chordal vocabulary on songs such as "Fantastic Planet of Love." My professor at UNC, Roger Hannay, wrote all kinds of music all his life; his outstanding final symphonies showed how he continued to expand artistically. Rehearsing with Kronos Quartet at Carnegie Hall in 2016 and seeing their attention to the smallest details, or watching my friends Karen and Shawn Galvin from New Music Raleigh practice, teach, record, and perform music at a high level eight to ten hours every single day—all this puts a different light on all the suggestions from labels to "spend time building up your social media presence." I got to stand next to a chamber orchestra for a series of international performances of Big Star's *Third*; I could hear my freshly penned arrangements, inches away, rosin on bows, which was mind-blowing, entrancing. There's nothing like hearing instruments that use just rather than equal temperament, which is to say, ones that are actually in tune, in the sweet spot, where the ratios really fall; it's the music of the spheres. And the more arrangements I wrote, the more I was able to vary them stylistically, to match bossa nova colors or countrypolitan or Nelson Riddle jazz highlights (which themselves connect to Ravel and Samuel Barber). I can hear music in a way I never did before. I'm still on this path, not sure where it will lead.

One of the boons of songwriting is that the process can be a kind of time travel. When I was a child, tapping away at the baby grand, I liked the unpredictability of Gershwin and Porter and the complexity and rhythmic freedom of Chopin as well, but the singsong of Irving Berlin and Harry Warren was easier for a kid to follow. I tried to find that breeziness again in 2016 when, to pen an opening number for my 1963-based fin-du-jazz musical radio play *Occasional Shivers*, I sat down to write "Manhattan Melody" . . .

> . . . *I close my eyes, stroll my fingers across the keys. And I am striding those cherished twentieth-century streets again . . . I cross over from the Plaza to now long-gone F.A.O. Schwartz, amble down to hear Mr. Gillespie on Fifty-Second Street, and grab a yellow cab to the fish market to watch the sky fill with fireworks that look like nothing so much as the notes Charlie Parker must have scattered so skillfully across the firmament of Birdland on that night Stravinsky came, Bird playing "KoKo" for him with bits of* The Firebird *mixed in. . . . I hear a ball* ca-rrrack *the bat, the cheers of a new year in Time Square . . . I see the skaters watched by golden Prometheus. . . . Now it's 3 a.m., and I'm on the A train up to Sylvia's, for collards and cornbread. . . . Trucks unload a new day's edition of* The New York Times, *as a gentle rain begins. Steam rises from manhole covers. . . .*
>
> *I am not there . . .*

. . . and I have never left. I step away from the keys, walk outside into the daylight, drinking in the blue Carolina sky—glad to be able to celebrate now, in some small way, the mythical, visceral town that has always loomed so large in my life.

Acknowledgments

Although it is hard to describe how to write a song, it's not hard to explain how to write better songs: *practice, practice, practice*, of course—that is, write a lot, learn the craft, learn music theory and poetics, and hang around with songwriters who know more than you. I learned a ton from playing with Don Dixon, Marshall Crenshaw, Alex Chilton, Peter Blegvad, Matthew Sweet, Jody Stephens, Jack Bruce . . . by repeatedly listening to songs by Ray Davies, Brian Wilson, Cole Porter, and Charles Ives (his *114 Songs*) . . . and yes, even from the Beatles. For lyrics, inspiration came from Stephen Sondheim's *Hat* books and Lewis Carroll . . . from all the artists I have produced, especially Le Tigre, Alejandro Escovedo, Tift Merritt, Skylar Gudasz, Ryan Adams, Yo La Tengo, and Roman Candle, whose approaches were all unique, all different from mine . . . and of course directly from Peter Holsapple, my off-and-on bandmate since middle school; if there is a music gene, he has it in spades.

I learned so much from Mitch Easter as well. Mitch, mind you, was the guy in our town who, at fourteen, could play Mason Williams's 1968 hit "Classical Gas" perfectly right after it came out, as well as all those high, fleet Townshend chords that ring over a drone-string pedal point in Who songs. And his abilities remain on display with his 2007 solo record, *Dynamico*, and all the Let's Active releases, the third of which, *Big Plans for Everybody*, he alone wrote, produced, and mostly played: It remains a brilliantly impressive disk even to this day.

Many thanks and superlatives galore go as well to all the team at the University of Texas Press—but especially my ever-so-patient and wise editor, Casey Kittrell, and my indefatigable graphic designer, Derek George; to my agent, David Patterson, at Stuart Krichevsky; to all the photographers who so generously "joined my band" here; to my Kitchen Cabinet, whose multitudes over the last two years included David Menconi, Laura Williams, Peter Holsapple, Elizabeth Van Itallie, Julia Gorton, Anton Fier, and Kathy Pories; to Ilene Beckerman, whose *Love, Loss and What I Wore* was the inspiration for this book; to my parents, Charles and Margaret, and siblings, Cindy and Kent; and, last in the list but first in my heart, Dana and Julia.

Appendix
A Listener's Guide

I F YOU WRITE SONGS, IT HELPS TO LEARN THE TOOLS OF the craft. Most folks eventually learn *roman numeral analysis* or the related *Nashville number system* (I learned figured bass, à la Bach, but it's similar). This will let you sense the "flavor" of chords by separating their harmonic function from specific pitch names. For example, if you know that G^7 in C functions the same as B^7 in E, you can start to hear what a V^7–I cadence is in all keys. Then listen for the IV chord, the ii, . . . Recognizing functional harmony by ear will increase your expressive options—and your enjoyment of others' music as well. And it will keep you from unwittingly writing the same chord progression over and over in different keys. The following examples show how I think about some of the songs referenced here.

You can listen to these on Spotify; just go to my artist's profile there and select the playlist for *A Spy in the House of Loud* or type https://lnk.to/chrisstamey into your browser.

Chapter 1: Don't Stop to Think
"On the Brink," Sneakers EP, Carnivorous (1976)

This song stays solidly in A major for the first part of the verses (with a momentary modal shift, a passing-note D♯, which is the ninth of the iii⁷, or the C♯-minor⁷ chord) and then modulates to E major for the second part with the help of an E♯°⁷ secondary dominant that starts a ii–iii–ii–IV–V progression. (I'm grateful to my brilliant high school music theory teacher, Bob Smith, for explaining the essence of this secondary dominant concept to me. Still wet behind the ears, I asked him about modulation, and he started a long, pedagogically correct explanation. Then he stopped and said, "Look, Chris, just somehow get logically to a dominant seventh chord [or a vii°⁷] of the place you want to end up, and it'll take you there." That was all I needed to hear.) The refrain sections leap to a D pedal bass with D, F, and G chords above and ends on an E (now a V⁷) chord to kick us back into A major for the next verse. It modulates unexpectedly right at the end, up a whole step, using an F♯, now major as a V, to get to that new key of B major. There is no guitar-solo relief from the words, a consequence of cramming three songs into a six-minute space on the vinyl EP. The line "was it cancer from the inside?" is unfortunate, but it comes from the Nixon era, as did so many things on that EP ("a cancer on the heart of the presidency" was a typical phrase at that time).

Chapter 2: I Love the Sound of the Traffic
"Manhattan Melody," *Occasional Shivers*, radio play (2016)

It's a bit "Hit the Road, Jack" (Ray Charles) in reverse; the bass goes up instead of down at the start of the verse. "Come On-a My House," the old Rosemary Clooney hit based on an Armenian folk song, has a similar bassline. I was writing ever more dense, chromatic songs ("The Woman Who Walks the Sea" as an example) that winter and, in contrast, wanted to just hit a stride for once, like Ellington would do ("Take the A Train," a masterful New York–centric tune). With verses in the key of C minor, the only slightly outside change comes at the end of the now C-major chorus, where it uses a temporary tritone substitution for the dominant—for example, over the words "with Charlie Parker stuck in my brain," it goes to the $\flat$II^7 (the substitution, D$\flat$^{7}, on "brain") before getting to the real V^7 (a G^7). This tour-guide song is about the words, so it's better to have the music simpler. In the recording, Branford Marsalis nailed it in one take. There are two versions of the lyrics, one contemporary ("High Line" and "Q Train") and another set in 1963 ("F.A.O. Schwartz" and "F Train").

Chapter 3: In Our Wildest Dreams
"14 Shades of Green," *Travels in the South*, Yep Roc (2005)

I've never attended any of my high school reunions. I did imagine doing so, though, in 2005 on the *Travels in the South* record, for "14 Shades of Green." In that song, I supposed that I was a guy who had never left the town and was in fact working as a tour bus driver assigned to the reunion party. Sent to meet their Lear jets at the airport, I went rogue and hijacked my more successful hedge-fund classmates for a sightseeing trip to places they didn't expect. Well, that was the idea! The chords here hang out mostly in the key of A major. It opens up melodically in the chorus, where the melody on "Here's where we [went to church]" has Es and a C♯ over a D chord, making it a ninth chord (with a major seventh yet no third) at that moment. And the melody comes back to that ninth, an E over a D chord, at the end, only to have it cadence $\flat$VII–I (G to A) with the melody still on the note E, so the G chord is really a G^6. There's a little suggestion of a modulation at the end, on the repeat of "What are we waiting, what are we waiting . . . for?" where it goes from E to A, as expected, and moves then out of the key to a secondary dominant, F♯ major followed by B major, to underline the sense of suspension, of "waiting." But then back to the key of A again for the walkdown to the final unresolving chord—an E major chord over a D in the bass.

Chapter 4: Have You Seen the Last Elite?
"Dearborn Street," unreleased, from Nokomis Court sessions

It's hard not to be sentimental about one's first augmented chord! The chorus of this very early song started on the tonic, E major, with the melody on a B. For the second chord, however, the note B in both the chord and the melody moves to a C♮, so with the bass now on G♯, we can call it a III+ (G♯–C–E), although it could also be called an E+ or even a C+ in other contexts. This moves up a half-step, to a IV, and the rest stays right in the key.

Chapter 5: The More You Learn, the Less You Know
"Condition Red," Sneakers seven-inch EP, Carnivorous (1976)

The verse starts cold (no intro) with a plosive on a A♯ minor, the vi chord in C-sharp major, the song's starting key. Then, five bars later, after a ii–IV–V–I passage, it uses a progression over an A pedal point to plow into a modulation to E major for a quarter note but then restlessly jumps from there with a subdominant modulation up to F-sharp Mixolydian, with a bluesy flat seventh in the melody, for eight bars. At this point, for all twelve bars of the chorus, it makes a modal shift to the key of F-sharp major until the next verse, where it goes through the shutter-quick changes of the verse once again. It was the bicentennial year, after all, and I was trying to convert my teenage Anglophilia into the Anglophobia of my twenties.

Chapter 6: Pavement Slapping My Feet
"The Summer Sun," Ork Records (1977)

Chordwise, "Summer Sun," in the key of C major, might be the first time I used the iv (here, F minor), which falls on the line "there's no way to tell," a somewhat corny but seemingly necessary step in the evolution of most songwriters—although I'm singing notes D and E over it, thus adding major sixths and sevenths to the ii; it's slightly hipper this way, and the rest of the melody also avoids the plain-jane notes, landing instead on suspended fourths and ninths. But the second part of the song travels a less-common road, first staying in C major but revolving around F (with some B♭s) and then walking down to a G, which then shifts to a G minor, the ii of what is to be the actual new key center, F major. The section ends with a plagal cadence (B♭ back to F), but the melody over the B♭ has a thirteenth (on "some are always *cold*") for a colder sound. Then back to G major at the end of the phrase, with that chord becoming the V of the original part, and we are back to the key of C for the next verse. So although it sounds like it's the harmonic language of the Shirelles, it's not quite the same as their typical I–vi–IV–V. And it ends with a "sunny" smile of a coda, abruptly pushing the ii to a major.

Chapter 7: Eyes Submerge Your Face
"If and When," Chris Stamey and the dB's, seven-inch vinyl single, Car Records (1978)

The Kinks invented a whole category of songs made from barre-chord guitar riffs, often traveling back and forth one whole step, "You Really Got Me" being one of many. You can add this tune to that list. The melody is built around parallel motion with a ninth: first the note C♯ over the tonic B-minor chord and then a B over an A major. The second half goes to the relative major of D and then ends up back in B minor. It's kind of like a rock blues, but it doesn't use the twelve-bar blues progression.

Chapter 8: Caress and Spite
"Dynamite," the dB's, seven-inch vinyl single, Albion Records (1981)

I don't know why that organ hook, which deceptively suggests the key of G major, is only three bars long! I'm sure it seemed like "a good idea at the time" to make it asymmetrical, to make the needle jump. I guess once we got back to the F chord, we were ready to start singing again. It's in C major, but it's hard to tell that for sure at the start; it sounds like A minor, as it goes F–G–F with a B♮ in the melody. It's only when it follows this with a D minor, an A minor, and an E⁷ (at first augmented, with the note C in the melody) that you realize the E⁷ (a III⁷) is a nonfunctioning secondary dominant usage that then walks us up securely a half step to the thrice repeated F–G (IV–V) resolution to C. (A nonfunctioning secondary dominant is one that resolves to any chord other than that rooted a fifth below it. In the key of C, a secondary dominant of D⁷ should resolve down a fifth to G major or minor, for example. If it resolves to F instead, it is nonfunctioning.) The middle section uses a B⁷ to modulate to E major (V to I) for a few bars and then walks down to the G-major chord. And we are back in C!

Chapter 9: I Loved You, and You Did, Too
"Soul Kiss," the dB's, B side of vinyl single, Shake Records (1980)

Too bad this record couldn't have come with its own "Fillmore" light show. It modulates after the Star Wars–derived instrumental. In the early sixties, it was very common to modulate up, a half or whole step, during a song; "Parchman Farm," by Mose Allison, a 1957 single on Prestige, which modulates several times by half steps, is where I learned this. I've been playing this one in recent years with a string trio arrangement (viola, cello, and acoustic guitar, with some added Bartokish licks), and it works surprisingly well that way.

Chapter 10: Exhilaration; or, Gorging a Neuronic Aperture
"Cycles Per Second," the dB's, *Stands for deciBels*,
Albion Records (1981)

Another connection between this song and Blondie's "Heart of Glass" is that both drop beats at times; that is, both have time changes inserted into the basic 4/4 pounding, to give a bit of a lift, a jolt. My song does this on the "having a good time" and "from y to b in" lines, with a 2/4 bar; theirs, in the instrumental in the middle of the song, where they drop a beat for a 3/4 bar.

Chapter 11: Just Like Yesterday
"Far Away and Long Ago," the dB's, *Falling Off the Sky*, Bar/None Records (2012)

This one has some twists and turns; it's not quite as simple as it sounds. Its intro is in C minor but resolves to a C^{sus4}, and then to a C major (a modal shift). The first note of the melody that comes in on top of this C chord is an A, a nonchord tone (the sixth). The C is revealed to be the V chord of the key of F, but the verse starts on B♭ (IV), the subdominant. After moving though a IV–V–I cadence (B♭–C–F), it uses a III^7 (A^7, another nonfunctioning secondary dominant) to set up a repeat of those first chords. The melody then introduces some more unexpected notes: the A over the E^{sus4} climbs to an E over D minor (a ninth). The D minor changes to a D^7 (with the melody on the C, the seventh), which then shifts to G major followed by G minor (with the melody on an E, the sixth); this G minor, as the ii of F major, lets us resolve and finish it all up with something akin to a so-called authentic cadence, I–V–I (F-C-F)—except the V is augmented (C-E-G♯) for an old-fashioned flavor. The bridge, in C minor, reminds me of the Zombies, harmonically, in the way it uses diminished seventh chords to move to a few different places. At the section's end, with "now the nights are long," the sense of the word *long* is reinforced by starting it on the ninth (B♭) of the A♭-major chord and sustaining it at length as the chords move up, underneath it, first to B♭ major and then to C major, at which point that B♭ in the melody has become the seventh of the V^7 (C^7) of the original key. And so we are back to F (and another verse). There's a slight "exit, pursued by a bear" zinger of a modulation at the very end, where, after a surprisingly minor B♭ chord, a G^{o7} drops us into a new key of A-flat in the very last seconds of the song. I'm not sure of either the how or the why of this, frankly, but it was always a part of the song to me.

Chapter 12: Who Will Baudelaire?
"The Seduction," *It's Alright*,
Coyote-Twin/Tone-A&M Records (1987)

Song beginnings are like chess openings. On the board, most everything has been done, but if you can take a road less traveled at the start and startle your adversary, you sometimes can seize the advantage. It's the same with songs—subbing "listener" for "adversary" of course. (Elliott Smith was so good at this kind of ambush.) This song establishes a little motif starting on the note G♯, almost "three blind mice," over the tonic chord of E major. But when the verse starts, that same melody is harmonized by a V chord (B major), so the G♯ becomes the thirteenth of that chord. And this use of suspensions in the melody continues, with a major seventh (A♯) over the B-major chord that starts the chorus ("Ev'-ry eye . . .") providing a Lydian modal shift, and a flat fifth (A♭) over the D ("who will buy . . .").

Chapter 13: Cut It Hot, Cut It Up, Cut It Clean, Cut It Slow
"Ask for Jill," the dB's, *Stands for deciBels*, Albion Records (1981)

The high notes at the beginning of the recording that sound like feedback are actually ghost tones on one of my beloved pre-CBS Fender Jazzmaster guitars, the only ones I used for most of the eighties. If you put down your finger on the fifth fret of those guitars but pick rapidly up and down (like tremolo picking on a mandolin) *behind* the bridge, the length of the string behind the bridge will resonate with the fretted part of the string before the bridge, and these high ghost tones will crescendo up out of nowhere, with no audible attack. You can then put vibrato on the string with the left hand, or even bend it slightly, as the bending will make the string stretch proportionately on both sides of the bridge. (This works as well on Fender Jaguars, which have similar bridges, but it's the fourth fret for them, since they have smaller, Gibson-scale necks.)

Chapter 14: Your Ballerina Curls
"Happenstance," the dB's, *Stands for deciBels*,
Albion Records (1981)

The verses here stay pretty solidly in A harmonic minor (whose penultimate tone is a major seventh, the middle note—G#—of the V, an E-major triad), but the water is muddied by often keeping the bass on the fifth or seventh of the chord for a slightly unsettling effect, even though it's nothing that Bach would have flinched at. The song goes to E minor for the choruses and then uses an E-major switcheroo (making it the V again) to push it all back into the A-minor territory. The quiet crickets section was typically elongated in live performance, with room for instrumental improvisations, guitars making noises of the forest. But again, for the vinyl release, every second was precious.

Chapter 15: She Took the Soda Pop
"Amplifier," the dB's, *Repercussion*, Albion Records (1982)

Dancing around on the guitar with dominant-seventh chords (found diatonically "in nature" as a V^7 chord) is part of the language of sixties funk. When you use them this way, they aren't necessarily expected to resolve in traditional ways. This song starts in the key of E major but uses these parallel sevenths to walk down to a D^7 and then a cool C^7 (that chord's seventh, the note Bb, is for sure not in the key of E major). This C^7 resolves to a G major (instead of leading to F major, as C^7 often does); the song then goes back to the C chord before walking up chromatically, D major to D# major to E major. The chromatic bit reminds me of "Hollywood Swinging," by the young Kool & the Gang, a group that influenced all of us when they played a memorable show at the Winston-Salem fairgrounds during our high school years. The choruses jump to a tonal center of G major with the helpful push of the bVII (F major).

After the song was recorded, Peter changed one chord for live performance, and it's even cooler with this alteration: On the very last quarter-note beat (beat "4"), the last chord before arriving back at the verse's E major verse became a passing A⁷! Which is a kind of IV chord in relation to the E that follows it, but with the added "funk" of the seventh. Or you can think of it as a sudden II⁷ in the chorus key of G major. Don't be afraid to try this at home. (This IV⁷–I move is essentially the same progression as the verse's C⁷–G.)

The other interesting detail: The end of the bridge throws in a bar of 5/4. There's one extra quarter note, on the "an" of the line "And all you've got to show for it's *an* amplifier." (I played that song about a million times before I realized this meter change was there.)

Chapter 16: Wine in Plastic Cups
"From a Window to a Screen," the dB's, *Repercussion* (1982)

The melody starts (in the original key of G major, before it was transposed up a step for recording) on a flat ninth, the note C on top of the B⁷ chord (the III⁷, a nonfunctioning secondary dominant), which was a bit bold for an indie rock song at that time. And on the next phrase, having moved up another third, to the V (D⁷), it resolves to a thirteenth (a note B on ". . . the wind") instead of a triadic tone. Otherwise, it's pretty straightforward. The bass plays the fifth of the chord in several places, notably on the word *mistake* the first time (G under a C-major chord). We probably liked that it sounded a little like a "mistake" to put the fifth of the chord in the bass like that. The primary-color shout-out to Ives, the quotation from the hymn "Shall We Gather at the River?," is played on a piano in the background of the second verse. The first two bars of it start on the word "stereo" and then two more bars are heard after the phrase "I remember when." This hymn, the opening superhigh bassoon line from *The Rite of Spring*, the theme of Ornette Coleman's "Dancing in Your Head," and the half-step high trill that cues the end of the intro in the Byrd's "Eight Miles High" were just some of the little motifs that would often get sprinkled into guitar solos in those days.

Chapter 17: The Distance That Surrounds Us
"Depth of Field," *It's a Wonderful Life*, DB Records (1983)

Again, that iv (an F minor in the key of C, just as was used in "Summer Sun"), this time after a passing first-inversion II (D/F♯) on the line "We were talking in the kitchen" (with the melody on "kit" hitting the note D, the sixth of the F minor). I think this song was the first time I used a half-diminished chord, which occurs on the lines "it's so simple, it's so straight"—in this case, it's a variation of D°, a chord we all learned from the second bar of the Big Star song "Back of a Car." And the C/D that comes right before this (one string fretted, on the first fret of the B string, with the low E damped) was probably lifted from Chris Bell's "I Am the Cosmos," where it falls on the last word of that song's line "I hate to have to take you *home*."

Chapter 18: The Air Is Full of Air
"Oh Yeah," *It's a Wonderful Life*, DB Records (1983)

This song constantly repeats a I–V–♭VII–IV (A–E–G–D) progression over a tonic drone but finally drops to a ♭VI (F♮) chord at the very end, still over the droned A. It seemed minimal to me at the time, but this was before radio waves of the twenty-first century became filled with such four-chord repetition, usually vi–IV–I–V or some variation thereof. I think my favorite version of this song was a live performance at the Knitting Factory's first location, around 1994, with Knox Chandler on cello and Ira Kaplan and Brent Lambert on guitars.

Chapter 19: Like a Party Balloon on the Strand
"27 Years in a Single Day," *It's Alright*,
Coyote-Twin/Tone-A&M Records (1987)

I've stated earlier that, in "The Summer Sun" and "Depth of Field," I used a iv chord in a major key (harmonically similar to a ii°). By "27 Years," I was using a "minor five," a v chord—the song, in the key of A major, has a chorus that abruptly moves from A major to E minor on the word "years," and the choruses end by moving first to the V and then back to the v on the way back to the tonic. ("Far Away and Long Ago" does something similar but uses a II/ii modulation instead of V/v). Paul McCartney, in Barry Miles's *Many Years from Now*, states that the Beatles learned this change from a Joan Baez song (which went from D to A minor in the key of D major). I learned it from "Expecting to Fly, a song by Neil Young on the second Buffalo Springfield record. It has the effect of "pulling the rug out from under you," because we expect the chord built on the fifth to be major. (Both "Expecting to Fly" and the band's collage tune, "Broken Arrow," were arranged by Jack Nitzsche, Phil Spector's arranger, and his contributions there were big influences on me.) My song's bridge modulates continuously, a kind of musical restlessness that impatiently contradicts the repeated lyrical suggestion to "take your time."

Chapter 20: Never a Time
"Something Came Over Me," *Instant Excitement*
(the acoustic version), Coyote-Twin/Tone Records (1984)

Musically, this song is pretty straightforward folk. Although solidly in the key of G major, it starts most lines on the V chord instead of the I, which gives it a somewhat modal sound. Also folky are the interspersed 2/4 bars (half-bars) that stretch phrases beyond 4/4. Harmonically, the use of the B^7 (here, a nonfunctioning secondary dominant) to pivot back to D major (the key's V) is probably the only real outlier. At the time, I had serious doubts about the "never a time" couplet, retaining it only at the insistence of my friends Lynn Blakey and Faye Hunter, who were visiting at the studio; but I'm glad they overruled me. In hindsight, it's clear that the instrumental section, over a pedal-bass G, took its rhythm from "See No Evil," by Television.

Chapter 21: Anyone Who Had to Laugh
"Occasional Shivers," B side of vinyl single,
Coyote-Twin/Tone Records (1985)

This songs cycles through three different minor modes: melodic, harmonic, and natural. Again, the opening move in the melodic "chess game" here is an unexpected note. After the intro solidly establishes the key as F minor, the melody of the first section begins on a note C, the seventh of a D$^\varnothing$ chord (a chord whose root is in the descending melodic minor mode), right away indicating a slightly enriched harmonic language. Then the next chord is a VI, a D♭^{maj7} (showing a shift to the harmonic minor), but the downbeat of the melody there falls on the note G note, the chord's flat fifth. After that, a C^{min7}, and we are in the harmonic minor. Then, a bit later, there's a C+^{7} (i.e., the notes C, E, G♯, and B♭) as a pivot to an A♭ chord (the relative major of F minor) and then to a G^{11}, at which point it repeats. The word "shivers," at the end of the song's second section, is set up by a chord meant to give shivers, a G♭ major with an F♭ (spelled enharmonically, an E) in the bass (a ♭II^7 with its seventh in the bass). This "surrounds" the key's tonic, F, from both above and below, with the bass note as the leading tone of the key, and then resolves to it. I would like to take lots of credit for this "shivers" text-painting moment, which is very successful in that regard. But really, it's another of those Pete Buck kind of chords on guitar, where you finger part of a chord but, lazily, let high strings ring, unfretted.

Chapter 22: The Whole World's Dirt
"Cara Lee," *It's Alright*, Coyote-Twin/Tone-A&M Records (1987)

Apart from the chorus's weak pseudo-plagal cadences of ii to I (here, A minor to G), something I had just learned from Peter Holsapple that gives it that flavor of emotionally exhausted, half-hearted irresolution, there's not a lot musically here that the Kinks hadn't done a thousand times. I was learning to end bridges with clusters, the "Good Vibrations" polychord effect, and this one's relative-minor Dorian mode climbing bridge ends with a left-turn F#-minor[7] and then up a tritone to C[maj7,9], nice stacked harmonies from Marshall and me hitting the plate reverb, before going back to the solid V at the start of the last choruses.

Chapter 23: Newspapers Collect on the Street

"The Newlyweds," *Fireworks*, A&M-RNA-Rhino Records (1991)

I tried to frame the muted, depressed nature of this divorcé's frozen life with moments where the narrator more passionately expresses the sadness he feels, secondhand. The first choruses end with, "he can't get over . . ." abruptly dropping you back into the plodding I–V verse progression on the line "the little things," where it would have been expected that there would have been two more bars before getting to that point. Then, once this expectation (of being dropped back into the stasis) is established on each chorus, it is repudiated at the end, when the line changes to "he can't get over the way she held his world up and . . ." over a climbing E minor–D/F#–G 6/4 bar that "drops" you back into the A major of the verse-progression coda on the words "let it drop." This final cadence is one of my favorite moments in my own songs, for what that's worth, because it fits the emotion and the lyric so tightly; it's only in this fleeting moment that the genuine anguish of the song's subject is revealed.

Chapter 24: I Want to Break Your Heart

"I Want to Break Your Heart," Peter Holsapple & Chris Stamey, *Mavericks*, RNA-Rhino Records (1991)

(a) The verses start with a F Lydian tonal center; there's a G major that slides down to F major twice and then adds an A minor for the third and fourth times. The choruses are more clearly in C major and pass through a descending progression in normal ways, but they use a IV[maj7]–iii[7]–V resolution at the end, with the melody on the seventh, instead of a ii–V, as might be more typical. As I recall, I had rarely used iii–V before, doing so previously only in "From the Word Go" (from *It's Alright*); in recent years, however, it has become one of my favorite moves (I use it, e.g., in both "What Is this Music that I Hear" and "I Fall in Love So Easily" from the 2016 radio play *Occasional Shivers*). The IV^{maj7} wrapped in distorted guitars (the melody on the note E over the F chord on the words "I wanna") is something else I associate with Neil Young. He was the guy who made the major-seventh chord into something less than totally wimpy for rock at the end of the sixties, at least when this major-seventh note was sung over a fuzzed-out Les Paul chord.

(b) And a note about "Angels," from that record: When I wrote the choruses here, to add to Peter's extant verses, I ended them on a II chord (G major), which resolves back to the tonic of F without going through the mediation of a V^7 (C^7) first. This is something I had learned from Peter; it's in a number of his songs. Most of the choruses get to this G by walking down from B♭ major (the IV) to a passing F/A. But to set up the repeat of the chorus at the very end, it gets to that G by instead walking down from B♭ major with a surprise passing A^7 (another of Peter's ideas), a nonfunctioning secondary dominant, as it would normally resolve to a D minor but doesn't (although a G^9 it does resolve to is very similar). This use of a sudden A^7 differs from that of the sudden A^7 Peter added to the live version of "Amplifier" (see chapter 15), but it's a go-to surprise chord in both cases. The song ends by putting in a ♭VII, an E♭, before the final F, which is something we liked on that album; "Geometry" does the same thing (in that case, using a D-major chord in the key of E major).

Chapter 25: All Around You Now the Stars Are Falling Down
"Close Your Eyes," Holsapple & Stamey, *Mavericks*,
RNA-Rhino Records (1991)

I wanted a "suspension of disbelief" here, so I have the climbing melody of "There is nothing in the world," over the tonic of D, resolve to an E-major chord with the D still in the bass (in effect, a D^{13} chord), which makes it seem to float up. This repeats and is then followed by a B-minor^9 that leads to a G major, all normal stuff. But the next time that B-minor^9 comes in, it's followed by an E^7, the two chords thus becoming a ii–V^7 progression, and you are finally clued in to the fact that the key is A major. Surprisingly, however, although I didn't realize it then, it *never actually has an A chord at all*. It *never* resolves to the tonic; instead, every time it seems ready to move there, it goes somewhere else instead. With twenty-twenty hindsight, I think I did this because so much in my life was also unresolved at the time.

Notes

1. For a fascinating insider's view of Morris Levy and Roulette Records, and for that matter the music racket in general as it played out in the sixties, read *Me, the Mob, and the Music*, by Tommy James (Scribner's, 2011).

2. Darling's curriculum vitae was not limited to starting the twelve-string invasion. After playing in the Tarriers (with actor Alan Arkin), he had scored a huge hit in 1956, with "The Banana Boat Song." He moved to Chapel Hill around 2000 and started recording at my studio, and we became friends. Even though he was now in a college town filled with indie-rock guitar distortion, he still felt that putting an acoustic twelve-string on a recording was a reliable way to hit the charts, and he would bring his out whenever a song we were working on needed some extra oomph. Surprisingly, though, his true ace in the hole, his overdub of last resort, was something else entirely: He told me during one session, with great sincerity, "Chris, the American populace has always had a great affection for . . . the banjo."

3. The Yellow Payges' underground credibility was crushed when they took an endorsement from AT&T that required them do phone commercials dressed in all yellow to match the printed business directories from which they took their name. They broke up soon after and have disappeared from the lexicon. Ham went on to work with another up-and-coming guitarist, Billy Gibbons, as the manager and initial producer for Gibbons's band, ZZ Top.

4. I was proud of some of the chamber pieces I wrote at UNC in the early seventies, and when I moved to New York, I carried all my student writing with me in a big white suitcase that had belonged to my grandmother (it contained my rare *Stack-O-Tracks* Beach Boys record and a few other treasured items as well). As I moved from one apartment to another, I always tried to make sure this precious collection was secure. When I started traveling a lot, around 1979, I left it with a woman who had worked with me at the Spring Street Bar. And there it stayed for years, until one day, when a new boyfriend of hers one day, with no attempt to contact me, simply set it out on the street as trash. All the music was gone without a trace. It was a punishing blow under which I staggered for a time, but it was also the gift of a clean slate. It was a pretty nice suitcase, however, and I've always wondered if someone grabbed it for the leather and then stuck the sheet music in the back of a closet somewhere, to be discovered one day in an archeological dig of the Lower East Side.

5. This blackout, and the attendant looting, is credited by some with having had a positive effect on the evolution of hip-hop in the Bronx. Looted electronics became tools for young DJs too poor to afford them, and the music grew at a rapid pace afterward.

6. Years later I was asked to sample the handclaps from Numan's "Cars" in Pro Tools for the Ben Folds Five 1997 breakout album *Whatever and Ever Amen*—although in the end, the samples were cut from the release.

7. When our daughter, Julia, was very young, one of her babysitters, in urging her to eat a balanced meal, told her that there were different "shelves" in her tummy for the food, and she

needed to have something on the fruit shelf, and the salad shelf, and the vegetable shelf. Her takeaway from this was that there was a dessert shelf that, no matter how much she had eaten, would still have room on it for some pie or ice cream.

I'm not certain that this is solid science. But it was a revelation to me when I applied it to arranging and mixing records. If you think about the sonic spectrum in terms of "shelves" of octaves, starting with the C below the lowest string on the bass, which at 32 Hertz is about as low as even the best speakers can reproduce, then things become much simpler. Shelf 1 can be 32–65 Hz; Shelf 2, 65–130 Hz; and on up to Shelf 8, which ends at 8372 Hz, and 9, ending at 16,744 Hz. So arranging becomes not about what instruments would be cool to hear but about what should be together on a given shelf at any one time. And if Shelf 4 already has a voice on it, you can consider it "full" and work off the others.

Speakers are not brilliant devices; they are air pumps. Like horses, they do best with simple, clear instructions. If you are telling them to play back three or four different instruments simultaneously on Shelf 2, say, they are going to get spooked and give you muddy sound.

If you are mixing a song that has been arranged without regard to shelves (careless of range conflicts), it becomes part of the job to make decisions so that you don't have song-defeating clutter, so that everything that's there can "speak." In some cases, this calls for filtering out frequencies on a given track that are taking up room on several shelves at once, even if that instrument, alone, sounds unnatural after the filtering. (It might also call for just taking some things off the shelf entirely—tough love.)

And there is also the concept of *tessitura*, which refers to the range in which each instrument "speaks" best. With the advent of close microphone placement, which became common with multitrack recording, lots of frequencies get captured that are not part of the most essential part of an instrument. Think about it: At a concert, we don't put our ear up to the lips of a flautist and hear all that huffing and puffing. We hear the flute from a distance, and the tones sound different; the frequency balance is different. So equalization (EQ) can re-create how natural or unnatural the instrument would sound if the mic had been placed farther away, where our ears might have been positioned in the sonic picture being created in the mix. For the flute, for example, perhaps everything on the lower shelves and much of the highest shelves can be cut, leaving only perhaps Shelf 5 or 6 in the mix. Of course, it's "to taste": Stravinsky went way up beyond the bassoon's normal tessitura, at the start of *The Rite of Spring*, and it's unforgettable. The Jethro Tull records were all about Ian Anderson's huffing and puffing on his flute, treating it as percussion. But it's good to know the rules before you break them. And it's good to leave room for pie.

8.   Now, to be clear: I'm not a Luddite. After twenty-five years of fun with analog tape, I started recording on computers in 1995, at Scott Litt's suggestion, when Pro Tools was just transitioning from the two-channel Sound Tools. He was using it on aspects of a project with R.E.M. and told me that I would love it, as he had heard some of the detailing I had done in my occasional midi computer work in the ten years previous. He was right: I took to it immediately, recording some of Ryan Adams's early material with Whiskeytown with the nascent version of the system at the first version of my studio, Modern Recording, then at 202 Spring Lane in downtown Chapel Hill. And I've never looked back. I am proud of my hard-earned computer-recording chops, go back to tape only rarely, and even with large budgets sometimes prefer the computer. I don't miss the way that tape sounds sparkly immediately after something is recorded but then, even forty-eight hours later, loses some edge as the magnetized metallic oxide bits relax their hold on the transients (the brief, loud parts of a note's attack). I don't miss the old days of all-night tape editing, either; they were fun in the first years, but ultimately, records made by sleep-deprived folks sound exhausted as well. And I don't miss the cost of two-inch tape, around two hundred dol-lars for every fifteen minutes. I do sometimes miss the minute speed fluctuations of the recorder motors, which add a slight "wow" or chorus effect to the music.

Digital recording also allows me to discuss a possible edit with a room full of musicians and then, after moving the cursor around for a few seconds on the screen, let everyone instantly hear what it will sound like; if it doesn't get the vote, I can "undo." This flexibility keeps sessions moving and inspiration firing. The problem is not this format itself but rather in the aforementioned now-unquestioned protocols associated with it.

On the plus side, the recording options that emerged at the end of the century let people who had great ideas and little money join the conversation early, before their chops had fully caught up with their concepts. This is huge and has made for a lot of unique music, some amazing and unexpected "indie" releases. On the minus, the instant gratification of laptop recording and the cosmetic fixes now available have removed a lot of the incentive for recording artists to put in the long hours of practice necessary to become a really excellent musician. Running multioctave scales in all keys? For far too many, that's gone the way of the dinosaurs. And albums now take longer to make, going from a few hours or days in the fifties and early sixties to weeks, months, and even years now. Despite these pervasive changes in process, though, most all A-list commercial records that have survived as perennials—the "canon," as it were, stuff on *Rolling Stone*'s "best of" lists—actually do feature a large percentage of highly skilled musicians at their core. The technological options seem to help more albums get up to baseline standards, to be palatable and enjoyable, so that we now hear few unarguably bad records. But real excellence most often still requires superb musicianship. Examples from those first years I spent in New York include David Bowie—not an accomplished guitarist, but already the author of many influential and sonically pioneering hit albums—who had his greatest success when he teamed up with the very accomplished Nile Rodgers and his stable of superb players at Power Station for the *Let's Dance* record. Or Talking Heads, who improved first by adding the versatile Jerry Harrison to their original trio lineup and then reached new heights when they added keyboard virtuoso

Bernie Worrell to their equation. And the first album by the band that drew me to Manhattan initially was created by many long hours of rehearsal, and only a short time in the studio: To even try to imagine Television's *Marquee Moon* (the title track of which was captured in the first—and the only—take) having been instead cut piecemeal to a click track and assembled bit by bit is beyond me.

9. On the subject of small audiences: I also treasured my memory of the night Karin Berg took Alex and me to see Charles Mingus at the Village Gate, probably the summer of 1977. That night, too, the crowd was small, yet the band burned. At one point in the middle of a solo, however, Mingus stopped cold and angrily chastised the guy running the PA, shouting, as I recall, "Hey, Mr. Soundman, goddamn, can you get some bass in the monitors here? I can't hear a thing!" We all looked at each other, agape, astonished that such an icon would stoop to recognize such a mundane issue. Chilton himself, though he often spurned sound checks, went on to stop innumerable shows and alienate innumerable sound men with his notoriously snide comment, "Hey, Mr. Soundman, can you get my voice in the monitors here?" Only years after that Mingus show did I realize that Karin and I were the only ones who could possibly know that he was actually just doing a secret shout-out to Mingus each time. It made me wonder what else was in his private lexicon.

10. Insects had always played a proportionally big part in the dB's oeuvre. When Easter signed up as the dB's soundman during a tour opening for Dave Edmunds in the UK, our set included several psychogarage improv moments, stuff evocative of the *Nuggets* series of psychedelic rock. I made him a cassette tape of insects and frogs and instructed him that if things were getting dull in the "jams," he was to just fade in some random chirps and burps with the PA mix. I'm not sure if the audience liked or even realized this, but it always cheered me up to hear Teddy the Toad in the stage monitors.

11. I recall talking to Ryan Adams about songwriting much later, in 1995, during one of our early sessions together when he was just starting out, and I told him that I thought Neil Young had

it right: you have to stop whatever you are doing, no matter what, find a quiet corner, and honor the song that is "coming on." One always thinks, "Oh, this is easy! But it's so easy, in fact, that I can finish it later! I need to go check the mail/do the laundry/walk the dog." Don't be fooled, I told him: It might be easy now, but if you don't go ahead and snatch that second verse out of the air right that very moment, you'll be pulling your hair out trying to find the "easy" rest of the song in the weeks to come.

At the time, I was never sure how much credence Ryan gave to any of my various in-studio "lectures," but when he later quoted my advice in *Time* magazine, I realized that from then on, his tour managers and bandmates might be blaming me if he ever put the world on hold or missed sound checks and photo ops because he was chasing a muse. He did manage to write quite a few good songs, however, using the "Whoa, stop the presses" method, so there's that.

12.   Peter reminds me that the title was a play on the Allen Toussaint song "From a Whisper to a Scream" (originally sung by Esther Phillips), with perhaps a bit of the Billy J. Kramer tune in there, too.

13.   The original 1978 lineup of the band has since come together intermittently over the decades, even releasing a new record together (*Falling Off the Sky*, on Bar/None [2012]) and an EP (*Revolution of the Mind* [2013]). And we continue to record together occasionally. In 2015 I was glad to have the chance to finally capture a dB's interpretation of "Depth of Field" at one of these studio reunions.

14.   Minimalism was a part of the CBGB scene I walked into. At the first show Alex and I played there, a young band called the Feelies were opening. I asked them backstage how their sound check had gone, and they excitedly said that they had written a brand new song during it, "Forces at Work." I offered congrats and made a point to listen for this during their set. It was indeed a minimal song and a maximum surprise: The writing consisted solely of the title chanted hypnotically in unison many times over just a rapidly strummed E chord. As if they themselves were the force. At work. (The later recording of this

had a section where it went to D, and there were some other words. But my memory—and it has been a while—is that, at its inception, there was literally just the single chord and the "forces at work" chant.)

15. Bob Mould, late of Minneapolis's Hüsker Dü, the most renowned indie-rock band out of Minnesota until the Replacements knocked them off the throne, had heard a rough mix of this before its release from our mutual friend Steve Fallon at Maxwell's, and Mould was enthused about the tune. We even played it together on occasion. He also told me that he had really liked the subdued, tasteful drum performance on this and that this was part of the reason he had asked Anton Fier to play on his first solo album, *Workbook*—the irony being that, although Anton had indeed played excellently on much of my record, "27 Years in a Single Day" actually featured a drum machine arrangement I had entered into a computer.

16. I had doubts about the "never a time" verse, retaining it only at the insistence of Lynn Blakey and Faye Hunter; I'm now glad they overruled me.

17. The "there's no single" speech is a familiar one, but it has become known as the "Dancing in the Dark" speech: According to a popular story, Bruce Springsteen, after spending two years cutting umpteen tracks for his *Born in the USA* album, thought he was done at last. (His band prayed he was done at last.) Then manager and coproducer Jon Landau gave him the bad news: Jon thought the record lacked a linchpin track. The tale concludes with Springsteen coming right back with "Dancing in the Dark"; it's a hit; everyone cheers. So Glenn's speech to me fell somewhat under this "D. in the D." category. In 2016, however, I met engineer John Davenport, who was an assistant at the Hit Factory in the early eighties, and he filled in the picture for me: The ever-sociable Bruce, late one night at the coffee machine as they were putting together the finished mixes reel for mastering, asked J.D. how it was going. He replied, perhaps too frankly, that he was "sick and tired of himself, exhausted all the time, things were going badly, he and his gal were not getting along . . . but sometimes the two of them would at least put on a record and"—you guessed it—

cut a rug with all the lights off. The very next morning, John insists, Springsteen, a Studs Terkel of song, walked in and told the band it was back to the trenches one more time . . .

18. John Noble Wilford, *The New York Times*, Jan. 8, 1986.

19. Ray Davies's multifaceted catalog was to me what Lennon and McCartney's was to others: a constant source of inspiration. It was a high-water mark, then, to work with him years later, as I did in 2012, at London's Barbican Hall during one of Big Star's *Third* concerts for which I was music director. We had come close to having Davies join us a few times before for this concert, as he'd been friends with Chilton when they both lived in New Orleans in later years, and Alex had helped him during his hospitalization and recovery from a gunshot wound during a street mugging in 2004. His slow recovery and his busy schedule had always caused him to cancel, though. Finally, in London, we were told Ray might really come sing with us, both "The Letter" and "Till the End of the Day," a song of his that Big Star had recorded. Or he might come by and just listen. Or say a few words. Or he might skip it, as he had a play in rehearsal. A few hours before his projected, possible, tentative (dubious?) arrival, with the band and chamber orchestra working through many complicated scores on a tight deadline, we got word from management—Ray's voice was tired from an earlier event and could we please rewrite the parts into a lower key? From A minor all the way down to E minor? (Note to nonsingers: This is a huge leap.) We scrambled madly to accommodate this, transposing parts for twenty people. But on his arrival, he said that, no, he felt fine, and we should stick to the original key. No problem; a new paper bucket-brigade went forth, and we swapped back to the original parts. We were just glad to have him there.

We had a total blast on the first run-through of the Kinks tune. Wow, he was the real deal. I wasn't playing on that one, however. I was musical director, and I didn't know the guitar parts, just the brass and strings. But he wasn't satisfied yet. He stopped the rehearsal and said, "It needs an acoustic. That's what it's missing! Here, Chris, you play." Not only had I never imagined I would ever play onstage with Ray, an absolute hero, but I had certainly never imagined I would have to do it standing right next to him strumming a song whose chords I didn't exactly know. A bit nightmarish, but a nice dream nonetheless; I faked my way through it, hiding my left hand from his sight on the sections where I was clueless, and afterward Mitch whispered that all those D major barres were really minors, but otherwise it would do.

Our other takeaway from that rehearsal was when Davies turned to Jody Stephens and said, "We need a big ending. Can you build a shed?" "Um, pardon?" "Build a shed, you know, a *shed*!" As Jody remained nonplussed, Ray mimicked taking a hammer and rapidly nailing imaginary nails into imaginary boards in all directions. Lightbulbs of recognition went off above the Americans' heads, and Jody "nailed" the ending with a triumphantly trashy drum solo that traveled frenetically around every corner of the kit for about a minute. The phrase "to build a shed" marched forever into our Secret Decoder Ring handbook, becoming gradually applicable to all aspects of celebrating life's unpredictable moments of exhilaration.

20. Dave and Paul would later expand their efforts into the spectacular Wild Honey Foundation concert series with the help of the Wondermints (who became Brian Wilson's band), guitarist Rob Laufer, pianist Willie Aron, and a host of others.

21. After that bright morning in 1990, I frankly didn't expect to have any further contact with Van Dyke. It was just one more disconnected Los Angeles experience. This expectation was happily confounded over two decades later. I was working as musical director and orchestrator for a concert version of Big Star's *Third* album, itself somewhat akin to *Smile* in that both were legendary and once-lost passion projects that had been surprisingly revived as concert arrangements by a younger band. My hands were fully engaged playing guitar for much of the *Third* set, so we always used a conductor for the chamber orchestra. In September 2014 we were slated for a Los Angeles benefit performance for the Wild Honey Foundation when our scheduled conductor, Willie Aron, had to cancel. He insisted that I at least call Van Dyke as a replacement, and so once again, I found that kindly raconteur on the other end of the line.

Lo and behold, Parks immediately accepted the assignment with joy and gusto; we worked closely together on that concert and then on several more the next year, including San Francisco's Hardly Strictly Bluegrass festival. It was a great validation for all concerned when he afterward described these concerts as "a real triumph of the human spirit." He and his wife, Sally, have become gracious friends and mentors. And I discovered they have close ties to the same Carolina-based Red Clay Ramblers group of players who showed me, back in 1975, how to make my first indie record. It may be a small world, but it's also a better one with the likes of Van Dyke in it. (I would be remiss if I didn't add that he also played piano and synthesizer on the fourth dB's record, 1987's *The Sound of Music*.)

Selected Discography

Sneakers
Sneakers (EP; Carnivorous) 1976
In the Red (EP; Car) 1978

The dB's
"I Thought You Wanted to Know" b/w "If and When"
   (single; Car) 1978
Stands for deciBels (Albion) 1981
Repercussion (Albion) 1982
Falling Off the Sky (Bar/None) 2012
Revolution of the Mind (EP; Orange Sound) 2013

Solo
"The Summer Sun" b/w "Where the Fun Is" (single; Ork)
   1977
It's a Wonderful Life (DB) 1983
Instant Excitement (EP; Coyote-Twin/Tone) 1984
Christmas Time (Coyote-Twin/Tone) 1985

It's Alright (Coyote-Twin/Tone-A&M) 1987
Fireworks (Coyote-Twin/Tone-RNA-A&M) 1991
"Let It Be Me" b/w "That's Why I Hate (the Replacements)"
(single; Carr Records) 1994
The Robust Beauty of Improper Linear Models in Decision-Making
(with Kirk Ross; East Side Digital) 1995
Alaska (with Alaska; EP; Hello Recording Club, 1995)
Travels in the South (Yep Roc) 2004
A Question of Temperature (with Yo La Tengo and Tyson Rogers;
Yep Roc) 2005
Lovesick Blues (Yep Roc) 2013
Euphoria (Yep Roc) 2015

Peter Holsapple & Chris Stamey
Mavericks (RNA-Rhino) 1991
hERE aND nOW (Bar/None) 2009